D1135857

WHO RUNS BRITAIN?

Also by Robert Peston

BROWN'S BRITAIN

WHO RUNS BRITAIN?

ROBERT PESTON

HODDER &
STOUGHTON

First published in Great Britain in 2008 by Hodder & Stoughton
An Hachette Livre UK company

3

Copyright © Robert Peston 2008

The right of Robert Peston to be identified as the Author
of the Work has been asserted by him in accordance
with the Copyright, Designs and Patents Act 1988.

A CIP catalogue record for this title is available from the British Library

Hardback ISBN 978 0 340 83942 3

Typeset in Plantin Light by Hewer Text UK Ltd, Edinburgh
Printed and bound in the UK by CPI Mackays, Chatham ME5 8TD

Hodder & Stoughton policy is to use papers that are natural, renewable
and recyclable products and made from wood grown in sustainable forests.
The logging and manufacturing processes are expected to conform
to the environmental regulations of the country of origin.

Hodder & Stoughton Ltd
338 Euston Road
London NW1 3BH

www.hodder.co.uk

To my parents

CONTENTS

CHAPTER 1
TOO MUCH MONEY

I didn't expect flying cars. But when growing up in leafy, salubrious north London of the 1960s and 1970s, I did expect that the UK would become a progressively fairer place as we hurtled towards the millennium. Ours wasn't a religious household in any sense. But we did have a faith (well, three, if you include support for the Arsenal and my adolescent, homoerotic obsession with David Bowie). My parents passionately believed that everyone should have an equal chance to make something of themselves. In my father's case, this was manifested in devotion to the Labour Party. My mother was less tribal, though just as committed to campaigning for education and health systems that did not discriminate against the disadvantaged. They weren't naive or doctrinaire enough to expect equality of outcome. There always had been, and always would be, gaps between the richest and the poorest. In fact, Mum and Dad might have manned the barricades to protect their right to have a Colston dishwasher or a Baird colour television before anyone else in our wide, airy, suburban road. But they had confidence that through a combination of progressive taxation, state education and the welfare state, the gap between the haves and have-nots would narrow – and would do so in a way that improved society. Little by little, there would be a greater sense of freedom and opportunity for the majority, at relatively minor cost or inconvenience to the wealthy minority. And statistics seemed to prove their point, because for the best part of the twentieth century, the gap between rich and poor had been narrowing.

My parents put their money where their mouths were. Actually, that is not quite right. As a matter of principle, they refused to spend a penny of their disposable income on our education (if you exclude the mountains of books that were everywhere). They were prominent in a campaign to close down selective schools and they sent me, my sister and my brother to local comprehensives. My school in Crouch End was a noisy, happy and cohesive gaggle of white kids, Greek Cypriots, Asians and West Indians. Those of us with professional parents and big estate cars were a smallish and thoroughly integrated minority. University and then a career in journalism would eventually see me return to a middle-class white ghetto. But, for my seven years there, Highgate Wood School was a haven beyond those invisible herding pens. It was what a comprehensive ought to be, even though its origins were not auspicious. Created as a secondary modern, it had been one of those dumping grounds in the 1960s for those who failed the 11-plus examination. When I arrived in 1971, the top of the school was still made up of teenagers who had flunked that exam and been rejected as academically inadequate at the age of just 11. But our aloof Welsh rugby-playing headmaster, Eurof Walters, did not write off anyone.

Mr Walters ran an institution with progressive ideals in a very old-fashioned way, putting an emphasis on discipline. Highgate Wood's backbone was a Taffia of teachers called Jones, Williams and Owen. The place was filled with staff passionate about Thomas Hardy and Oliver Cromwell and isosceles triangles. These were teachers with a vocation, many of whom stayed at the school for 30 years. So although the adverse conditions which make it difficult for London state schools to thrive these days were present – there were punch-ups with gangs from rival schools, drugs were commonplace and we were boisterously obsessed with sex – Highgate Wood worked very well; it improved the life-chances of hundreds of children.

It is probably unsurprising that I too would take it for granted, once I ventured into the world, that Britain would continue to become a more equal place. It stood to reason: progressive values were palpably the rational ones; most human beings were evidently sensible intelligent people; ergo any democracy would obviously evolve into a place where the gap between the privileged and the deprived – as manifested in wealth and income – would narrow. For me in 1979, aged 19, the election of Margaret Thatcher's Conservative Party as the new Government was a weird and temporary aberration, a blip, an anomaly. It would be years before I realized that the Pestons as members of a British egalitarian species were dinosaurs faced with extinction. Little did I know it, but more or less from the moment I became a full voting member of our democracy in the late 1970s, the gap between rich and poor started to widen and would never narrow again. Increasing inequality was to define the Thatcher years from 1979 to 1990. But more than that, her way of seeing the world became the establishment view. What was at first a right-wing minority view captured the centre ground of politics. In her world, striving for equality and economic success were antithetical aspirations, so equality must die – and it did.

During her decade in power, the real incomes of the poorest fifth, or quintile, of the British population grew by less than 0.5 per cent a year, while those of the richest 20 per cent rose by almost 4 per cent. It was a return to Darwinism for the distribution of income: the more anyone earned, the bigger the increase in earnings he or she secured. In the words of the Institute of Fiscal Studies, the respected economic think tank, in *Poverty and Inequality in the UK: 2007*, the magnitude of the rise in inequality under her Conservative Government was 'unparalleled both historically and compared with the changes taking place at the same time in most other developed countries'.

Here's the oddity: I gradually came to see that much of what Margaret Thatcher did was necessary. For much of the post-war era, the British economy was sliding into a mediocrity of below-par growth punctuated by periodic crisis. Perhaps there was a cure that would not have led to growing inequality. But that is an academic point. The medicine administered by Margaret Thatcher created a less fair UK, but also an economy that – after she had left – would start to grow faster than its main European rivals' and would continue to do so right up to the present. Hers was radical surgery: a systematic reduction in the power of trade unions which reduced the bargaining power of employees; cuts in income tax to provide increasing rewards for incremental effort; reductions in benefits to create stronger incentives to take any kind of job; privatization of swathes of the public sector that improved basic services but also precipitated significant pay rises for those who ran the former nationalized industries. A lot of people were bruised or more seriously harmed along the way. However, the economy became more competitive. And the majority of us have become richer in an absolute sense, even as those at the top have scooped a disproportionately large win.

So I am not going to resort to hand-wringing hypocrisy. My teenage conviction that it is *always* in the national interest for the gap between rich and poor to be reduced was wrong. As a journalist reporting on the business and political elite from 1983 onwards, it is clear to me that Britain has benefited from what was a cultural revolution under Thatcher. It was not just that she changed the tax system so that those who create wealth from which we all benefit could keep more of it for themselves. It was also that she was on their side, willing them to create that wealth in a way that the Labour Party of the 1970s and 1980s was not.

The caricature of the 1980s new entrepreneur, Harry Enfield's 'Loadsamoney', should possibly be a national hero, Margaret Thatcher's Stakhanov. It has been good for the UK that businessmen, footballers and even civil servants have had their pay linked much more closely to how well they perform. And also, perhaps, that some have been able to earn colossal sums for superlative performance. For 25 years, in a series of different media jobs – Business Editor for the BBC and the *Sunday Telegraph*, Financial

Editor and Political Editor for the *Financial Times* – I've been an advocate for wealth creators being able to retain a generous share of the incremental wealth they create. I've argued that we should all cheer when a chief executive pockets millions so long as he (occasionally she) has significantly increased the wealth of the relevant company's shareholders. Why? Well, those shareholders are us, because they include the pension funds that most of us rely on for a decent income in retirement. And we therefore benefit when a company boss boosts the value of a company's shares. Further, any company should be prepared to pay almost whatever it takes to secure and retain the services of the best chief executive on the market, so long as his or her remuneration rises and falls with the returns generated for us as shareholders.

In practice, it has proved very difficult to design formulae for executives' pay that aligns their interests in a perfect way with those of shareholders. The recent history of British and US companies is littered with sorry tales of companies being damaged by executives' fraudulent or near-fraudulent attempts to manufacture profits in the hope of boosting their personal earnings. But the principle of trying to secure that alignment of interest between shareholders and managers is a sound one.

Even if Thatcher's ideas were to gain near-universal acceptance, she never stopped being a divisive figure within the UK. What is more, by 1990 the country wanted a breather from its reinvention as an unpolluted neo-liberal paradise, where notions of equality are toxic. However, it did not need the election of an ostensibly left-leaning Labour Government for there to be a hiatus in the Thatcherite trends: between 1990 and 1997, when the Tories were in power and led by John Major as Prime Minister, there was a modest distribution of income to the poorest fifth of the population, those who could describe themselves as the victims of Thatcherism (although they probably didn't feel much richer, since this relative rise in their earnings stemmed in part from a recession which precipitated a rise in social-security payments). However, it was in Major's latter years that Britain became a slightly more equal place again, according to the conventional measure known as the Gini coefficient. This is a measure of income inequality that condenses the distribution of income into a number between zero and one, where zero corresponds to a world in which all households have identical income, and one would be a place where all income goes to a single person. During Thatcher's years, Gini had risen (and how). It fell a bit as her successor steered their party towards electoral massacre and more than a decade in the political wilderness.

What happened to income distribution under Major turned out to be an anomaly. A swing in the political pendulum away from the Tories was not a manifestation of public clamour to soak the rich. Tony Blair's New Labour won a landslide election victory in 1997 in part because he had made an explicit promise that he would not seek to redistribute income and wealth in a conventional left-wing way. He and his Shadow Chancellor, Gordon Brown, calculated that their party could not be elected unless they pledged not to increase personal tax rates – and, having given that pledge, they've never gone the whole hog to become ideological tax-cutters, but they have been generous in their tax treatment of wealthy individuals.

So although you would expect Gini to fall under a Labour Government, after Tony Blair became Prime Minister and Gordon Brown became Chancellor it actually rose: inequality worsened during New Labour's first few years in office. This was a period of strong economic growth when Brown was determined to demonstrate his muscular love of capitalism to the City by keeping public spending in check. The Gini coefficient reached a record high in 2000–01. On that measure, the rich had never been better off. However, from then onwards, the billions of pounds which Brown allocated to tax credits for those on low earnings, along with an increase in means-tested benefits for pensioners and rapid growth in public-sector employment, started to have an impact. The gap between rich and poor closed a bit and returned to levels Labour inherited from John Major.

Even so, by the standards of most of the years since the Second World War, Britain was still an unequal place. And, latterly, inequality has actually increased again. In 2005–06, for the first time in many years, the pattern of income growth replicated what went on during the Thatcher years, with the richest fifth of the population seeing the highest income rise, and pay increments becoming progressively smaller for the lower-income groups. There has even been a deterioration in the measure of equality on which the Labour Government has performed best. That is the 90:10 ratio, which is the ratio of incomes between those at points 90 and 10 in a classification of earners from 1 to 99, where point 1 is the 1 per cent of the population who earn least and point 99 is top of the heap.

The 90:10 ratio tells an important story about the distributive impact of the policies of Gordon Brown and Tony Blair. For most of their time in office, they have given a significant boost in income to those who are not quite the poorest in the land, at a cost of a deceleration in earnings growth for those who are not quite the richest. If that were the test of being a modern socialist, then Brown and Blair passed it – though, whether by accident or design, they have failed to stem the impoverishment of the very poorest or the enrichment of the super-rich. But even their funny version of socialism, which pretends that the very richest and the very poorest don't really exist, was nowhere to be seen from the end of 2005 or so. Since then the poor have become relatively poorer again on the 90:10 ratio and as measured by most other yardsticks.

The really striking social phenomenon under New Labour has been the triumph of the super-rich. To be clear, it is a worldwide phenomenon and not something unique to the UK. But the presence on British soil of a disproportionate number of immensely wealthy people, who are becoming wealthier by the minute, has been encouraged by Tony Blair and Gordon Brown. They have nurtured a welcoming environment for billionaires of any nationality, who can live in the UK and pay relatively little tax thanks to benign rules for those who classify themselves as domiciled or resident in another country (usually a tax haven) for purposes of paying tax. And Brown as Chancellor was, as a matter of deliberate policy, strikingly generous to the City's new plutocrats – the owners of hedge-fund and private-equity firms, the partners of Goldman Sachs – by cutting from 40 per cent to 10 per cent the tax they pay when selling their more important assets.

Under Gordon Brown and Tony Blair, there has been an extraordinary increase in the income of the top 1 per cent of earners, an even bigger increase for the top 0.5 per cent, and a still bigger rise for the top 0.01 per cent. Brown's Britain, the UK of New Labour, has been very heaven for those in a whole range of businesses and industries where the talent of individuals is rewarded in tens of millions of pounds. At the apex of the income scale, what has been going on is a supercharged version of the trends promoted by Thatcher. The rate of increase in remuneration rises almost exponentially as you subdivide that top 1 per cent into smaller and smaller groups on higher and higher earnings. In this jungle where the super-predators feast best, some 30,000 people earn more than £500,000 per annum, or the proverbial million dollars at current exchange rates, and their average income is £1.1m (according to an analysis by David Goodhart and Harvey Cole in the August 2007 edition of *Prospect* magazine). They are the top 0.1 per cent of British earners with a combined income of £33bn, or about 4 per cent of all personal earnings in the UK. On those figures, Britain is a much less equal place than France, where this top 0.1 per cent scoop half as much, or 2 per cent of all personal income. But the UK is still more equal than the US, where the gap between rich and poor is at its widest for more than 60 years, with the highest-earning 0.1 per cent taking 6 per cent of personal income, and the top 1 per cent taking a remarkable 21.2 per cent of economic output.

Such figures give only a skewed picture of individual life-chances in those countries, and of whether their economies are constructed in a way that most of us would think fair. Those statistics say nothing about equality of opportunity or social mobility – about how easy it is to break out of poverty. However, that £33bn earned by 30,000 British individuals is, by any standards, a big number. It is, for example, considerably more than the value of the entire economy of Vietnam, a country with a population of 84m.

That said, it could be misleading to rely on just one set of statistics, because the super-rich are so adept at hiding offshore for tax purposes much of what they own or what they earn. So here are a few other snapshots of rich Britain. As one example, it became an accepted truth, cited even by the Deputy Governor of the Bank of England, Sir John Gieve, that 4,200 people in the City of London pocketed £1m or more in bonuses during the financial year 2006–07. Meanwhile, the form guide to the fortunes of the super-rich, the *Sunday Times* Rich List, estimated that in 2007 there were 68 billionaires living in the UK. And you needed at least £70m to be included in that newspaper's list of the 1,000 wealthiest people. The aggregated wealth of these 1,000 was £360bn, or about 50 times the size of the Uruguayan economy. It is also much more than treble what they possessed when Tony Blair became Prime Minister in 1997, in contrast to a doubling in the average net worth of the typical British citizen.

As it happens, I know many others who ought to be on that list but aren't, because they don't like flaunting what they've got. And there are thousands living in the UK who have a net worth of at least £10m. To give some idea of what might be called the democratization of riches, an annual survey by Merrill Lynch and Cap Gemini showed that in 2006 some 485,000 people in Britain had net financial assets of at least $1m (around £500,000). Extrapolating from global trends, their data indicates there may also have been around 5,000 individuals in the UK with net financial assets in excess of $30m (roughly £15m) – although, once again, that feels to me like a bit of an understatement. But according to this survey, the so-called 'high net worth' population – those whose financial wealth was more than a million dollars – increased by 8.1 per cent in 2006, double the rate of increase in Germany and a third faster than in France. British dollar millionaires are being created at more or less the same rate as in America, which would have been unthinkable just a few years ago.

We are reconstructing a UK where the share of national income taken by those at the pinnacle of the income scale is at levels not seen for a century. Research by the Centre for

Analysis of Social Exclusion showed that as long ago as 1999 the best paid 0.5 per cent and 0.05 per cent were pocketing almost as large a slice of national income as they were in 1937, having seen a steep decline that was dramatically reversed after 1979. Since then, there has been an almost unprecedented boom in earnings for hundreds of thousands of people, most of whom work in the City or in businesses connected to the City – although footballers, celebrities, entrepreneurs and corporate bosses have done pretty well too.

There are lots of other ways of showing this growing gap between the very rich and the rest. One way is to look at the ratio of bosses' pay to that of employees in general. An annual review by Income Data Services showed that the median total earnings of the chief executives of the FTSE 100 companies – the UK's 100 largest quoted companies – in the financial year 2005-06 was £2m, up 20 per cent on the previous year. (If you lined up chief executives and put them in order from lowest paid to best rewarded, the median would be the one right in the middle.) By contrast, the gross median pay for full-time British employees in April 2006 was £23,600, up a mere 3 per cent on the previous year. So the typical FTSE 100 boss earned 75.2 times what the typical employee was paid – and just one year's pay rise for that typical boss was £400,000, equivalent to 17 times the total pay of the typical employee. To put that into some kind of historical context, in 1989 the average (not median) pay for senior directors running the top 10 per cent of British companies was £222,000 (according to a survey by the Institute of Directors and the Reward Group), when the median pay for employees was £11,648. So, less than 20 years ago, the ratio of bosses' pay to that of the employee was 19:1. Since then, pay for the majority of employees has just about doubled, whereas bosses' pay has risen by a factor of 9. And there is reason to believe that the income gap will widen further. In an international market for senior managers, the US determines where we are going on remuneration: right now, US chief executives earn 300 times what the average US worker makes.

But those who run our largest companies, the members of the FTSE 100 index, are not by any means the best paid in the UK. And since there aren't that many of them anyway (though you wouldn't guess that, given all the media attention devoted to exposing their allegedly excessive remuneration), they don't feature much in this book. Among the new generation of plutocrats they're pretty low down the hierarchy. The high-earning elite is to a large extent found in the financial sector, where a combination of globalization and a technological revolution has allowed a talent for making money to be rewarded in ways that are breaking all known barriers. Millions of pounds, tens of millions, even hundreds of millions are accruing to brainy individuals who create and trade almost incomprehensible new financial products. These individuals may have the nous to spot and buy entire companies that are undervalued. Or they may be computer whiz-kids who build complex computer programs to exploit minute, temporary anomalies in financial markets. The best-paid director of a British FTSE 100 company is actually the number two at Barclays, the 'president' of the bank, Bob Diamond, who runs all its investment banking and fund-management businesses. He earned £22m in 2006 and has accumulated shares in the bank worth at least £70m. However, there are several executives at the world's most successful investment bank, Goldman Sachs, who earn more than that. And there are hundreds of people in London working in hedge funds and private equity making that kind of money every year. A couple of partners of a UK-based hedge-fund firm called GLG, Noam Gottesman and Pierre Lagrange, have been reported by the house magazine of the hedge-fund industry, *Institutional Investor's Alpha*, to have earned £120m each in 2006 – although that was paltry compared with the billion dollars plus pocketed by a handful of their US-based rivals. Also, a few individuals are generating hundreds of millions of pounds for themselves as more or less sole traders in the business of buying and selling entire companies. The most successful of those is Sir Philip Green, owner of Bhs, Topshop and quite a lot of the rest of the high street, who paid himself a tax-free dividend of £1.2bn in

2005 (technically the dividend went to his non-resident wife, to avoid the payment of tax).

The forces at work are powerful and global. It is not just happening in the UK but all over the world, especially in the US, Russia, India and China. In a way it's wrong to look at this trend in terms of nationality in any sense. These inordinately wealthy people are British, or American, or Russian in name, but they are essentially stateless, living where the taxes are lowest and where the opportunities to increase their net worth are greatest. For a variety of reasons – technological, regulatory, economic – increasing amounts of wealth are sticking to individuals with special talents rather than being dispersed to the owners of public companies or being siphoned by the state in the form of tax. That's true whether you are a footballer born in Madeira, like Cristiano Ronaldo, or an Indian steel magnate, like Lakshmi Mittal, or a British hedge-fund superstar whose father was a car mechanic, like Chris Hohn. Why is that? Well, capital was – until the meltdown in money markets in the summer of 2007 – plentiful and cheap for those who could demonstrate they could make big profits in the way they deploy that capital. In the UK, for example, Philip Green was able to borrow £10bn from the world's biggest banks for his failed attempt to buy Marks & Spencer, with minimal negotiation and with few strings attached. What counted for the lenders was his track record of making fortunes from buying and selling other businesses.

And the marketplace for an individual's talents – whether as a manager or an inventor or a performer – is the whole world, which means that the returns generated by the relevant talent can be huge. Take David Beckham. The 'Beckham' brand is a global brand: his name sells more around the world by a substantial margin than that of his new employer, the Los Angeles Galaxy. That's why he can negotiate a contract with his Californian football club supposedly worth £125m to him. And it's why a hard-nosed financier such as Philip Green is prepared to pay millions of pounds to the supermodel Kate Moss to borrow her brand for use at his fashion chain, Topshop.

Also, many of the newly created businesses can go global remarkably rapidly. Based in the UK, Permira – a private-equity firm that buys and sells whole companies – has in just a few short years become an international powerhouse controlling many billions of pounds, even though it employs just 103 professional staff. Faster still has been the wealth creation among the younger generation of internet businesses, the Web 2.0 gang, from You-Tube to MySpace to Facebook.

In other words, globalization has been wonderful for anyone with a special talent capable of generating incremental revenues. The crucial word here is 'incremental'. If you can demonstrate that you have the magic to generate additional revenues, then you can do very nicely. The reason is that the market for the fruits of your talent is bigger than it has ever been. That market is the whole world. There are, of course, still regional and local markets. But, for many products and services, an almost seamless, all-day-and-all-night, worldwide marketplace with billions of customers has been created by the internet and the dismantling of barriers to trade. The rewards of succeeding in that marketplace, for a multinational maker of snacks, or a social-networking website, or a football club with a brand, are immense.

There are two sorts of winners in the transcontinental souk. There are those who make millions by demonstrating to an established business – from Goldman Sachs, to Tesco, to Manchester United – that they can make a difference to corporate success or failure. These can include bankers, or engineers, or footballers, or professional managers. But the enormous spoils accrue to those who do it for themselves, by going direct to the market as owners rather than employees. They might do this by setting up a new financial business, such as a hedge fund or a private-equity firm, or – like Mark Zuckerberg at Facebook – by seeing the international potential of an online meeting place for university students.

But precisely the same trends are terrible news for those with no special skills. Builders and cleaners in the UK are being undercut by migrants from Poland or Slovakia. And a British cleaner had better hope that the company which employs him or her is not taken over by a private-equity house – because in that case the pressure to work harder for the same basic pay becomes remorseless, while the new owners scoop a gigantic jackpot. The best that a British cleaner can hope for is to become more productive in order to keep his or her job, all the while hoping that inflation in many of the basics of life, such as food, energy and housing, leaves something left over for pay TV and a mobile phone. Recently, according to research by the supermarket group Asda, those hopes have been cruelly crushed, as price rises in the essentials have squeezed the living standards of thousands and thousands of low-paid people.

What is worse is that the bar is being raised all the time for what qualifies as an economically useful skill. It is a cliché that manufacturers in the Midlands have been, and are being, squeezed by Chinese rivals – though it can be highly profitable to own a basic business in low-growth, high-cost Europe if your special genius is driving down costs. Lakshmi Mittal has become a billionaire many times over by becoming the very biggest in a very basic industry – steelmaking – and ruthlessly increasing the productivity of his European operations. But even being talented at software development and maintenance is no guarantee of a decent income, as Asian universities crank out armies of maths and engineering graduates. In the worldwide battle for economic supremacy, it's best not to be cannon fodder – but the qualifications for becoming a general or even a captain are becoming more demanding all the time.

But even if there is a global inevitability to this widening in the gap between haves and have-littles, for the first time in my career I'm finding myself rather less enthusiastic to be a cheerleader for the uber-capitalists. The sums of money now accruing to top talent, especially in financial services, have become absurdly large. Significant numbers of individuals are earning in a single year sums that they would not be able to spend in a lifetime, or indeed the lifetimes of their children and children's children. Well-heeled dynasties are being created in a way that we've not seen since the Victorian era.

Why should any of us care? For one thing, it's not healthy for democracy. The new super-rich have the means through the financing of political parties, the funding of think tanks and the ownership of the media to shape Government policies or to deter reform of a *status quo* that suits them. More or less whenever I talk to a minister or a Tory politician or a senior civil servant, I observe a neurosis on their part not to do or say anything that might upset the wealthy, that might prompt one or two of the super-rich to stomp off in a huff to another country. It could, for example, be expensive for Labour as a political party to upset many in the City by imposing seriously higher taxes or tougher regulations on the operation of hedge funds and private equity in a way that curtailed their profitability, even if there was a strong public-interest reason for doing so. How so? Well, since 2001, the private-equity doyens Sir Ronnie Cohen and Nigel Doughty have contributed £1.8m and £1.005m respectively to Labour, the former Goldman Sachs partner John Aisbitt has given £750,000 and the hedge-fund executive William Bollinger has handed over £510,000. Tony Blair decided it was preferable for Labour to be financially dependent on wealthy individuals than on the party's trade union founders; but both forms of dependence can create conflicts of interest in the formulation of policy.

Perhaps more dangerous for democracy would be the potential mischief-making of the bored offspring of those who generated the great fortunes. They may have strong ideas about how whole countries should be run, and would have the economic muscle to turn ideas into influential campaigns.

But the biggest cost from the swelling of the super-rich class is an erosion of the fabric that holds together communities and the nation. The plutocrats who live here behave as though the UK is permanently on probation. They pay the least amount of tax they possibly can, a fraction in percentage terms of the tax most of us pay on the income we earn. They rarely allow themselves to be comfortable in their Britishness, whether they have been born here or have adopted the country. And they would never surrender their right and ability to move somewhere else should the financial tariff for staying in the UK rise above an unspecified threshold. What's more, Gordon Brown's actions when Chancellor underpinned this idea of the super-rich doing us all a favour by living here, since he very carefully shied away from ever alienating them; which explains in part why the burden of tax increases has fallen on the vast majority who are not quite wealthy enough to relocate to Monaco or the Caymans.

Brown may be right that the presence on British soil of wealthy entrepreneurs who pay little tax in their own right is beneficial, in that they create or expand businesses and employment. But it is demeaning to the authority of the state and insulting to the majority of taxpaying citizens that so little in tax is collected from them. Many of the super-rich actually feel it is their moral duty *not* to pay tax. This is not malicious hearsay. I know these guys pretty well, and they regularly moan about paying any tax. But whatever you think about the waste and inefficiency of public services – and I would certainly be one of those who would criticize Gordon Brown and Tony Blair for failing to make the public sector demonstrably more efficient while pumping huge amounts of cash into it – my strong conviction is that no one should use a club's facilities who is not prepared to pay the subscription fee. Here's the point. Any particular wealthy individual may have used state schools and hospitals when growing up. Or their employees may still use them. And their ability to generate wealth today depends in large part on the stability of the state and an expensive physical infrastructure. All of which costs money. So their determination to make the least possible contribution to what underpins their ability to enrich themselves – not even paying Gordon Brown's slashed, paltry rate of capital gains tax – is grotesquely selfish.

One group who wholly legitimately avoid paying much tax are those that live here but claim that they are non-domiciled for tax purposes. In order to qualify for this privilege they would typically have been born abroad – but these 'non-doms' have frequently lived in the UK for decades and some have generated impressive fortunes from a UK base. They include financial supporters of the Labour Party, such as the private-equity pioneer and friend of

Gordon Brown, Sir Ronald Cohen (whose colleagues say that he pays substantial tax in the UK on his British earnings, even though he is a non-dom) and Chai Patel, the healthcare entrepreneur. Our rules on the treatment of these notionally foreign individuals are more benign than those of most other developed economies. I can be confident of this because relevant billionaires have told me so. In theory, non-doms are supposed to pay tax to Revenue and Customs on their earnings generated in the UK, though there are clever ways around this and they can almost always avoid capital gains tax. According to Treasury figures, around 25,000 non-doms pay no UK income tax at all (there is no suggestion that Cohen or Patel are among the zero-tax non-doms).

Here are a few other relevant statistics, which imply that they run rings around the tax man. Some 112,000 individuals indicated on their self-assessment tax returns for the year to April 2005 that they are not domiciled in the UK for tax purposes. That's 72 per cent more than in 2002 – which may reflect the expansion of the City and is a pretty stupendous growth rate. Now those 112,000 were liable to tax in 2004–05 of about £3bn on taxable income of £9.8bn, according to the Treasury. That may seem quite a lot of wonga, but it equates to an average tax liability per non-dom of just £27,000 on declared income of £90,000 a year. In other words, they are being taxed as though they were middle-ranking civil servants, not successful wealth creators. The Treasury says the reason for the relatively low yield of tax per non-dom is that many are not particularly wealthy or well paid. Many of them, it claims, are foreign doctors or even nurses recruited by the National Health Service. Which is probably correct. But the Treasury also acknowledges that a significant number are very well-remunerated temporary émigrés working in investment banks, private-equity firms and hedge funds.

There was a time when Gordon Brown was hell-bent on cracking down on the non-doms and also on those British-born people who continue to operate businesses and own assets in the UK but become resident offshore for tax purposes. But, around 2002, his zeal to tax them on their total worldwide earnings evaporated – largely because he became persuaded that the non-doms, especially those in financial services and the City, were making an important contribution to the economy. He became anxious that merely insisting the super-wealthy pay the tax that most of the rest of us pay – such as the top 40 per cent rate of income tax on all their global earnings and 10 per cent on realized capital gains – would lead to a flight of valuable capital and brains abroad.

However, if they weren't to flee these shores, the sums that could be raised from them would be quite something. If the wealth of the UK's 1,000 wealthiest on the *Sunday Times*'s list were rising at 10 per cent per annum – and it's probably been increasing more than that – and if Her Majesty's Revenue and Customs could get its hands on just 10 per cent of the capital gain as and when crystallized, and could also secure 40 per cent of the income earned by these individuals, the 1,000 would be paying about £12bn per annum in direct taxes or about £12m each every year. What these individuals actually pay is a fraction of that. In 2006, the accountants Grant Thornton estimated that 54 UK-based billionaires were paying income tax of just £14.7m on a combined fortune of £126bn and only a tiny number paid any capital gains tax at all. Of these, at least 32 of the billionaire dynasties had probably not paid any personal taxes on their wealth.

The difference between what they pay and what they perhaps ought to pay, if the tax rules that applied to most of us also applied to them, would run to billions of pounds. Capturing these billions would not transform the public finances. But they would allow a useful cut in the basic rate of income tax or even in the top rate of income tax – which, in theory, would be good for wealth creation in the UK, in providing stronger incentives for all of us to work more and accumulate more.

However, for years both Labour and the Tories were too afraid of the super-wealthy – or too close to them – to campaign that they should pay their fair share of tax. Senior politicians of both parties have been fearful that they could be painted by the media (much of it owned by the super-rich) as somehow 'anti-success'. And they tend to enjoy being in the company of business winners. Tony Blair, when he was Prime Minister, valued the friendship of successful business magnates, from Rupert Murdoch to Charles Dunstone, the founder of Carphone Warehouse. Both parties also benefited from the generous donations of fabulously wealthy individuals – which they would not have wished to jeopardize. But overlaying all of this is that mainstream politicians accept as a fundamental truth that there is an inverse relationship between the amount of tax that could be raised from the super-rich and economic activity: it is seen as self-evident that the world's most talented entrepreneurs would relocate themselves and their businesses offshore to a more benign taxation environment if they were asked to pay the same proportionate amount of tax as the rest of us.

That fear of the economic costs outweighing any immediate gain in tax revenues is almost impossible to prove or disprove. It is certainly the case, for example, that some of the hedge funds that have been created in the UK provide a surprising amount of high-skilled, high-remunerated employment in London, which at a stroke could go elsewhere. The hi-tech trading floors of CQS or Marshall Wace, which I have visited, are filled with lots of people who spend money and pay taxes in the UK. And if those businesses were moved to Geneva, or Dublin, as they could fairly easily be, the jobs would be gone too. But the politicians' fear of this flight may well have lost a sense of proportion.

There has also been a cynicism in this Government's exploitation of one of the harsh realities of globalization, which is that millions of people on middling incomes in middling jobs do not have the clout to demand tax reductions that the super-rich have or that big companies have. Only a limited number of very big businesses or stunningly talented entrepreneurs can actually up sticks to anywhere in the world, if the tax rates here are not to their liking. So tax increases have tended to be directed towards those who cannot escape them: the most important measure in Gordon Brown's last Budget as Chancellor in 2007 was to cut corporation tax for big companies, to deter them from moving abroad, while increasing it for small companies, most of whom would find it almost impossible to emigrate.

Even so, politicians in all parties began to spot in 2007 that much of the electorate was becoming exasperated at how little was being paid by those making enormous sums. The turning point was the remark to the *Financial Times* by a senior and respected provider of funds to private equity, Nick Ferguson, to the effect that it wasn't really cricket for his cleaner to be paying more tax than those pocketing millions in a particular corner of the City. Ferguson's cleaner became a totem of the unfairness of the system. It is not overstating the matter to say that his cleaner panicked the Treasury into reforming the entire system of capital gains tax (CGT) that was in part responsible for the injustice. Treasury officials discussed plans to increase CGT explicitly in terms of the 'Ferguson premium'.

But in the end the Treasury used a sledgehammer to crack a nut. In the pre-Budget report of 2007, the new Chancellor, Alistair Darling, announced there would be an 18 per cent rate of capital gains tax for everyone. By doing so, he infuriated hundreds of thousands of small businessmen who had created proper businesses over many years of toil and were now being told that the tax they would pay when selling all or part of their life's work would rise by 80 per cent. The Treasury claimed that the tax being paid by those explicitly in Ferguson's sights, the partners of private-equity firms who can make millions when assets are sold by their funds (what is known as their 'carried interest' or 'carry'), would also see an 80 per cent tax rise. But in the furore, one rather important detail was widely ignored. The Treasury had totally rejected the argument of principle about the 'carry', which is that it has the characteristics of income rather than capital gain and should perhaps be taxed as such at 40 per cent. Once again, the Treasury had bent over backwards to protect the high earners in the private-equity industry, because it was persuaded that they were great for Britain and would move abroad within seconds if forced to pay 40 per cent tax.

The partners of private-equity firms tell me that they are more than happy paying 18 per cent. Apart from anything else, most won't pay as much as 18 per cent even if they are UK taxpayers, thanks to the way they construct their deals. And a good many of them are not UK taxpayers.

To be crystal clear, Darling had mollycoddled the private-equity industry again. And, in a second sense, he did it once more in the way that he belatedly took action to extract a bit more tax from non-doms and non-residents. Darling, an immensely cautious politician, had come to recognize that the non-dom had become a distasteful character for many voters, and not only among Labour supporters. In fact, he has been accused of shamelessly stealing from the Tories in respect of the non-dom reform. It was striking how on 1 October 2007, the Shadow Chancellor, George Osborne, announced that a Tory Government would impose an annual levy of £25,000 on all those who register for non-domicile status, which would be on top of whatever other tax the non-doms pay to the Exchequer. It was a bold initiative for a Tory party which had been financed for years by donations from non-doms and those not resident here. But Osborne had been aware for months that his party's core middle-class vote was increasingly fed up at what it perceived as the free ride being given to the rich. This was quite a shock for a Labour Government which in theory was more committed to redistribution through the tax system than the ostensibly right-wing opposition. Darling responded by announcing a very similar non-dom levy, one that was just a bit higher at £30,000. But once again, the party founded by industrial trade unions bent over backwards to keep the City and private equity sweet. The levy would only apply to those resident in the UK for seven years. So the high-earning clever-clogs financiers working for global banks and financial firms, who come to London for just a few years before relocating to New York or Tokyo, could continue to be non-dom at no additional cost at all.

That was no accidental omission. By design of a Labour premier, Gordon Brown, and a socialist mayor, Ken Livingstone, London is now the capital city of the borderless world of the super-rich. But the reinvention of Britain as a giant tax haven also brings costs, for all the contribution of the immensely wealthy to economic growth (which is real, though often exaggerated). I shall look at the longer-term costs in the final chapter of this book. But among the conspicuous immediate annoyances for the majority of Britons is the inflation generated in the price of residential property – which has created wealthy ghettoes in parts of London and the south-east where no one earning less than a few hundred thousand pounds per annum can contemplate living. The ratcheting up of all property prices, stimulated by the prohibitive pricing at the top of the housing market, has contributed to the exclusion of younger people and those on low earnings from home ownership in vast swathes of the country.

That is a small example of a modern paradox: at a time of unprecedented prosperity, young people face greater financial uncertainty than they have for decades and many of those in middle age and on middle incomes would be justified in believing that the current economic and stock-market boom had passed them by. In Chapter 7, I explore the collapse of a British private-sector pensions system that had been the envy of the world. The super-rich may be effortlessly becoming richer, but millions of people have been obliged to contribute more cash than they have ever done to guarantee even a modest income in retirement. And, what's more, some of the hard-pressed company pension schemes that were once a model of enlightened paternalism are now being transferred to specially created new companies backed by the super-rich – who see in them an opportunity to make a fortune for themselves, though not for pensioners. There is something unseemly in the way that the retirement hopes of millions of people – who have saved all their lives – can be bought and sold as though they were no different from Mars Bars.

But the point of this book is certainly not to argue that free markets are in general a bad thing. The chapter on the travails of Royal Mail (Chapter 9) is something of an indictment of the Government's refusal to privatize the postal service. What the book tries to do is provide a tourist's guide to a new world in which financial opportunities are limitless for a minority of individuals with specific talents. The chapter on private equity (Chapter 2) tells you how to make a couple of billion out of buying and selling entire companies, while the ones on hedge funds (Chapters 5 and 6) are about how the world's brainiest mathematicians and scientists are designing computer programs to beat financial markets rather than finding a cure for cancer. You can rail against what you may perceive as a waste of talent. And you may be infuriated that billions of pounds are being hoovered up by a few individuals, rather than being deployed to alleviate poverty. Or you may simply decide that you would rather join them than beat them – and will therefore endeavour to acquire the analytical skills and ruthlessness that might ultimately secure your entry to the plutocracy.

However, the Philip Green story (Chapter 3) shows that natural flair accounts for the difference between an entrepreneur who makes a few bob and one who makes a few billion pounds. And, indeed, some of that flair may be genetic – which is sobering. Just look at what has been achieved by the Tchenguiz brothers, Robbie and Vincent, whose family has within their lifetime been driven by turmoil in the Middle East from Iraq to Iran and then from Iran to here. With no roots in the UK, but buckets of drive and charm, they generated hundreds of millions of pounds, first through property investment and more latterly by buying and selling whole companies. But although in one sense they created their own respective business empires from very little, they come from a long line of Middle Eastern Jewish traders: Robbie Tchenguiz told me proudly that his great-grandfather owned and worked 2,000 camels along the main Arab trade routes. At the time of writing, a number of Robbie Tchenguiz's more ambitious investments were not performing brilliantly. The turmoil in financial markets took a toll. But his story remains one of remarkable personal reinvention a world away from his birthplace.

But I do not believe that conventional public companies – in which millions of us have stakes through our pension funds – are condemned to wither and die, that there is no future for businesses listed on stock markets rather than owned by wealthy individuals or by private equity. In a world of growing competition, there are problems with the stock-market model of ownership that has served us relatively well for decades. In a nutshell, there is a question about whether the traditional split between ownership and management in a stock-market-listed business allows those businesses to react speedily enough and boldly enough to the growing challenges and threats they face. The great advantage of ownership by private equity or by Philip Green is that if a serious problem at their respective businesses requires fixing, there is no need for lengthy agonizing about how shareholders would react before action is taken. Philip Green is both owner and manager, so if he wants something done, it is done; and the power to take decisions is only marginally more diffuse at a private-equity-owned firm. By contrast, chief executives of listed companies have relatively little time to actually run their businesses, because they have to devote vast effort and resources to communicating financial results and strategy to thousands of shareholders – who want to know everything but are rarely prepared to provide any guarantees of support to those managers, and who rarely speak with a single, coherent voice. Little wonder that private equity can recruit the very best executives. Even so, the crisis of confidence at publicly listed companies can be overcome. They can thrive again under determined, motivated leadership, as shown by the gloriously theatrical events at Marks & Spencer over the past decade (Chapter 4).

M&S and other companies are being shaken up and revitalized in part to ward off the threat of being captured by a Philip Green or a private-equity firm or to pre-empt pressure from hedge funds. So, in that sense, the rise of these new tools of the super-rich is a good thing. But what concerns me is the lack of serious public debate about how globalization and deliberate Government policy has empowered those with particular financial talents to make vast sums of money for themselves, while disempowering the rest of us.

The financial crisis of the summer of 2007 – manifested in the run on Northern Rock, the first run on a substantial British bank for 141 years – was a direct consequence of the pervasive and orthodox Anglo-American ideology that the liberalization of global financial markets is both intrinsically good and unstoppable. The extraordinary creativity of participants in these markets has spurred growth over many years, by directing money or capital to places where it can best be employed. But some time over the past two or three years, their success bred complacency. Innovation became malign: trillions of dollars of financial products were created and then sold to banks and investors, many of whom did not understand the risks they were taking on. It was not unlike a pyramid-selling scheme, which could be seen from the mass panic that took hold in August 2007 when a big French bank said it could not put a value on these products. At that moment, and for weeks afterwards, banks and other financial institutions became deeply reluctant to lend to each other. Why? Because in the climate of fear and uncertainty, it was rational for any individual bank to hoard its cash, even if it was irrational for the system as a whole.

When the going was good, investment bankers, hedge-fund managers and partners in private-equity firms all did very nicely from the bonuses and the capital gains and the fees generated by the frenetic manufacturing of deal after deal after deal. Many of them are now paying a price for failing to understand the risks they were taking on. But it is often a small price, in the form of reduced future remuneration. Don't weep for them. They have already extracted fortunes. It is most of us who are paying for their foolhardiness, as the pricking of a financial bubble they created has a negative impact on all our prosperity. Months, possibly years, may go by before banks are prepared to lend as freely as they had been doing. In a way, that is a good thing. Banks and other financial institutions were lending too much too cheaply, thus encouraging individuals and businesses to take on excessive debts. But in reducing how much they will lend, by increasing the cost of that debt, and in withdrawing credit completely from some borrowers stigmatized as poor risks, there will be pain for companies and consumers. The price of money is going up for all of us, and the economy is slowing down, because regulators and governments did not dare stop the over-exuberant behaviour of greedy traders, bankers and financiers. In fact, to an extent the Government encouraged the excesses of these super-rich individuals and their financial servants, because they were thought to be good for London and good for Britain. And, as of now, there is collusion between most politicians, bankers and investors to avoid asking the big question: has the freedom of investment banks, private-equity firms and hedge funds to buy and sell what they like, when they like, gone too far? That would be to threaten the return to full throttle, whenever it comes, of the most successful machine in the history of the world for expanding the clone army of the super-rich.

Now, I don't believe there is some secret conspiracy between plutocrats and governments to sustain a mutually beneficial status quo. But I do believe that politicians are too fatalistic about their ability to shape globalization – and naturally it is in the interest of the super-rich to encourage such fatalism, to have it widely believed that the current system is more or less the best available.

That said, there is a plausible argument that for all the growing concentration of money in fewer hands, we live in a world where power in a broader sense is more evenly and more fairly shared than hitherto. The internet has turned up the volume on the voices of millions of citizens – through blogs, social websites and online campaigns. And politicians and businesses are using ever more scientific methods to measure what voters want and then supply them with it. There is a question about the determination of what we think we want, which is well beyond the ambition of this book. But to argue that money and power are not connected would be absurd. Many of the new super-rich are not currently using their immense wealth to buy politicians and influence political decisions. That's largely because they are too pre-occupied with making themselves even wealthier. Even so, the dismal tale of the Labour Party's attempt under Tony Blair to reduce its financial dependence on the trade unions by raising money from wealthy supporters is a stark warning of how the credibility of the political system can be threatened when there is a perception of power and position being bought by the privileged few (Chapter 8).

And it would be to ignore all history to presume that the super-rich, or their trust-fund children, or their plutocratic children's children won't endeavour to convert a fraction of their fortunes into control of the media, sponsorship of lobby groups or seats in parliament. Their big financial boots will become big political boots. It is irrelevant whether you think that they will do ill or good with their new political power. The accumulation of vast wealth by a growing class of super-rich – who owe no allegiance to any state – is a regressive trend for the distribution of power. It will taint governance and distort democracy.

CHAPTER 2

THE ELIXIR OF BORROWED MONEY

When any of us buys a house and it rises in value, it's hard not to feel pleased. But there's no great sense of achievement, because over the last 15 years or so the price of all houses has risen in a fairly straight line. In fact, over the past decade, a typical British house has trebled in value. Over that time, it has required particular stupidity or bad luck to lose money on a house purchase. In other words, there is nothing terribly clever in making a profit on a house sale. And few of us would expect the Treasury to give special tax breaks to encourage each of us to buy and sell houses by the score. However, there is a bunch of clever financiers in London, New York and San Francisco who have been generating colossal profits doing something that is in a fundamental sense very similar to the way you and I generate a capital gain on the house we buy with a mortgage. They are the founders and partners of private-equity firms. And Gordon Brown, as Chancellor and as Prime Minister, has done all he can to make them comfortable in the UK – first with a generous tax break on the biggest part of their remuneration and then, when that became politically unsustainable, with a tax reform designed not to upset them.

So what do private-equity firms do? Well, although in detail their activities can seem bewildering and very complex, the essence is simple. They borrow money to buy companies, not a few shares in companies, but whole companies, in deals called 'buyouts'. In Britain, for example, the most famous private-equity firm, Kohlberg Kravis Roberts (or KKR), bought Alliance Boots (owner of Boots, the high-street chain of chemists we've all used since childhood) for £11.1bn in the spring of 2007. That was the biggest private-equity takeover in the history of the UK, for which KKR – and its partner, the pharmacy magnate Stefano Pessina – borrowed £9bn. A private-equity firm would then typically hold the acquired company in its portfolio of businesses for between two and five years, after which it would hope to sell it for a substantial profit. And thanks to the magnanimity of Gordon Brown when he was Chancellor, the tax that the partners of these firms have been paying on their share of this profit has been at most 10 per cent. In fact, due to clever tax planning, some pay just 5 per cent and others pay nothing at all.

You may think I am being silly, unfair or patronizing in comparing the daunting undertaking of buying a company like Boots with purchasing a house. But here is where the analogy is appropriate: it is in the use of borrowed money, or what private-equity and investment bankers call 'leverage'. This is how to think about it. Let's say you buy a house for £100,000 of your own money and it rises in value to £110,000 over the course of a year. If you were then to sell it, your percentage profit or return would be 10 per cent. But if you had bought it in the way that most of us would do, with a mortgage – well, then your return would go into the stratosphere. For example, if you borrowed £90,000 of the purchase price and used only £10,000 of your own money – which in City lingo would be your "equity" in the deal – then the sale at £110,000 would turn that £10,000 of equity into £20,000. In other words, you would make a return of 100 per cent on your personal investment. Borrowing money to finance an investment has a magical effect on returns. If the market is rising, the magical effect is to magnify the returns. That is why so many people have become dealers in buy-to-let properties. Although some may kid themselves they are doing it for the rental income, quite a number are buying and selling residential properties with their bank's money to generate a capital gain. But there's a catch. As hundreds of thousands of people found to their cost in the early 1990s, the magic can be quite deadly when there is a generalized fall in house prices. In a downturn, any house can quickly become worth less than the value of the outstanding mortgage, wiping out the equity in the house and destroying the owner's personal investment.

The important similarity between private-equity purchases of businesses and house-buying is in the use of borrowed money. During the halcyon private-equity years of the past two decades, the partners of private-equity firms have made huge personal fortunes – the American giants of the industry have become multibillionaires – in part because they used the simple technique of purchasing companies with borrowed money at a time when the value of all companies was rising and the cost of that debt was falling. Here is the analogous calculation to the house-purchase one. Let us say a private-equity firm buys a fictional company – we'll call it United Shoes – for £11bn with £9bn of borrowed money and £2bn of their own money. Actually, that £2bn typically comes from other investors in the funds they raise – and we will explore that nuance later. If they were then to sell United Shoes for £13bn, hey presto they have turned their £2bn investment into £4bn. And, under standard profit-sharing arrangements agreed with their investors, the partners in the private-equity firm would pocket 20 per cent of the £2bn profit, or £400m between them. Most of that £400m might be shared between just two or three senior partners, on which they would pay minimal tax. Not a bad day's work.

It is not that the private-equity profits are somehow undeserved or shameful. Some private-equity firms display real talent in the way that they improve the fundamental efficiency and growth prospects of a business, just as a superior buy-to-let investor will enhance the intrinsic value of a property. But, for many of them, their competitive advantage lies in their ability to persuade banks and other financial institutions to lend them stupendous sums. It is – of course – riskier and more stressful to buy a whole business than it is to buy a house. In a house, there is the plumbing and the dry rot and the insulation to worry about. But if you buy a company like Boots, there are 100,000 employees and product-liability issues and relationships with suppliers to keep you awake at night. That said, there is no great secret in the City about which businesses are fundamentally solid. And most private-equity firms take enormous pains to vet any business before buying it: they run away double-quick from any whose foundations do not look sound. The important point is that if stock markets happen to be on a strongly rising trend, as they have been for the past five years, the value of an acquired business will tend to rise even if that business is not managed outstandingly well. Or, to put it another way, a substantial proportion of the colossal profits made by private-equity firms over the past few years is no more the result of business genius than the profits made by someone who bought a house in central London in 2000 and sold it last autumn.

If there is a single point I want to get across here it is that many members of the super-rich have created their fortunes by borrowing money to buy assets at the right time. That is true of many private-equity firms. It is true of an individual tycoon, like Philip Green, who bought store groups at the start of the consumer boom. It is true of hedge funds, which use borrowed money to magnify any returns they make on their investments. Cheap debt – or leverage – has been the single most powerful tool of the new super-rich.

But in the summer of 2007, debt also became the great cloud hanging over the global economy. Throughout that year, financial institutions became increasingly anxious that they might have become too euphoric about private equity's apparently stunning successes. They became fearful that in the finance that they had been providing for private-equity deals – known as buyouts – they had been lending too much, too cheaply and with too few strings attached. Concerns were raised about whether these lenders had been taking false comfort from their ability to insure their loans against default using the special financial insurance of credit derivatives or credit default swaps. Initially, these concerns were not shared by the big banks. In what appears in retrospect to be an extraordinary example of greed-induced short-sightedness, the banks continued to lend billions and billions for the financing of private-equity deals, in the mistaken belief that they would then be able to sell on this debt in a repackaged form – as collateralized loan obligations, for example – to hedge funds, pension funds, insurers and other banks. What is more, they lent this money with fewer and fewer strings attached, in the form of 'covenant-lite' loans, which gave them diminished rights to seize control of a borrower or its assets in the event that it ran into difficulties.

Suddenly, in July 2007, there was a rude awakening when all the big banks found that no one wanted to take off their hands the loans they had made to private-equity deals. Try as they might, they simply could not sell on this debt. They were stuck with somewhere between \$300bn and \$400bn of this unwanted leverage or loans. Much of this unsellable debt related to US buyouts, but it also included billions of pounds of bank loans to Alliance Boots and to a merger of two British private-equity-owned companies: Saga (the financial services, travel and publishing group aimed at the over-50s) and the AA (the roadside-recovery business).

At the time of writing, attempts are being made to re-create a market for this private-equity debt. Some banks are trying to sell it to investors for prices below 100 cents in the dollar – which means that those banks are suffering a loss on those disposals. Even banks that are not selling are recognizing that they lent the money too cheaply and are therefore writing down the value of the loans in their balance sheets – which is their way of saying that they have been stupid and expect to make losses on these loans. Collectively, the banks which made these loans – led by the world's biggest bank, Citigroup, and also including UBS, JP Morgan Chase, Barclays and Royal Bank of Scotland – will suffer billions of dollars in losses, probably somewhere between \$10bn and \$20bn in aggregate (my estimate is that they will lose around £13bn). And note that those specific losses stem only from the foolishness of the banks in providing the credit too cheaply. They are in effect suffering from an adjustment in the market price of debt. If any of the actual buyouts, the acquired companies, were one day to run into difficulties – which well they might in a prolonged or severe economic downturn – then the losses on loans could escalate painfully.

Until the banks have cleared their books of this debt, none of them are prepared to provide new substantial loans to private-equity firms wanting to make big takeovers. Which means that, for now at least, the private-equity deal binge has come to a juddering halt. It is as though an entire, enormous financial industry has gone on an extended sabbatical. The partners of private-equity firms had been manically, frenetically busy over the previous few years. Now, in their offices in Mayfair or St James's, they seem to have all the time in the world to chat. It is almost as though they are living in a ghost town after a gold rush.

THE NEW ROCK AND ROLL

How different it all seemed in January 2007. London had probably never seen more wealth gathered in one place. The eminences of British private equity, together with their lawyers and bankers, had – for the first and perhaps only time – gathered together to celebrate their mutual success and to 'give something back'. The glittering throng met on 24 January 2007 at north London's magnificently refurbished performance venue, the Roundhouse – which was famous in the 1960s for dope-infused, avant-garde, psychedelic circus and rock, and now supplements its income by selling hospitality to Britain's uber-class of pluto-crats. What a symbol of a changing Britain and a changing world. It would be tempting to say that it's not rock and roll, but that's not true either – since U2's Bono has become a substantial investor in a private-equity fund, Elevation Partners, which in 2006 bought a 40 per cent stake in Forbes, publisher of the monthly magazine that celebrates, calibrates and ranks the wealth of the plutocracy.

Many of those at the Roundhouse were worth several tens of millions of pounds each, some were worth comfortably more than £100m. According to one banker who was there, the collective net worth of attendees was well over £10bn. They were launching the Private Equity Foundation, a new charitable trust endowed by private equity's leading firms and individuals. It was part of a charm offensive by an industry that was suddenly attracting attention and criticism. The private-equity executives were demonstrating that some of the fat returns generated by their wholesale purchase of companies would be ploughed back into good causes. But the start-up funding received by the charity, of £5.1m, didn't look particularly generous in the context of the industry's colossal net worth. 'It was a bit of PR disaster,' says the banker. 'These guys have been in denial about how the world sees them. I'm not sure it particularly helped for them all to be out with their glamorous wives. But the food was pretty good for such a big affair.'

The real theatre was happening outside the Roundhouse, where members of the GMB trade union were handing out sick bags. For over a year, the GMB had been protesting on behalf of members who felt they were victims of the ownership of their respective businesses by private-equity funds. It was trying to raise awareness of job cuts at the AA, the roadside-breakdown business, after it had been bought by two private-equity firms, CVC and Permira, and of a factory closure at Birds Eye, the frozen-foods business owned by Permira. The trade unionists have focused much of their campaign on Damon Buffini, who was then the managing partner of Permira and has since been appointed chairman. They've put his face on posters, they've picketed him close to his home in south London, they littered Labour's last annual conference with leaflets alleging that he targeted the AA's disabled workers in a redundancy campaign (which he denies). They even took a live camel to his local church, to make a biblical point about rich individuals and the kingdom of heaven. So when Buffini left the Roundhouse that evening in search of a taxi to take him home (unlike many of his peers, he didn't go for the chauffeured limo, though he could afford a fleet of them), he wasn't surprised that his face was on the GMB placards.

But Buffini is hardly a traditional target for a trade union campaign of humiliation. He is the antithesis of lazy inherited privilege. Brought up on a council estate in the Midlands by a single mum, he's black and he went to local state schools – before winning a place at Cambridge University and then embarking on a long career at Permira, where he's become one of the most powerful capitalists in the UK as the head of Europe's largest private-equity business. An Arsenal-supporting family man, he lives in south London and does his best to lead a normal life, when he's not in some far-flung part of the world overseeing Permira's sprawling network of acquired businesses, whose value at the time of writing was €65bn (£46bn). It has been quite a career trajectory, and even the Prime Minister, Gordon Brown, is a Buffini fan. He has co-opted Buffini on to his Business Council for Britain – which brings together the UK's business superstars to advise him on how to improve the competitiveness of the UK – and on to the National Council for Educational Excellence, where business leaders discuss with educational representatives how schools can be improved.

Buffini himself was bowled over to be recruited to Brown's New Establishment. It demonstrated how both he and his industry had made it into the mainstream. However, he hates publicity and has given only one broadcast interview (an interview with me on the BBC's Today Programme in February 2007): he won't bow to pressure from his private-equity peers to become the figurehead for his industry. How easy it would be to cast Buffini as a role model for young, disadvantaged kids, who could see in him an alternative path to magnificent riches than that offered by Wayne Rooney or David Beckham. But he seems profoundly uninterested in becoming the pin-up for a can-do, new meritocratic UK, in which anyone can become wealthy beyond their wildest dreams. Perhaps it would be too much of a distraction from the day job.

CREATURE OF THE AGE

For all the passions aroused by the private-equity boom, it was largely the product of the market conditions of the past 15 years or so. Until 2007, the availability of capital increased exponentially and the cost of that money dwindled. There was an ocean of money available to private-equity firms (and hedge funds), which took two forms: equity from international investors for their funds; and various forms of debt. Although that is an important distinction – on which I shall elaborate – more important is that the price of all the forms of capital (with the occasional blip upwards) just kept on falling. It is analogous to the glut of cheap credit available to most of us as consumers, which saw the halving of the mortgage rate since the early 1990s.

As with hedge funds, private equity has benefited from what's often referred to as the 'search for yield' – or the desire of wealthy investors to earn more than the small returns available from lending to governments, which for a while was zero or close to zero in Japan and the US. Private equity's track record of earning superior returns looked terribly attractive in that context. That is why British-based private-equity firms were able to raise £34bn for investment in 2006, almost four times what they raised in 2003 (according to figures from the BVCA, the British Venture Capital Association). And US funds raised a breathtaking £152bn in 2006, up from £24bn in 2003. There are two important qualifications to make here. The first is that the £34bn would be the equity portion in the financing for any deal, so it buys companies worth a great deal more than £34bn. Equity is always augmented by debt, which may be between two and five times the value of the equity. So £34bn would buy businesses with an aggregate value well in excess of £100bn (just to provide context, Tesco – by far the UK's biggest retailer – has a market value of £36bn). It is why, until the credit crunch of the summer of 2007, it was fair to say that very few businesses were too big to be acquired by private equity.

There is a second important qualification, which is that money raised by UK firms would not necessarily be invested in the UK.

Permira, for example, buys companies all over the world. Equally, US funds – like Blackstone and Texas Pacific – frequently buy in the UK. So these numbers indicate the massive fire power of private equity – without saying terribly much about how many British businesses have been, or will be, bought by private equity.

In fact, for the 20 biggest UK private-equity groups, only 38 per cent of their investment was in the UK during 2004 to 2006. However, it still represented a significant investment. In that three-year period, the total value – including debt – of private-equity deals in the UK was somewhere between £80bn and £120bn (based on figures from the BVCA and the Centre for Management Buyout Research at the University of Nottingham). By the end of 2006, private-equity-controlled businesses employed some 1.2m people in the UK, or 8 per cent of UK private-sector employment. And, following the deal mania of the first half of 2007, which included the takeover of Alliance Boots, private equity now accounts for rather more of the British economy.

It is arguable, in fact, that private equity has for a few years been more important than the London Stock Exchange in supplying capital to businesses. A review published by the Financial Services Authority, the City watchdog, pointed out that in the first six months of 2006, UK-based private-equity fund managers raised £11.2bn of capital, but that companies coming to the stock market raised just £10.4bn from initial public offerings, or IPOs. However, there are cycles at work – and at the time of writing, in the aftermath of the credit crunch, the stock market is once again a more fruitful source of capital for big companies than private equity.

TWO AND TWENTY EQUALS FABULOUS RICHES

The giants of the private-equity industry are American firms, notably Blackstone, Texas Pacific, Carlyle and Kohlberg Kravis Roberts. In the US, even the division two firms, such as Apollo, Bain and Warburg Pincus, are pretty colossal. The grand-daddy is

KKR, which made billionaires of its three founders (two of whom, Kravis and Roberts, are cousins). It is still run by Kravis, one of the most influential financiers of the post-war years. For 18 years, KKR's 1988 purchase of RJR Nabisco for $31.4bn held the record for the world's largest-ever buyout – and it has been beaten only a few times and only very recently. Kravis's great rival is Steven Schwarzman, the founder of Blackstone. For years, the battle between KKR and Blackstone seemed a personal competition between Kravis and Schwarzman to create the biggest funds, carry out the biggest takeovers and take home the biggest number of billions of dollars. Schwarzman is probably slightly out in front right now.

In 2007, Blackstone raised a world-record $22bn for a new investment fund and it became the first of the elite private-equity firms to secure a stock-market listing for its management company. When floated on the New York Stock Exchange, Blackstone was valued at $32bn, valuing Schwarzman's personal stake at around $7.5bn. Schwarzman also pocketed more than $650m from the share sale, having earned $398m in the previous year. Oh, and Rod Stewart provided the cabaret at Schwarzman's 60th birthday party. Since the money-markets crisis of the summer, Blackstone's shares have performed poorly – and its revenues in the third quarter of 2007 were well below what analysts had hoped and expected. But Schwarzman can afford to sit and wait for the market to recover.

The third member of the global private-equity elite is Texas Pacific Group (TPG). A recent fund-raising document issued by TPG – whose headquarters overlook Alcatraz and the Golden Gate Bridge in San Francisco – show that it has generated a breathtaking $20.1bn from $7.2bn put into 67 investments, which is a return of 2.8 times. It employs 300,000 people in its assorted companies across the world and the combined revenue of these companies is $65bn.

However, in the UK and Germany it has rubbed up against the political establishment. Its ownership of Grohe, the German bath-room appliances and products business, meant it was dragged into the controversy in that country about the impact of international private equity and hedge funds on domestic industry – during which a leading politician branded such funds as 'locusts'. And in the UK, it received unwanted publicity through its ownership of Gate Gourmet, the airline catering business where a strike in August 2005 brought British Airways to its knees. The man who helped to facilitate a settlement of that industrial dispute – at the request of TPG's founder, David Bonderman – was Lord Stevenson, a businessman with fingers in more pies than most (he is governor of the Bank of Scotland and chairman of its holding company, HBOS; and he features in this book both as the chairman of the House of Lords Appointments Commission, whose rejection of three Labour nominees for peerages helped to precipitate the cash-for-honours police inquiry, and as an ally of Sir Philip Green in his bid for Marks & Spencer).

To digress momentarily, Sir Philip Green once retailed a vignette to me about private-equity egos. He and Bonderman – whom he had never met before – were giving a talk in October 2005 to students at Oxford University's Said Business School. During the question-and-answer session Green made a characteristic spur-of-the-moment decision to offer £500,000 to help finance the best business plans from students at the school. Green then said mischievously, in front of the audience, that he was sure Bonderman would match the offer. Bonderman was apparently stunned, taken aback by Green's bravado. Green extracted the cash from Bonderman when they talked later.

Only one British private-equity firm, Permira, is in the global premier league – though others, notably CVC and Apax, are not far behind. Established in 1985, Permira has, to date, raised €21.6bn ($32bn) in five separate funds for the acquisition of businesses. At the time of writing, companies currently in its portfolio employ more than 220,000 people, which puts it on a par with some of the world's very biggest companies. What's important for our purposes is that it has just embarked on a massive expansion phase, having raised €11.1bn or $16.3bn for the Permira IV Fund, Europe's largest-ever buyout fund. With that $16.3bn, it should be able to buy businesses worth $80bn (£40bn) in aggregate.

What can the investors in the Permira IV Fund expect to earn from Permira? Well, Permira says that after the deduction of all fees and costs, its funds have generated an internal rate of return of 33 per cent every year on average – which is vastly better than could have been obtained by investing in the stock market over the equivalent period. And, Permira claims that statistics demonstrate how it improves the quality of the businesses it buys, in that the unadulterated magnifying effect of borrowing or leverage would not have generated as much as 33 per cent per annum. Which is probably correct, although Permira has not supplied enough data on what it bought and when for me to be able to test its assertion. Even so, any investor in its fund would probably be profoundly grateful for 33 per cent, however it was achieved, and wouldn't begrudge Damon Buffini and his colleagues their rewards.

Not all British private-equity firms perform quite as well as Permira, according to data published by Calpers, the giant Californian public-sector pension fund, which invests heavily in them. One of Permira's great British rivals, CVC, has generated returns ranging from 19.7 per cent per annum to 41.7 per cent on three European funds launched between 1996 and 2001. And the performance of Permira's own funds is far from uniform. Calpers shows that one of Permira's funds, Permira Europe 1, has generated an annual internal rate of return of 74.5 per cent since it was launched in 1997 – which is stellar. The internal rate of return of a smaller UK fund launched a year earlier is 14.4 per cent – while a couple of others have been returning around 30 per cent a year. But on the basis of Calpers's extensive data, the performance of both Permira and CVC is good by international standards.

Permira, like all private-equity funds, does not disclose the remuneration of its partners and other executives. However, when I put it to Damon Buffini in an interview for the BBC that its charging structure was typical of the industry at around 2 per cent for an annual management fee and a 20 per cent 'carried interest', he didn't demur. So I'm going to do my sums on that basis. Also, I'm going to apply that charging structure simply to the new $16.3bn fund, and ignore the €10.5bn in other funds. So if all investors pay 2 per cent a year on $16.3bn, that generates a breathtaking $326m a year (or around £160m) to cover Permira's rent on its assorted offices, the salaries of its mere 103 professionals and partners, its IT expenses, research and so on. Even if I'm wrong, and Permira is actually charging 1.5 per cent a year, that's still £120m per annum. Now it's difficult to be sure where all the cash is going, because its head office in Covent Garden is distinctly unflashy. It's far less grand, for example, than most Government offices, such as the newish home of the Department for Environment, Food and Rural Affairs. On the other hand, Permira's utilitarian offices are unusual – those of the US private-equity giant Kohlberg Kravis Roberts just off Pall Mall, for example, are done up in the predictable *faux*-country-house style favoured by many financial firms. And Blackstone occupies some of the most desirable real estate in London, overlooking Berkeley Square.

But the big spoils come from the carried interest. Obviously, what it pays out depends on the gains made by the fund. But I'm going to be generous to Permira and calculate on the naive assumption that there won't be diminishing returns from the increased size of Permira's investments and the growing competition from its rivals. I shall assume that it will continue to make 33 per cent per annum net of costs for its investors. Depending on where Permira has set the hurdle rate of return that has to be passed before the carried interest kicks in, my estimate is that Permira's 28 partners (the top bananas in the firm) could expect to share £5bn in cash gains if the fund lasts about ten years. That's around £175m per partner from just the one fund – but, of course, the rewards would not be shared precisely evenly, and some would do better and some worse. It's not as much as Philip Green, but there's only one Philip Green.

CLEANING UP

Permira's Buffini manifests not a scintilla of doubt about the public benefits of what he and his peers do in the process of enriching themselves. He believes that businesses bought and reconstructed by private equity become more efficient, that their long-term growth prospects are enhanced, that for any short-term pain caused to employees while a company is knocked into shape there are future benefits in the form of improved job opportunities. He's not sentimental or emotional about the process of rehabilitation. If a loss-making division has to be closed, so be it. To him, it's dishonest to prop up an operation that can never thrive. And what remains should have a more prosperous future by concentrating its resources where it has a competitive advantage. Permira typically combines a ruthless drive to improve efficiency with investment to generate growth – as can be seen from the story of its ownership of Travelodge, the budget-hotel chain.

Permira bought Travelodge in early 2003 from Compass, the catering group, for £712m. Within a couple of years, it had sold its Irish hotels for £15m and raised around £400m by selling 135 freehold properties to a consortium led by Sir Tom Hunter, the tycoon philanthropist, with Nick Leslau, the property entrepreneur. In October 2005 it sold its weakest business, the chain of Little Chef roadside cafes, for £52m in cash. The disposal of the 235 restaurants came to look particularly shrewd, because in early 2007 Little Chef ran into serious difficulties. For reasons that are not altogether clear, Little Chef's apparent death throes became a matter of widespread public concern. There was a moral panic in the media about the possible disappearance of this post-war symbol of every household's dream to own a motor car. Eventually, a small private-equity house, R-Capital, rescued 200 of the totemic greasy spoons but 41 were closed.

In total, Permira raised about £500m from a series of asset sales, which presumably paid off the money it would have borrowed to buy Travelodge. So when in August 2006 it sold Travelodge to Dubai International Capital, a Middle Eastern private-equity firm, for £675m, it probably trebled the value of its initial equity investment, a 200 per cent return – although my hunch would be that it may have done even better than that. Was this a brilliant example of how Permira directs capital to businesses where under-valued assets can be liberated and operating performance can be improved by shrewder management and selective investment? Or was it an example of what trading unions have been lambasting as cynical asset stripping to yield a fast buck at the risk of weakening the fabric of the business?

Well, I am minded to give Permira the benefit of the doubt. Whatever its ability to spot a bargain, it does do a good deal more than buy cheap and sell dear. Under Permira's ownership, the management of Travelodge – led by the chief executive, Grant Hearn – significantly improved its operational performance and expanded the chain. It had 12,500 rooms in 2003. By 2006, that had increased to 20,000. And every room and public area was redecorated over 18 months. But perhaps more important were efficiency measures that seem trivial but can yield significant savings – and thus significantly enhance cash flow. Permira, for example, has given me data on Travelodge which shows that the time allocated for the cleaning of each room was reduced from 40 minutes to 25 minutes – which in theory would allow each hotel to operate with 40 per cent fewer cleaners. My back-of-envelope calculations are that for 20,000 rooms, an increase in cleaning productivity on that scale could save around £10m a year.

Also, Travelodge adopted the kind of computerized system used by budget airlines for making sure their flights are always packed (it's called a 'yield management system') – and there was a remarkable shift to the internet for bookings, from 17 per cent in 2003 to 73 per cent when the business was sold by Permira. Certainly, the new owner, Dubai International Capital, believes that Travelodge has great prospects for future growth (its chief executive, Sameer Al Ansari, talks of continuing 'an aggressive expansion plan').

There's nothing either heroic or scandalous about what hap-pened at Travelodge. It's a story of a business being managed better than its rivals and better than it had been under its previous owners, Compass, which is a large publicly listed company. So if that's what private equity does, why all the fuss? There are a bewildering number of possible answers. But I think the important ones are in fact implicit in Travelodge's rehabilitation – and they tend to be related to how the employees in companies bought by private equity frequently undergo massive and unsettling changes in their working practices for which the rewards go disproportionately to senior managers and owners.

Now, it looks to me as though in the relatively brief time they owned Travelodge, Permira and investors in its fund made a cash profit of around £450m. And under the normal division of spoils, the share for Permira's partners would be around £90m (though they would not necessarily pocket this immediately). What's more, thanks to the generosity of the Chancellor in cutting the rate of capital gains tax on such investments, Buffini and his colleagues would pay no more than 10 per cent tax on the millions they would each make from the deal (in practice, they would probably pay just 5 per cent, as a result of the way that notional costs are imputed to them).

Compare their rewards with the experience of the cleaners at Travelodge. As I mentioned, Permira says that the time taken to clean a room has been reduced from 40 minutes to 25 minutes. Grant Hearn, Travelodge's chief executive, tells me that the cleaning time is coming down to 20 minutes (as the cleaners learn from a specially made DVD produced by the company that shows them how to become super-cleaners). So the cleaners' productivity will have doubled, it will have improved by 100 per cent. But only a fraction of this improved productivity will have been distributed to the cleaners in the form of higher pay. That's inevitable in a market where there is no great shortage of cleaners – and it's either fair or unfair depending on whether you measure fairness according to the personal experiences of employed cleaners or the frustration of unemployed ones who would be prepared to work for less.

But what if the Travelodge cleaners were rewarded better than most? How would the tax system then treat them, how much of any increment would they have kept? The Government provides billions of pounds to augment the pay of those on low earnings, largely through tax credits. But, understandably, it provides less financial support to the young and single. If Travelodge's cleaners are in that category, they would have suffered from the abolition of the 10 per cent starting rate of income tax in the Budget of April 2007. Also, as a general rule, those on low pay can find themselves taking home less than 50p of every additional pound of pay they earn, because of the withdrawal of tax credits as income rises. So Travelodge's cleaners probably keep a much lower proportion of any incremental pay they make than Mr Buffini and his colleagues retain from their spectacular gains. Is that fair? Is it appropriate for the tax and social-security system to be tilted to that extent in favour of private-equity executives and against those earning least? A fatuous question, perhaps.

Here is another reason why the passions excited by private equity are understandable. It is about the sharing of risk and reward. When a company is acquired and is burdened with vast amounts of additional borrowings, the risks of it running into trouble increase a good deal. And if the company – heaven forfend – were to go bust, there would be damage for the private-equity firm which did the deal, for the investors who backed it, for the lenders, for the management and for the employees. To state the obvious, the employees would probably be out of a job. However, when these deals go well, the rewards for private-equity partners, for the investors, for lenders and for management tend to be generous, bordering on the lavish. But, except in rare cases where private-equity management is unusually enlightened, there are slim pickings for most employees, even when the business does superlatively well. Naturally, the job security of staff will increase and their pay should too. But only rarely are they able to acquire any meaningful investment in the reconstructed business – so they are excluded from the juiciest recompense. And that does not seem just, given that – whether they wanted to or not – they are forced to bear much of the increased risk taken on in the buyout. A relatively small group of executives at Travelodge, for example, enjoyed the fat rewards when it was sold by Permira. And what happened at Travelodge has been fairly typical (although there are signs that private-equity firms are at last taking steps to share at least a portion of the spoils with employees in the businesses they buy).

It offends against the British sense of fair play when the majority is excluded from even a sliver of the riches that they helped to generate. But, until recently, private-equity firms did not seem to notice – or, if they did, they decided fair play did not matter. What I have found shocking over many years of observing the leaders of this industry is that many – not all, by any means – view businesses in a very impersonal and blinkered fashion. For them, a company is property and chattels, and statistics about cash flows and market shares. Often there is little empathetic understanding of a business as a social institution wholly dependent on its people. The single-minded determination to pay off debts and earn a fabulous profit has a propensity to dehumanize the private-equity owners. To be fair to Permira, it does recognize its wider responsibilities, and is a supporter of an imaginative project, Breakthrough, to help the growth of enterprises with an explicit social objective. But, in general, there has been an unattractive, cold calculation to private-equity firms' style of acquiring businesses. And no one, not even the grandees at the companies they are thinking of buying, seems to be treated with much charm and warmth. One business leader, who knows the private-equity industry intimately, put it like this to me:

> They are ruthless. They'll say they want to buy a company, insist the company opens its books, create all sorts of uncertainty for management and staff. But if they see or smell anything they think is funny, they'll simply walk away. My advice to anyone dealing with private equity is: don't believe a word they say till it's written down in a legally binding document. [Interview with business leader, May 2007]

PRIVATE EQUITY'S GAIN IS OUR PAIN

The cold logic of their approach to running companies made private-equity firms more vulnerable to the GMB trade union's campaign against them. The GMB's complaints about the scale of cost-cutting and the handling of redundancies at the AA, for example, left a taint on its two owners, Permira and CVC. Which was partly their own fault, because they were hopeless at managing their public relations and – in an arrogant way – they refused to respond to the charges. They took the 'private' element of their nomenclature far too seriously. As it happens, the GMB may well have been motivated to an extent by its unhappiness that it no longer represented AA employees – it had been supplanted by a specially created trade union, the AA Democratic Union, and was fighting for official recognition by management. But the idea that Permira and CVC were caught in the crossfire of a trade-union turf war never entered the public consciousness, even though that was the firm belief of the AA's chief executive at the time, Tim Parker, and of Alistair Maclean, national secretary of the AA Democratic Union. Instead, the AA became associated with the notion that private equity was making a bundle from the fear and insecurity of its workforce.

For Parker, Permira and CVC, the criticisms of how they reorganized the AA and of the treatment of staff were unfair. Parker felt he was simply doing what was needed to ensure that the AA could prosper over the long term. He closed down loss-making operations, such as service centres, a vehicle-inspection unit and a tyre-fitting business. He invested in new kit for AA vans. And he put in place new working practices that permitted the patrolmen to go to the rescue of more customers during any shift. My view would be that the AA has probably emerged stronger from what he did. However, it turned out that innuendo about the spoils being reaped by Permira and CVC were – if anything – understated.

In June 2007, it was announced that the AA would be merging with Saga, the provider of assorted financial and travel services to the over-50s. The deal valued the combined businesses at

£6.15bn. For the owners of both the AA and Saga, that valuation would deliver a vast profit. The AA had been bought from Centrica, the owner of British Gas, in the summer of 2004. At that time, CVC and Permira each invested in the business around £250m from their funds. Less than three years later, that £250m had been turned into £890m – generating a profit for each of them of around £640m. They had more than trebled their money. As for Chaterhouse, the private-equity owner of Saga, it had done just as well. It bought Saga towards the end of 2004, a little after CVC and Permira had acquired the AA. It then turned just under £500m of investment into £1.73bn. Like CVC and Permira, Charterhouse had generated a return of around 3.5 times in less than three years. And, in theory, that is not the end of the spoils for the private-equity troika, since they have all reinvested some of their profits in the merged operation.

As I have already explained, 80 per cent of the gains on these deals goes to investors in the private-equity firms' funds and 20 per cent is the 'carry' taken by the partners of the firms. Now in the case of the AA/Saga deal, I estimate the partners of the three private-equity firms would share around £450m, a colossal amount. They would not pocket all of it immediately. Precisely when they receive it – and also how much per partner – depends on the arrangements they have with their investors. But a relatively small number of executives at CVC, Permira and Charterhouse will do very nicely indeed. Which highlights one of the basic problems for their industry. Although much of the criticism it faces is ill-informed, the sums being earned by the partners in the biggest firms is hard to put into any kind of context that makes the rewards seem reasonable to most of us.

The fat returns being earned from the takeovers of great British companies would perhaps seem less outrageous if the spoils were also going to millions of British people through their pension funds. And surely, if private equity is such a good thing, our pension funds would be channelling our hard-earned savings into it. As it turns out, this defence is not available. Take the new $14.2bn Permira fund, raised from 180 different investors. Of this, only 31 per cent came from pension funds, 45 per cent from other sorts of investment managers and 24 per cent from assorted financial institutions. But it gets worse. Although one of Permira's favourite statistics is that the largest single group of investor beneficiaries in Permira funds are teachers, it is not the whole story. Your children's teachers are not the beneficiaries. The teachers in question are American teachers, whose retirement plans are managed by American pension schemes. The point is that overseas pension groups and foreign investors supply most of Permira's investment capital. Very little of its funds come from the likes of you and me, very little comes from British pension schemes.

Permira's dependence on foreign funding is typical of its industry. According to the British Venture Capital Association, more than 70 per cent of funds flowing to UK private equity over the past six years came from abroad (or about £50bn of inward investment into private equity in total). And for the 20 largest British private-equity groups, 79 per cent of new funding came from outside the UK during 2004–06. So the purchase by private equity of British businesses represents a transfer of ownership to foreign interests. Now, on the assumption that they are buying wisely and generating capital gains, it also represents a distribution of wealth from millions of British people to overseas investors. The reason is that most British public companies are owned by British pension funds, which (sorry to repeat this) in turn look after the financial interests of millions of British savers. The beneficiaries may be thoroughly deserving foreigners. But it is impossible for Damon Buffini or any other private-equity titan to argue that the enrichment of private-equity partners is simply reward for providing all of us with investment gains and a more secure retirement. That said, for historical reasons, Permira may have more British funding than most, because of its close ties to SVG, a UK-listed investment vehicle which always makes substantial investments in Permira's funds. But the general point holds true: when a British business is sold to Permira, it typically represents a sale directly or indirectly by British pension funds representing millions of British people to funds representing millions of American people.

There is a great variety of reasons why British pension funds invest relatively little in private equity (and in hedge funds too). According to pension experts, probably the most important reasons are that pension-fund trustees lack confidence and expertise and also that they are more reluctant than their American counterparts to spend money on hiring executives for the time-consuming task of monitoring the performance of private-equity investments. Explicit Government policy has also played a role, in that new regulation has tended to deter pension funds from taking risks, even where they offer superior rewards. In a sense, therefore, Government attempts to protect our long-term savings have had the effect of widening the gap between the rich – who are able and willing to take the risks offered by this sort of investment – and the rest of us. All that said, pension funds have been gradually increasing their exposure to both private equity and hedge funds. But, arguably, they did so at just the wrong time, right at the top of the market as returns started to shrink.

PENSION FUNDS ARE WIMPS

The billions of pounds already earned by private equity should be seen as the loss of a golden opportunity for British pension funds and therefore for millions of us. So who should we blame? Should we rail at private equity? The Government? Or would it be more appropriate to vent our anger at our pension funds? In part, the success of Permira and its ilk highlights the inadequate stewardship of public companies by the funds on which we depend for our retirement. Take the AA again. Between 1999 and 2004, it was owned by a large quoted company, Centrica. It is now clear that Centrica did not run the AA as efficiently as it should have done. So why on earth didn't the pension funds exert pressure on Centrica to fix the business on their behalf, rather than sell it? If they felt Centrica's management was incapable of fixing the AA, perhaps they should have sacked that management – which had bought the AA in the first place. By contrast, private equity rarely hesitates to dismiss underperforming managers. But such bold remedial action is not the way of the pension funds that manage our money. They only like to take on that kind of responsibility in the most extreme of circumstances, when a company is already in the direst of straits.

Also, part of the AA's fantastic returns under the ownership of private equity stems from the way its takeover was financed, using well over £1bn of debt. Now, in theory, Centrica could have kept the AA and borrowed £1bn against the value of the business – which it could then have distributed to shareholders. That way, its shareholders – our pension funds – would have received much of the capital gain that instead went to Permira and CVC. The point is that it is always open to publicly listed companies to 'gear up' or take on additional borrowing, while remaining as listed companies. But although their indebtedness has been rising in an attempt to increase their returns to share-holders, they still remain much less indebted or geared up than their private-equity-owned peers. Why? Largely because pension funds signal to the boards of public companies that they don't like the risks which would be taken on by companies if they borrowed substantial sums.

Funnily enough, pension funds' averseness to debt may be rational, in the sense that there are obvious dangers to individual companies and to the economy from borrowing too much. And as a matter of economic theory, the value of a business over the long-term should not – in theory – be affected by how it's financed in respect of the balance between debt and equity. But the important phrase here is 'long term'. Pension funds are only being rational if they tend to keep their investments for many years. Instead, pension funds are often fickle owners. And they have routinely and systematically sold businesses to private equity too cheaply or allowed them to be sold – which means that their business model is irrational and means they deliver much lower returns to all of us than they should.

THE FLEECING OF THE GOVERNMENT

But don't worry. It's not just your pension fund that sells out too cheaply to private equity. The Government does it too. When the Ministry of Defence (MoD) wanted to modernize and expand Qinetiq its research arm in February 2003, it struck a deal with Carlyle – one of the world's leading private-equity firms, which should be famous for the stupendous profits it generates from its investments (which are often in the defence industry) but is probably better known for its links to the US presidential Bushes and for its unwanted starring role in Michael Moore's film *Fahrenheit 911*. Carlyle bought a third of Qinetiq for £42.2m, of which 90 per cent was in the form of redeemable cumulative preference shares. Now, these preference shares were quite a lot like debt – and they were redeemed (purchased and cancelled) by Qinetiq pretty quickly. So there is an argument (one which Carlyle disputes) that Carlyle really only had £4.2m of its funds seriously at risk – which was its investment in the ordinary share capital of Qinetiq.

It did pretty well out of its £4.2m. These ordinary shares gave it 51 per cent of the voting rights over Qinetiq. In other words, for a payment of £4.2m the Government surrendered management control to Carlyle of a sizeable and strategically important company. And when Qinetiq floated on the stock market just three years later, in early 2006, Carlyle's stake had risen in value to more than £400m – though in the event, the private equity firm says that it returned "only" £372m to investors (it sold some of its Qinetiq shares at less than the peak price). On Carlyle's own sums, it made a return of 8.8 times its original investment. My calculations show it did rather better than that. But I'm not going to quibble. The story is unambiguous: Carlyle and its backers made a fortune; the Ministry of Defence and the Treasury, which negotiated the deal with Carlyle, short-changed taxpayers; and there was a transfer of taxpayers' wealth to offshore interests.

The MoD and the Treasury gulled themselves. At least that is the implication of an investigation by the National Audit Office into whether the public purse obtained value for money from Qinetiq's privatization. The Ministry's naive error was to run an auction and then select Carlyle as the preferred bidder before nailing down precisely what was being sold. Having won the auction, Carlyle was able to negotiate down the price it would pay, by pointing to a hole in Qinetiq's pension fund and citing the terms of a new service contract with the MoD. At the time of this crucial last-minute haggling, there was no other acquirer in sight to whom the MoD could turn for a better bid: the Department's bargaining position was undermined by a lack of competitive tension.

The deal was also done in the least favourable market conditions, when stock markets were in a slump. So credit is due to Lord Moonie, who at the time was a defence minister, because he pressed for any transaction to be delayed. As he told me in an interview for the BBC, it was the Treasury which was as keen as mustard on a transaction and – as ever – won the day. To be fair to the Treasury, the uplift in the value of Qinetiq since Carlyle acquired its stake has been a benefit to the taxpayer, because the MoD kept a majority holding. Realized and unrealized proceeds total about £800m for the Exchequer. And much of the gain was due to the greater commercial freedom obtained by Qinetiq after Carlyle took control. However, the distribution of rewards between public sector and private sector was unbalanced. For the MoD, according to the National Audit Office, the internal rate of return on this deal was 14 per cent a year – which is respectable, but not a triumph. By contrast, Carlyle's internal rate of return was a magnificent 112 per cent per annum.

The rewards for those who run Qinetiq were even better. The top ten executives in the business made £200 for every £1 of their own cash they invested in the company. Sir John Chisholm, Qinetiq's chairman, turned £130,000 into £26m; Graham Love, the chief executive, scooped £21m from £110,000. They deserved to do well, because they transformed a public-sector cost-centre into a profit-making, international, hi-tech business with great prospects – and the UK has too few of those. But there was an element of windfall or good fortune, in that they bought their equity at a bargain basement price, courtesy of the Treasury's and MoD's decision to sell off a healthy chunk of Qinetiq at the bottom of the market. And what is perhaps more embarrassing for the Treasury and MoD is the National Audit Office's conclusion that the proceeds of the sale to Carlyle were less than what could have been achieved even in the depressed climate.

WE ARE ALL SUBSIDIZING PRIVATE EQUITY

The Exchequer has not just lost out from the sale of a controlling stake in Qinetiq at too low a price. Every time a big company is sold to private equity there is a significant erosion of Government revenues in the form of corporation tax, simply because of the way that private-equity deals are constructed. It's all about debt, again. The interest on debt is deductible from profits. That is true for all companies, not just those owned by private equity. But the point, as I've explained, is that private-equity-owned businesses typically borrow far more than any other kind of business. So when companies are acquired by private equity their taxable profits disappear – and so does their liability to pay corporation tax. Just to be crystal clear, when a private-equity company stops making taxable profits, that doesn't mean it is doing badly. Quite the reverse, in fact. Private-equity owners deliberately load up their acquired businesses with just enough debt to wipe out the tax charge, because that allows them to take control of those businesses for a smaller outlay from their investment funds. In that sense, the taxpayer is providing a very significant subsidy to the capital gains that are eventually made.

Now, in theory, the taxman gets much of that money back, if those who lend to private-equity-controlled businesses pay tax in the UK. For example, if a British bank receives interest on loans to a business owned by private equity, that bank pays tax on the profit it makes from the loans. But most of the lenders to private equity organize their tax affairs so as not to pay tax in the UK. Don't take my word for it. This is what an influential private-equity executive,

John Moulton, founder of the buyout firm Alchemy, told the Treasury Select Committee on 3 July 2007:

> The domicile of debt providers is not an abuse issue, it is a simple statement of fact. If we have large amounts of debt providers having their interest deducted in the UK and the people who receive that interest are being taxed somewhere else, that is a statement of fact. It is not an abuse and I have not alleged it to be an abuse. It is a transfer of revenue from within the UK to outside on one view of life. That is a fact which needs to be added up by the Treasury in their total tax take.

One striking example is what happened to the tax liability of Debenhams, the department-store group, after it was bought by the private-equity firms CVC, Texas Pacific and Merrill Lynch at the end of 2003. In its last full year as a listed business, it paid £40m in tax on profits of £144m. But when Debenhams transferred to private-equity ownership, it appears to have stopped paying corporation tax and seems to have actually become a creditor of the Government. Its profit-and-loss account for the following year shows a tax credit of £9.3m and there's a further tax credit of £13m in the 12 months after that to 3 September 2005. As for its cash-flow statements, these show a similar picture of Debenhams being a net beneficiary of payments from HM Revenue and Customs. Thus, in the 53 weeks to 3 September 2005, Debenhams actually paid £10.4m in tax, but then received £18m in the following half year, to leave it a net £8m in credit. Debenhams has now been refloated on the stock market and has not been performing brilliantly – which rather gives the lie to the notion that private equity always improves businesses. But the important point for our purposes here is that during the brief two years that Debenhams was owned by private equity, HM Revenue and Customs ended up paying money to it.

Both Saga and the AA stopped paying corporation tax too, after being taken over by private equity. Remember that in June 2007 the two of them were valued at £6.15bn. They are big businesses.

But for the two previous financial years, Saga's accounts show a zero corporation tax liability in aggregate. In fact, it claimed a net tax refund of £18.7m (however, Saga insists that many of its lenders do pay tax in the UK, so in its case the effective loss to the Exchequer would be less). As for the AA, its accounts show that it ended both 2005 and 2006 with the taxman owing it money, £67.5m and £11.9m respectively. And it is unlikely that the AA and Saga in their new unified form are going to start paying large amounts of corporation tax any time soon. The merger in 2007 of the two businesses involved them borrowing £4.8bn from Barclays and a Japanese bank, Mizuho. The trend to more big companies being owned by private equity has eroded the tax base of the UK, and reduced the amount of money available for schools and hospitals.

BROWN HEARTS PRIVATE EQUITY

Why hasn't Gordon Brown, when Chancellor or, latterly, as Prime Minister, taken steps to squeeze more corporation tax out of private-equity-owned companies? The reason is that he and the Treasury became convinced in the late 1990s that the economy would benefit from what was then known as venture capital. Brown has been a consistent friend to the British venture-capital industry, partly because he seems to have confused it with the very different US venture-capital industry. In the US, venture capital means putting capital into new and young businesses. Great venture-capital successes of the past 20 years have included Google, Amazon, Netscape, Cisco, Sun Microsystems, America Online, YouTube and Yahoo, to name just a few. Venture-capital firms like Sequoia Capital and Kleiner, Perkins, Caufield and Byers (commonly known as Kleiner Perkins) have been the source of much of the US economy's amazing dynamism during its economic renaissance since the early 1990s. It is no exaggeration to say that venture capital has reinforced the world-leading position of the US economy. Understandably, Brown and the

Treasury believed that the UK could benefit from a bit of that. And they have changed the tax system in a fairly fundamental way to help venture capital.

But what they've ended up helping is what the US – and increasingly the rest of the world – would call private equity, rather than American-style venture capital. Although there are venture capitalists in the UK who try to do what Kleiner Perkins and Sequoia do in the US, which is to provide seed capital to risky young outfits, most British venture capitalists purchase more mature businesses. They've only recently styled themselves as private-equity firms, but they've been engaged in private-equity financing for years.

These days, however, the Treasury has made a virtue out of what may have been a bit of a cock-up or a case of mistaken identity. It is convinced that companies become fitter and stronger from receiving the private-equity treatment – and also that, once these companies have been sold back to the stock market or to a public company, they'll actually end up paying more tax over the longer term. But they are taking quite a lot on trust, because the evidence is by no means conclusive. Much of the research 'proving' that private equity is good for business is of questionable depth and robustness. And the anecdotal evidence is mixed. A number of retailers, for example, do not seem to have been strengthened by private-equity ownership. Debenhams' trading performance since returning to the stock market has been lacklustre and its share price has plunged. Jessops, the photographic retailer, experienced a serious profits fall in 2007. And Unwins, the off-licence chain, collapsed at the end of 2005. But even if most private-equity deals have, to date, tended to improve the prospects of the relevant individual businesses, there have been so many more buyouts during the past few years, involving so much more debt, that the historic experience may not be a reliable guide to the future.

In private conversations with Treasury ministers and officials over many years, I have been struck by their admiration for private-equity firms, including the big firms that purchase substantial public companies and which are the subject of this chapter.

The Treasury doesn't take the soft option of reserving its love for the saints of capitalism beloved of politicians of all parties: the smaller private-equity firms that help medium-size companies, or the brave venture-capital firms which finance risky start-ups. No, the uber-class of Blackstone, KKR, Permira and the rest have also been nurtured by the Treasury, to the extent that it granted them a hugely valuable tax break on capital gains and – when that became politically unpopular – it reformed the capital gains tax system in a fashion that was explicitly designed to limit the damage to them.

The financier who more than anyone else converted Brown to the merits of private equity was Sir Ronald 'Ronnie' Cohen. Knighted in the New Year Honours list at the end of 2000, Cohen was the founder and chairman of a successful British private-equity firm, Apax – which he left in 2005 – and is a pioneer of private equity in the UK. These days, he is chairman of Portland Capital, a hedge-fund operation, and also styles himself as a social entrepreneur, having created a new fund, called Bridges Ventures, which endeavours to combine conventional for-profit commercial investment with a 'social purpose'. Bridges invests in what it hopes are proper businesses but only those that it believes will have a positive social impact on deprived parts of the country. But it is pretty small-scale compared with Apax, which has invested billions: founded in 2002, Bridges' first fund raised £40m, £20m from the private sector and £20m of matched funding from the Government – and in total it has now raised more than £100m. This substantial Labour donor was close to Tony Blair but is closer to Brown. On 11 October 2006, Gordon Brown hosted a party in 11 Downing Street to celebrate Bridges' initial successes.

Cohen left Egypt as a child after the Suez crisis of 1956 and went on to become president of the Oxford Union. For years he has mixed business and politics. A Jew, he created the Portland Trust, whose aim is to promote businesses in the Palestinian Territories with the aim of fostering better relations between Israelis and Palestinians. And Cohen is proud that he has been pressing Tory and Labour Governments for years to give greater support to private equity. He believes passionately that private equity is good for the economy and has lobbied tirelessly for favourable tax treatment for the industry he helped to create. I have spoken to him several times about all this, and I have no doubt that he sincerely believes that what private equity does is good for everybody, even if it's been particularly good for his own bank balance.

Brown was a sympathetic listener, and in 2002, as Chancellor, he made the big leap by announcing that the tax on capital gains accumulated on 'business' assets held for just two years would be a mere 10 per cent. It was the culmination of a progressive lightening of the burden of capital gains tax by Brown, which started in 1998 after he inherited a 40 per cent uniform rate from the previous Conservative Government. Brown gave to the UK one of the most generous tax regimes for creators of businesses, for entrepreneurs, of any developed economy. It was an incredibly powerful symbol of his intent to be a friend to business. And for venture capital and private equity, the great news was that the tax rate on carried interest – the millions earned by private-equity partners from their share of the gains on big deals – would also be 10 per cent. At the time, Cohen was over the moon. His lobbying had been extremely effective.

But when in 2007 the sheer scale of the remuneration of private-equity partners began to attract attention, that 10 per cent tax rate began to look rather generous – to put it mildly. In fact, Cohen himself started to be embarrassed by it. He suggested that the beneficiaries of the biggest private-equity deals should pay significantly more tax than so-called 'real' venture capitalists – or those who invest smaller sums in smaller companies. Such was the mood of public outrage that even the Shadow Chancellor, George Osborne, hinted that he wanted to see partners of private-equity firms pay a good deal more tax. In June 2007, Osborne said he thought that the 'carry' looked more like income than capital gain and should be taxed as such – which would have implied an increase in the tax rate payable to 40 per cent.

But all the way through this heated debate the Treasury remained robustly on the side of private equity. It was sympathetic to Osborne's argument that the 'carry' had many of the characteristics of income, but it was terrified of imposing the 40 per cent top rate of income tax, because it believed that the giants of the industry would relocate abroad in an instant if forced to pay it. Treasury ministers and officials also knew that the status quo was unsustainable. As late as September 2007, however, they were reluctant to go for wholesale reform of the capital gains tax system or abolition of an advantageous rate for gains made on certain assets held for two years. The message given to me was that nothing would be rushed, because too much was at stake. The great fear within the Treasury was that the great private-equity firms would be so offended by any ill-considered reforms that they would flee these shores with the minimum of delay. The next stage would probably be a formal consultation, I was told.

Within a month, however, everything changed. In the excitement of preparation for a possible general election – which Gordon Brown notoriously decided not to call at the last moment – a decision was taken to snuff out any allegation that the Government was being soft on the private-equity panjandrums whose earnings had become notorious. It would be done by way of an initiative to simplify and streamline the entire capital gains tax system. There would now be just one rate, of 18 per cent, payable on all capital gains generated on all assets, and that rate would apply whether the gain was built up in a second or over a lifetime. And it would be presented as an initiative to extract a fair rate of tax from private equity. However, it backfired in the most spectacular fashion. It caused outrage among many thousands of genuine entrepreneurs and those who had lovingly tended their businesses over many years. The tax they would pay if they sold some or all of their respective companies would rise 80 per cent. But partners of big private-equity firms could not believe their luck. They had expected much harsher treatment, to be asked to pay much more tax. As one said to me with a chuckle, 'I can live with this.'

The entire capital gains tax system had been turned upside down with the apparent aim of capturing a relatively small amount of additional tax from the modest number of private-equity executives at the big international firms who pay any tax in the UK at all.

As it happens, five senior partners at CVC each received £50m in the autumn of 2007, according to *The Sunday Times*. But there are not many in their league. And if you've earned £50m, you can probably cope with paying £9m in tax rather than £5m. Also, 18 per cent remains a lot less than most people pay on their earnings. What is more, with careful tax planning, they would probably not even pay 18 per cent on the entire £50m, according to private-equity experts. The effective rate might be considerably less. And then, of course, there is the important nuance that many partners at leading international private-equity firms do not pay tax in Britain on the bulk of their earnings, either because they are not domiciled here or because they are not resident here for tax purposes. Sir Ronnie Cohen, for example, has non-domicile status and pays UK tax on just some of his global earnings. On my calculations, there are only 30 or 40 private-equity superstars in London who earn fortunes here and pay tax here.

Arguably, therefore, the increase in capital gains tax to 18 per cent was of little significance to the super-rich of the private-equity industry – although the reform of the tax would not have happened at all if there had not been public outrage at how little tax they pay. Or, to put it another way, a tax change aimed at them has caused them little discomfort, but it would be seriously painful to genuine entrepreneurs (including partners of venture-capital firms financing start-ups and owners of small businesses). In its zeal to protect the big boys of private equity, the Treasury and the new Chancellor, Alistair Darling, caused a good deal of collateral harm. Which is why at the time of writing the Treasury was frantically trying to tinker with the tax reform to make it less onerous for those who have created small businesses or want to create such businesses.

TOO SUCCESSFUL FOR THEIR AND OUR GOOD

This is not to argue that private equity is intrinsically a bad thing. Private-equity firms buying substantial mature companies can and often do improve the efficiency and prospects of the businesses they acquire. For all the upheaval inflicted on the workforce, the AA is a stronger business for having been bought by Permira and CVC and then reorganized by a new management team. And there are plenty of less controversial examples of established large companies being improved by private equity. But in the past two or three years the rewards being earned by private-equity partners and their investors were too great, for their good and ours. What I mean is that they became a super-magnet for capital. They attracted too much new money from investors desperate for a piece of the action. So the buyouts became bigger and bigger, especially in the US, but in the UK too. It was a classic bubble, created – as they always are – when greed triumphed over reason.

The bubble has since burst. There will now be a hiatus in mega takeovers by private-equity firms. But the scale of the damage wreaked by all that exuberant deal-making is yet to be determined. That depends on whether the global economy slows sharply and how many businesses burdened with huge borrowings – foisted on them by their private-equity owners – have difficulty keeping up the payments. Private-equity-controlled companies will go bust. That's not a probability. It is a cast-iron certainty. Too many deals were done in 2006 and the first half of 2007 for all of them to be sound as a pound. By the autumn of 2007, the debt of several British buyouts completed only months before was being bought and sold at prices well below 100 cents in the dollar – which implied that their private-equity owners had paid far too much to buy these businesses.

Just as serious is the weight of all that debt on the global financial system. Anxieties about whether too much had been lent to too many big buyouts too cheaply contributed to the seizing up of financial markets in the summer of 2007 and a contraction in the amount of credit which banks and other institutions are prepared to provide to all and any of us – which is having a negative economic impact. And if the bad times really start to roll, as they just might, quite soon, you can be sure that some of the superstars and super-rich of the private-equity industry will be sitting pretty

on their mega-yachts, having cashed in quite enough over the past
few years. Which should come as no great surprise. The precipi-
tators of great financial shocks often prosper through those very
shocks. As for those who have not taken the money and scarpered,
they are actually anticipating a return to glory days sooner than
you might think. They expect to profit from the market mayhem
they in part created. There is a broad expectation that stock
markets and the price of companies will fall, as a direct consequence of the new shortage of credit. So any firm with funds to
invest – and Permira, Blackstone and Goldman Sachs have all
raised record-breaking sums that they have not yet used – should
be able to pick up businesses at attractive prices. They will not be
able to borrow as much from banks and other investors as they did
in the past couple of years. The providers of debt have been
burned too badly. In any deal they would have to put in a greater
proportion of equity from their funds. Which means that, in order
for them to make a decent return, there would have to be a very
steep drop in the stock market – a rout – and in what they have to
pay to acquire companies. However, the history of this industry is
that the best profits are always made on the deals transacted after a
market slump. '2008 could be a great vintage year,' one private-
equity veteran told me, with a twinkle.

We should of course celebrate the resilience and creativity of
capitalism and capitalists. But what should perhaps be of concern
is that Gordon Brown provided generous tax incentives that
helped to pump up the market excesses. Here is the stinging irony
for Brown. He was bamboozled by the lobbying of venture
capitalists into providing them with tax breaks. His hope was that
these venture-capital firms would put the UK on the path to a
productivity revolution and create new global businesses to rival
those of the US. But the new global businesses that have been
created aren't Britain's answers to Google or Apple. Funnily
enough, they are the enlarged venture-capital firms themselves,
now styling themselves as private-equity firms, which are holding
him to ransom, threatening to move abroad if he dares to ask them
to pay what many would perceive as a fair amount of tax. Brown

has become the economic prisoner of the super-rich class, whose ranks he swelled through providing them with tax breaks. What a curious epitaph for a Labour Chancellor and Labour Prime Minister.

★　　★　　★

TOP PROFITS FROM THE BOTTOM SHOP

Maddeningly, banks and international investors will not give all of us a billion or two to invest. But in the scale of human achievements, there is nothing terribly special or challenging in doing a private-equity deal and making a profit from that deal. It is a lot easier than scoring a goal in the Premier League, or carrying out brain surgery, or even – probably – improving standards in a large urban comprehensive school. Here's how you do it.

My own private-equity fund, PestieCo Partners V, has decided to buy the Bottom Shop – the UK's leading retailer of knickers and pants – which is listed on the stock market. Its market price is £1.6bn, but I cannot get it for that because the fund managers who control it at the moment demand a takeover premium. So I will need to pay £2bn. However, I only want to put in £400m of equity from my fund, so I persuade Megabank to lend me the other £1.6bn. You should note that very little of my own money is actually at risk. PestieCo Partners V contains a bit of my own wealth, but most of it has been raised from US public-sector pension schemes and Ivy League university-endowment funds. And not only am I using other people's money, but I have demanded and received a cov-lite loan from a group of banks led by Megabank – so if it all goes wrong, the banks still won't be able to wrest control from me, unless and until I turn the Bottom Shop into a basket case.

There's one small problem: I know nothing about running shops. That said, it's pretty easy to seduce a couple of experienced retailers away from their jobs at public companies. All I have to do is dangle in front of them the prospect of making them rich beyond their wildest dreams – by sharing with them a small portion of the enormous capital gains I anticipate making from this deal. To earn those rewards all they have to do is generate a bit more cash from the Bottom Shop than it was making under its previous owners. How will they squeeze more out? Well, they'll reduce the amount of stock held in the shops, which means less precious capital will be tied up. Also, they will force suppliers to reduce what they charge us for underwear, and to wait longer for payment. All this means that even if we don't increase sales, we will be generating a lot more cash from the same turnover. This sort of improvement in the financial efficiency of the business may not be pretty but there is a genuine skill in finding the right balance between screwing the suppliers and incentivizing them to provide the best goods at the keenest prices. Getting it right could be life or death for a private-equity-owned business. Remember that we've saddled the Bottom Shop with £1.6bn of new debt – and it would be curtains if we fail to keep up the interest payments.

However, I am super-confident that I will come out of this deal in pretty good shape, even if my managers do not perform quite as well as I expect in cutting costs and maximizing cash flows. The reason is my knowledge of the Bottom Shop's properties. Most of its shops are in prime high-street positions. In addition, most are freeholds while the others are on long leases. I estimate they are worth many times more than the out-of-date valuation in the company's publicly available balance sheet. In fact, one of my main motivations for doing this deal was my conviction that the Bottom Shop's shareholders did not really understand what they owned. So more or less as soon as the business is mine, I sell the freeholds to a specialist property company for £1bn and rent the premises back on long leases. And with that £1bn I reduce what the Bottom Shop owes the banks from £1.6bn to £600m.

But what about the business itself? How's that going? Well, the general climate for consumer spending is very strong. And we also make a brilliant marketing decision: we run a 'green' advertising campaign, encouraging people to combat global warming by turning down the heat in their homes and offices. They can spew less CO_2 in comfort and style by wearing our new range of 'cosy but sexy' thermal underwear. The campaign is a big hit and sales rise.

It's all going swimmingly, so much so that I am confident I can borrow from banks on even better terms than I did when I bought the *business. So the Bottom Shop obtains a new £400m loan from a group of banks. And then it pays that £400m to PestieCo Partners V in the form of a dividend. In other words, my fund has received all its money back in just a year. And here's the magic: it still owns 100 per cent of the Bottom Shop – and the Bottom Shop, not the PestieCo fund, owes the banks £1bn.*

So far, so profitable. I then spend the next year planning to sell the company – to a retailer, to another private-equity fund or even back to the very fund managers who sold it to me in the first place. I need to create a climate of excitement around the business in order to do this. So I appoint one of the huge US investment banks to sound out possible buyers and persuade anyone who might remotely be interested that buying the Bottom Shop is a once-in-a-lifetime investment opportunity with 'humungous upside'. And in order to maximize the buzz around the company, I also hire a leading firm of public-relations advisers. On their advice, I give the occasional newspaper interview – which the newspapers are over the moon about because I am regarded as something of a recluse and also because I possess all the glamour that goes with being wealthy beyond anyone's powers of comprehension (and no one seems to notice that I am vain, rude and arrogant). Oh, and we periodically place 'scoops' with grateful journalists about how brilliantly the business is performing.

It all goes better than I could possibly have hoped. So I decide to refloat the Bottom Shop on the stock market. In other words, the sappy pension funds that sold me the business in the first place are going to buy it back for vastly more than I paid for it. Here's the great thing: the stock market has risen by 25 per cent in the two years since I bought the Bottom Shop and the retailing sector has risen by 30 per cent. What's more, the company's profits (before interest payments) have more than doubled in the period thanks to our stringent cost controls and the buoyancy of consumer spending. Also, my brilliant thermal-underwear campaign – 'heat your body, not the planet' – has persuaded the City that the Bottom Shop is a growth company. So if the business was valued at £1.6bn on the stock market when I bought it (excluding the 'takeover premium' I had to pay), it would now be valued at £1.6bn plus 30 per cent (for the inflation in the value of store groups in general) plus a bit more (for the magic dust I have sprinkled on it). So let's say I can sell it back to the stock market for £2.2bn. That doesn't look like a huge profit on the £2bn we paid for it. Does that make me a klutz? Au contraire.

If we can sell the Bottom Shop for £2.2bn, the profit for PestieCo would be enormous, largely because we financed the takeover with £1.6bn of borrowings. Here's how it all works. There is £1bn of borrowings left in the business. So we have to deduct that £1bn from the £2.2bn to calculate the capital gain available to PestieCo Partners V. And then we have to take into account the £400m dividend that the fund has already pocketed from the business. In other words, PestieCo's initial £400m investment has yielded £1.2bn plus £400m, or £1.6bn in total. However, we promised some of this profit to the retailing managers who helped maximize the Bottom Shop's cash flow. We're feeling generous, so we will give them £100m – which is probably five times what they would have earned in an entire career had they stayed at public companies. So that reduces PestieCo's return to £1.5bn. Even so, I have turned £400m into £1.5bn, almost quadrupling my investors' money in just two years, which is a very respectable return. The total capital gain is £1.1bn – and I, of course, receive my 20 per cent share of that, my 'carry'. Which is a tolerable £220m.

Here's the crucial point. Very little of what PestieCo did to earn this return required exceptional skill or imagination. The bulk of the profit stemmed from the decision to borrow a vast amount – which is something that, in theory, the Bottom Shop could have done itself as an independent company listed on the stock market. And although we hired decent managers, even if we had done next to nothing to improve the business, we would still have made a handsome capital gain just so long as the economy in general continued to improve and the stock market continued to rise. All hail the miracle-working properties of leverage.

CHAPTER 3

THE KING OF JACKPOT CAPITALISM

Sir Philip Green's greatest coup was to receive a dividend in 2005 of £1.2bn from Arcadia, the retailing business he had bought in the autumn of 2002 with just a few million pounds of his own cash. Actually, it would be more accurate to say that his wife received the dividend. He is the grafter, probably the greatest retailer of his generation, and she's the owner. Why are the superlative assets in her name? Well, as luck would have it, she became a resident of Monaco before he set new records for extracting cash from old-established businesses. So by vesting ownership in her hands, any dividend paid would avoid the payment of tax to the British Exchequer. On this one dividend – probably the biggest dividend ever paid to an individual in the history of British business – there was therefore a colossal tax saving, estimated at £300m by tax experts. That would have been enough to build around ten state secondary schools capable of educating around 13,000 teenagers in total. But although you might think that depriving the public purse of such a sum might put him in baddish odour with the Government, there has not been so much as a hint of unpleasantness. In fact, the lovable rogue of the British billionaire class was even knighted – for his services to retailing – just a few months after dancing around the tax man. Green is the matchless hero, the nonpareil of the new monied class. Understand him and how he made his pile and you understand twenty-first-century jackpot capitalism.

Just thinking about this one dividend payment – let alone his other billions – induces mild vertigo. Here is how I like to visualize it: if he collected the dividend in pound coins stacked one on top of another, the apex of the column would be 2,350 miles above the earth. It is also equivalent to what would be earned in a single year by 54,000 people on average earnings. And if Green were to be boring and put the lot in a building society account paying 5 per cent, the interest each year would be £60m. Nice work.

You think Green has done well? Here is the extraordinary thing: Stuart Rose, the chief executive of Marks & Spencer, who has had a volatile relationship with Green, believes he could have pocketed even more. Rose says Green could have bought Arcadia even cheaper. When Green purchased Arcadia – the owner of some 2,125 outlets, including Topshop, Topman, Dorothy Perkins, Wallis, Evans and Burton – the takeover price was £850m. But a couple of years earlier the business could have been bought for about £100m. Rose ought to know, because he was chief executive of Arcadia at the time.

Rose recalls his arrival as the new chief executive of Arcadia in November 2000. The business was perceived by the City to be in serious trouble. Sales were stagnant and profits were tumbling. Arcadia's shares had been priced at more than 500p each three years before. But in 2000 they fell to a low of 38p and were at 51.5p when Rose took the helm. At that price the whole of Arcadia was valued at £91m.

'Philip had certainly sniffed around it when the total value was around £100m and the share price was around 45p or 50p,' says Rose. And within a very short time of Rose being installed in Arcadia's West End headquarters, Green was bantering with him in his characteristic way:

His first words on the phone, ten minutes after I got in there, were: 'Have you found it?' And I said: 'What?' And he said: 'The black hole.' And I said: 'I've only been here ten minutes, Philip, but I think it just needs managing, I don't think there is a black hole.' And he said: 'No, no, son, you don't understand. There is a fucking black hole in there; I'd be careful you don't fall down it if I were you.'

And week two he would ring up and say: 'Well, have you found it yet? Well, you are not looking very hard. Get yourself a fucking torch, son.' Week three, he would do the same. And over a six-month period the share price goes from 38p to 50p to 60p to 70p to 80p to 90p. When the share price went to £1.20 it dawned on Philip that there wasn't a black hole, that this was actually quite a good business that had been badly managed. [Stuart Rose interview, 22 June 2006]

However, it was no longer quite so simple for Green to buy Arcadia. In early 2001, an Icelandic retailer, Baugur, started to acquire shares in the company and by May had accumulated a 20 per cent stake. Although Baugur was a fraction of Arcadia's size, in October 2001 it said it wanted to buy the whole business for between 280p and 300p per share.

I then played that long game, which went on a bit longer than people know or think, because I had a play-off between Philip and the Icelanders who were trying to buy the business. [ibid.]

Rose entered into negotiations with Baugur, which was created and run by a flamboyant Icelander, Jon Asgeir Johannesson. However, Johannesson had difficulty raising the finance for a full takeover, so Rose announced in February 2002 that Arcadia was no longer cooperating with Baugur, which effectively stymied Johannesson's hopes of buying the business.

Even so, with a 20 per cent holding Baugur had significant influence over Arcadia's future. It could determine whether anyone else could buy it outright. Which is why, in the summer of 2002, Philip Green decided to team up with the Icelandic group. Having tracked Arcadia closely for years, in mid-August he informed Arcadia's board that he would offer £690m for the group. In return for Baugur's support, Green was prepared to sell it three of Arcadia's brands, Miss Selfridge, Topman and, the absolute jewel among Arcadia's store chains, Topshop.

Now, had Green sold Topshop, he would be a significantly less powerful force on the high street than he is today. In fact, Topshop was to become his most cherished asset. But he was set to let Baugur have it, until fate intervened. On 29 August 2002, Baugur's offices in Reykjavik were raided by the Economic Crimes Department of the Icelandic Police. They were investigating alleged malpractice relating to 33 invoices. In the event, there was nothing untoward proved against Baugur. But at the time it complicated Green's plans because he had been working on the assumption that the costs of the acquisition would be reduced by making the significant disposal to Baugur – and that disposal was now in doubt. 'We anticipated most things but you wouldn't believe this unless it was an April 1st joke,' Green said at the time [*FT*, 30 August 2002].

It turned out to be a blessing in disguise. The incident forced him to put together an offer for the company that allowed him to keep Topshop, which is at the heart of the business he controls today, and which is central to his long-term hopes of being able to expand outside the UK. On 6 September 2002, Green secured the agreement of Arcadia's board to a revised offer of 408p per share plus a promise to pay a 4p dividend the following February. This valued Arcadia at £775m, or £850m including share options. Characteristically, Peter Cummings of Bank of Scotland provided much of the finance for the offer. Apart from the loan it provided, Bank of Scotland also acquired an 8 per cent holding in Taveta, the specially created company that was taking over Arcadia; Bank of Scotland would make a spectacular return on this investment.

Argument has raged subsequently about whether Rose and Arcadia's board, chaired by Adam Broadbent, a former merchant banker from Schroders, were right to advise Arcadia's shareholders to accept Green's offer:

I read in the *FT* that Philip bought a buggered-up business which he spectacularly turned round. Well, I can tell you it was all set up. Topshop was running . . . Did we sell it at the right price? Citigroup [Arcadia's financial advisers], ourselves, the board, all sat down and said this exit multiple [the valuation of the business in the form of the ratio of its price to its annual profits], given where the business had been and all that, looks about right. Hindsight: do I regret it? No. Did Philip get a good opportunity with some upside? Yes. [ibid.]

This was Green's own analysis, from a chat he and I had in October 2003:

People say I am 'lucky'. I am lucky enough to get my timing right: £775m that I paid [for Arcadia] a year ago against the mooted £700m for New Look [a smaller fashion chain that was to be bought by the private-equity firms Permira and Apax] or £1.789bn for Debenhams, with similar turnover. Everyone then was calling the top of the market. I got all the [newspaper] cuttings out the other day. The valuation of Arcadia was quite simple: £4 [what he paid for each Arcadia share] was a lot of money based on the fact it had come from 50p. At 50p it was bust.

To be clear, it was not just a good opportunity for Green, it was a great one. As Rose says, he could have bought the business much more cheaply if he had moved earlier – but there was, nonetheless, a spectacular return to be made. He had paid roughly half for each pound of Arcadia's sales than what was subsequently paid by the giants of private equity, Texas Pacific, CVC and Permira, in their takeovers of store groups. And here is the thing that stuns those to whom the buying and selling of companies is a wholly alien practice: the profit made by Green from Arcadia has been massively more than simply the difference between the £1.2bn dividend he received and the £850m price of the company. The reason is that one of Green's great skills is to borrow vast amounts from banks to finance his acquisitions rather than use his own savings.

Green is the unchallenged king of British buyouts. And two of his deals stand out for the sheer size of the profits he made from them. In the first, Green paid £200m for Bhs in the spring of 2000, of which he put in just £20m of his family's money and borrowed the rest. By 2004, he had received £400m in dividends from the group – so he made a return of 20 times his initial £20m outlay just from dividends; and he continued to own 94 per cent of the business. As he said in October 2004: 'It's not bad, is it? It's pretty good for a £20m investment, isn't it?' But Bhs has not continued to grow sales and profits with consistency. Green took his eye off the ball and in the year to 1 April 2006 sales dipped by 7.1 per cent on an underlying basis and profits fell by more than half. At the time of writing, Green is trying to revive the company by refurbishing stores, moving the business up-market and launching celebrity ranges. There are signs of progress and Bhs is far from valueless: via Bhs, Green has turned £20m of his family's money into more than £1bn.

But it is the return he made on Arcadia that set records. What is astonishing is that he put even less of his family's money into Arcadia than he did into Bhs. His equity investment was just £9.2m – and from that he reaped a dividend of £1.2bn in 2005. That represents a return on his initial investment of 130 times. The dividend was made possible by increasing the cash-generating capacity of Arcadia and then in June 2005 persuading six banks led by Bank of Scotland to refinance the business by making new loans to it of £1bn. Green calls these banks 'the proper banks' and 'not some bank out of Austria' [Philip Green interview, 20 October 2005]. Or, to put it another way, they are the mainstream British banks we all use. With Arcadia generating operating profits of £300m on sales of £1.8bn in 2005–06, the business is probably worth more than £1.5bn. So, in less than three years, he turned £9.2m into estimated family wealth of close to £3bn (the dividend plus the current value of Arcadia).

It is worth putting that return into historical context. To do that, we have to look at the performance of Burton Group, the company out of which Arcadia was created.

Burton was a fast-growing retailing conglomerate in the 1980s, built up in a series of takeovers by Sir Ralph Halpern, a charismatic entrepreneur who for a period had an enthusiastic City following. Halpern and his ilk – the 1980s generation of wheeler-dealer executives who specialized in using the shares of their respective companies to finance a succession of takeovers – were great corporate players, the equivalent of today's private-equity partners. The leaders in this takeover-for-shares game were Lord Hanson of Hanson Trust and Sir Owen Green of BTR, along with the disgraced head of Guinness, 'Deadly' Ernest Saunders. At the height of Halpern's reputation, Burton owned Topshop, Debenhams and Harvey Nichols – along with the eponymous menswear chain, *inter alia*. It employed 50,000 people and had a market value of £2bn. But investors' euphoria gradually gave way to concern that underlying growth in the individual businesses was not what they hoped it would be: in 1990 Halpern quit as its chairman and chief executive with a pay-off of £2m.

But the Burton built by Halpern paid £446m in dividends in aggregate from 1985 to 1998 (according to data supplied by the financial analysis firm, Quest). Or, to put it another way, Burton – which owned Arcadia's stores and some others – paid out over 13 years less than half what Green received in a single year. Burton's average annual dividend in those years was just £34m, a tiny fraction of Green's £1.2bn. It is also possible to bring the comparison closer to the moment that Arcadia was sold to Green. In 1998, Debenhams was demerged from Burton as a separate stock-market company and the rump of Burton was renamed Arcadia. If the dividends paid by Burton and then Arcadia over the 16 years from 1985 to August 2001 are added together, the total is £471.2m, which was £729m less than Green's mega-dividend.

There are two ways of looking at these numbers. One is to say that the £850m price negotiated by Rose from Green does not look too bad, given the lowish dividends paid out over many years. The other is to marvel at how much cash has been extracted by Green. How did he do it? Partly by improving the operating performance of Arcadia. But, as I have already mentioned, he also did something fairly simple. He calculated that Arcadia could afford to borrow much more than it had been doing, that its prodigious cash flows could support interest payments on a substantial amount of debt. So he persuaded a group of banks to lend Arcadia £1bn, which he then took out of the business as a dividend. In other words, probably the most significant difference between Burton Group as a public company and Arcadia under Green's ownership is that Green was less averse to borrowing than were Burton's executives (he is also a world-class operating manager). In fairness to Arcadia's and Burton's previous management, Green benefited from the much lower interest rates prevailing over the past few years than were being charged in the 1980s and much of the 1990s. What's more, Green was able to take advantage of remarkably stable economic conditions in the UK and a consumer boom of almost unprecedented duration. So his success doesn't mean borrowing vast amounts is a successful corporate strategy for all seasons. But it does show that the owners of public companies – or you and me, through our pension funds – pay a significant price in terms of lower returns because public companies on the whole have a much lower tolerance for debt than Green and his imitators.

To reinforce the point, let us quickly look at the returns made by a trio of specialist private-equity houses from their investment in Debenhams, the other half of Halpern's old Burton Group. A consortium of Texas Pacific Group, CVC and Merrill Lynch acquired the department-store chain Debenhams in December 2003 and then floated it back on the stock market in the spring of 2006. They invested £600m of their own funds in the business (as opposed to the debt raised from banks and external financial institutions). And they received £300m back within five months of buying Debenhams and a further £1bn in June 2005. In other words, they took out £1.3bn over 18 months, more than doubling their money. I am ignoring the proceeds of the shares they sold when Debenhams was floated back on the stock market in 2006 and the value of their residual shareholdings. In total, they may eventually turn their equity investment of £600m into more than

£1.8bn – although, notoriously, as a company quoted on the stock market again, the business is not performing brilliantly and the share price has halved.

Here's the final unbelievable calculation about the financial transformation of Debenhams and Arcadia under their recent owners. These businesses that were in the 1980s and 1990s generating an annual average dividend of £34m a year have paid out 76 times that amount – or £2.6bn – to Green, his bank and the private-equity threesome (that's Green's £1.2bn dividend, some £100m to HBOS from Arcadia plus the £1.3bn taken out of Debenhams by the private-equity troika before it was floated). Arcadia and Debenhams cannot possibly yield £2.6bn every year. But even if Green and the private-equity houses in effect pocketed five years of dividends rolled into one lump, they have not done a bad job of turning mainstream retailers into great gushers of cash.

Apart from loading them with debt, Green, CVC, TPG and Merrill all drove their businesses harder than their public-company competitors. The private-equity troika at Debenhams and their management team – Rob Templeman, Chris Woodhouse and John Lovering – have had to sweat the assets harder than Green because they paid relatively more for their business. The Debenhams' team may have been more aggressive than Green in renegotiating terms with suppliers and in seeking operational efficiencies. And, unlike Green, they have sold and leased back properties – Green prefers to retain ownership of good property, but will mortgage it to obtain cheap finance (his particular pride and joy is the enormous Topshop site at Oxford Circus, which is worth hundreds of millions of pounds). But the respective techniques of Green and the private-equity group are broadly similar and none of it is rocket science. And here is what should shock: there is little that Green, TPG, Merrill or CVC have done that could not have been done by the managements of Arcadia and Debenhams when they were listed companies. Working capital could have been reduced; better terms with suppliers could have been arranged; the property assets could have been mortgaged or sold; and borrowings could have been increased to pay huge dividends to the pension funds that owned the companies. The profits generated by Green and the private-equity troika could have gone to you, me and the millions of others who depend on those pension funds for our income in retirement.

Arguably, Debenhams' lacklustre performance in 2007 after returning to the stock market shows that its new management is rather better at financial engineering than at running a fashion business over the long term. Even so, there are lessons for listed business. Plenty of quoted companies – including some regarded as absolutely top rate – are still not working their assets as efficiently as they should be, largely because they are irrationally fearful of increasing their debt. The losers are all of us as the beneficiaries of pension funds. The fund managers employed by pension funds in effect work for us. When they sell businesses like Arcadia too cheaply, they short-change us. And when they fail to put the right kind of pressure on the businesses they continue to hold, we lose out. Over the past decade, they have given away billions of pounds of our wealth. The lucky beneficiaries are either wealthy individuals or the overseas investment institutions that tend to finance private equity. There has been a massive transfer from the have-littles to the have-loads.

There is a further cost to all of us from the rise and rise of private equity, in the form of reduced revenues for the Exchequer, as private-equity firms are super-adept at reducing the tax paid by the businesses they own. When Debenhams was owned by private equity it did better than pay no tax: it actually received tax credits from Her Majesty's Revenue and Customs. By contrast, Arcadia has paid around £290m in corporation tax since Green bought it. Green says he deliberately did not take his tax planning to the limit. There was an alternative way of reorganizing Arcadia that would have wiped out its £80m annual corporation tax liability as well and allowed Green to take out even more cash. It would have involved borrowing more money, which would have exhausted all its profits in interest payments. It is what most private-equity owners do. But Green decided against despite being urged to do so by his advisers. As he said to me in the autumn of 2005:

Let's say a VC [venture-capital or private-equity firm] came along tomorrow to buy Arcadia off me. And I'm paying £80m a year in corporation tax, which I am. Today it might be £72m or whatever. In their [private-equity] capital structure, they look to use that £72m as part of their financing. And the answer is, which would shock the world, I could take £3bn out of Arcadia [using the private-equity approach]. There is another structure I could use where I could strip all the tax.

But I took a view with both Bhs and Arcadia, recognizing that . . . my wife is offshore and I get a big win on that side, I took a view not to poke their eye out, the Revenue, not to be greedy and try and strip the corporation tax. It was a conscious decision. I have files and files. All these accountants said: 'You are mad.' I said: 'I am not mad, I don't think it's correct. We are getting a big win on the dividends, we are going to pay our tax.' That was a conscious, open-ended view I took.

For me, the quintessential Green scene was Topshop in Oxford Circus at 7 p.m. on 30 April 2007. It was the great unveiling of the fashion range developed by Green's firm in partnership with Kate Moss, the supermodel. More than anything else, he is a schmutter mogul, and that particular branch of Topshop is the cathedral of mass-market British fashion. But he is also a risk-taker – and there was undoubtedly a risk in working with Moss. On the one hand, she generates extraordinary excitement among fashion-conscious young people. Women were queuing around the block to be the first to pick up a Moss garment. But it was less than two years since she was savaged by the press and dropped by the leading fashion businesses Chanel, Burberry and H&M after photographs of her in close proximity to cocaine were published by the *Daily Mirror*.

Green has a love-hate relationship with the media. And before the crowds of shoppers swarmed in for this night-time spending binge, there was a media circus inside the store: five film crews; fashion photographers; the paparazzi; a couple of senior business journalists; and a leading fashion writer. Green never knowingly spends when he can get something for free. And he is a genius at generating free publicity for his businesses by staging events that attract reporters and cameras. Also, unlike the secrecy-obsessed partners of private-equity firms, he has largely avoided personal criticism of even his more controversial business decisions by forming close relationships with journalists over many years and making himself available for questioning by reporters and commentators. But he can really blow his top on the rare occasions when newspapers put the boot in.

The Topshop performance gave a glimpse of the trappings and restrictions of the billionaire high life. As always, Green was accompanied by his bodyguards whenever he toured the public spaces of Topshop. But on the basement floor he had constructed a softly lit, lavishly appointed, *de facto* nightclub, open for just this one night, where Moss and her gang could drape themselves on divans, drown themselves in Louis Roederer Cristal champagne and wade through mountains of caviar. It's a tough job but . . .

So just how has he succeeded in enriching himself on a scale and at a speed that are probably without precedent in Britain? Well, as entrepreneur he has two salient characteristics. He is an unusually talented retailer. And, perhaps even more importantly, he has won the confidence and trust of British lending banks to an almost unprecedented extent. Collectively, they have been prepared to lend him billions with more alacrity than they will lend a few thousand to most people. For little more effort than talking through the outline of a desired deal over one of the two chunky, old-fashioned Nokia mobile phones that are always somewhere about his person, he can borrow enormous sums from the best British and American banking names. What bankers have been impressed by is his ability to see the big picture – the financial structure of what he builds – while at the same time not neglecting the detail of his business, which is rare. Oh, and he has a history of making good money for them.

When he is knocked down, as he has been a few times, he picks himself up, learns from the experience and does a bigger and more profitable transaction the next time. This determination is

very un-British, which helps to explain why for years the mainstream conservative elements in the City of London were wary of
him.

If you want a mental image of Green, think Toad of Toad
Hall with an Estuary-accented roar loud enough to knock down
walls. He is stocky, opinionated, fast-talking and endowed with
one of the best analytical brains in business, a natural talent like
a top-class footballer's rather than one acquired in the modern
way through a business school and a management training
scheme at a multinational company. His eye for the main
chance reaped a handsome dividend at a garden party held
on 28 June 2007 by Roland Rudd, the founder of the public-
relations firm Finsbury, at his Kensington home to raise money
for the NSPCC. There was a charity auction, in which Green
did not participate, because he had come up with his own fund-
raising wheeze. Also at the function was Paul Dacre, the editor
of the *Daily Mail* – which has riled Green by periodically
criticizing him (for not paying tax on his dividend and for
doing business with Kate Moss after she was photographed in
the company of cocaine). Green always found Dacre elusive
when he contacted the paper. So now, in front of assorted
business leaders, he shouted out that he was prepared to offer
£10,000 to have lunch with him – which was an offer that
Dacre found hard to refuse. However, Paul Myners, Green's
nemesis as erstwhile chairman of Marks & Spencer (see Chapter 4), made a counter bid of £11,000. Green then upped his
offer. In the end, Green suggested that he and Myners each
honour their bids and that they have lunch with Dacre together.
It was a classic Green gambit. Dacre had been discomfited.
Myners had been forced to dig into his own pocket. And Green
had turned the £10,000 he was prepared to pay into more than
double that for the NSPCC, by some last-minute quick thinking.

Green makes better-than-normal returns because he sees opportunities missed by others. And he is concerned as much with
the microscopic detail of his companies as with the daily cash flow:

he immerses himself in the selection and positioning of stock for his stores. When he walks through a Bhs branch, he can spot when stuff is in the wrong place and he makes sure it is moved straight away. Allan Leighton, the chairman of Royal Mail, and a business partner of Green – as chairman of Bhs – says that he can look at any item and give an uncanny estimate of what it costs to make, where it was made and what it should be priced at. Finding the lowest-cost stock has been part of his métier for over three decades. He discovered the manufacturing potential of China years before most British companies.

I have rarely come across anyone with greater and deeper knowledge of a chosen industry or with more commercial insights. He leaps from subject to subject. When he lets rip in an habitual stream of consciousness, it is hard to keep up with him. But it's worth the effort because his seemingly unconnected statements usually do join up to form a view of the business world that is worth seeing.

Green knows what he is good at:

> I have always been confident that I would make money . . . Obviously, getting up to this sort of scale you don't think about. But I've got a gut feel for it. I didn't even think about how much, to be honest [when he started out]. I've never thought like that. I was just always confident that I would live well and I would make money. [Philip Green interview, 31 May 2006]

With a low boredom threshold and a voracious appetite for deals, Green is an enthusiast for business who borders on the obsessive. He can appear to be a bully and many find him intimidating. But he recognizes that his business would be doomed if he surrounded himself with patsies. The chairman of Arcadia, Lord Grabiner, is a distinguished barrister and nobody's pushover. His cousin, Ian Grabiner, has been an important lieutenant for Green over many years. And then there is a network of powerful independent deal-makers and grandees who periodically work with him, such as Leighton, Lord Stevenson, Sir Tom Hunter and the Barclay dynasty, headed by Sir Frederick and Sir David Barclay. Not everyone stays the course with him: in the autumn of 2006, the woman credited with much of Topshop's phenomenal success, Jane Shepherdson, quit.

Among his very many stocks-in-trade is information. He always seems to know what his rivals are up to or what deal is about to be negotiated in the City. He is the man who knows, a one-off. Why do people confide in him?

> Because they know confidential means confidential. I know of three deals going on at the moment, but people trust me. They come to me for advice, help. A guy came to me this morning saying: 'Need a bit of help, bit of guidance.' It is about help, about trust. But I am not, for example, contrary to what everybody thinks, I am not a networker.
>
> I go either to odd things, which I think are polite, things you need to go to, or basically so I've got access [to individuals who might be useful to him], so that if I do call I'm not a pesterer and I get a hearing. I think being a prominent businessman is about you being available. Two Fridays ago, somebody called me up – wanted to invite me somewhere – and couldn't believe they got a call back in an hour. He was completely in shock and said: 'People like you don't return calls.' I said: 'What do you mean "people like me"?' Ninety-nine per cent of calls I get that day I return that day.' That's how you get knowledge. [ibid.]

Born in 1952, Green is not the cockney who pulled himself up by the bootstraps of his in-your-face public image. Both his parents were successful, entrepreneurial business people, who moved from Croydon to salubrious, middle-class north London when he was growing up. His father died of a heart attack when Green was 11. It is tempting to attribute Green's voracious hunger for success to the tragedy of losing a father while still a child. When I wrote weekly profiles for *The Sunday Times* in 2001 and 2002, I was struck by the disproportionate number of business leaders whose fathers had died or walked out when they were young. Green talks about his mother as his strong and abiding influence:

> Some people are academic. I'm not. I left school with no qualifications, learned about business by working with my mother in her businesses at weekends. I enjoyed it. Business was in the family. That was much more important to me than school. She had petrol stations, self-service petrol stations, car showrooms, coin-operated launderettes at the time. She was in business all her life, still is. I went everywhere [in the business]. Learned. Enjoyed talking to the people running the businesses, seeing what they were doing, listened, learned. It seemed more appealing [than school]. I wasn't going to be an academic. [ibid.]

In fact, if he has a prejudice it is against those who have been to university. This was on display in September 2006, when the two Grabiners, Patience Wheatcroft, who was then editor of the *Sunday Telegraph*, and I sat with him in the shiny black decor of Arcadia's boardroom. He was choosing young employees for the fast-stream management training programme at Arcadia. I don't quite know how he persuaded me to join his selection panel since it is difficult to see Arcadia as a charity. But it provided me with an insight into him and his business. The applicants – largely women – were spirited and passionate about shops. Few seemed to come from privileged backgrounds, and most displayed commercial nous. Green was trying to behave like a consensual boss – not wholly convincingly – rather than *le patron*, an autocrat. My contribution was to try to prevent him rejecting the rare university graduate on the list.

Green thinks that spending three years studying for a non-vocational degree is a sign of lack of focus and ambition:

> It seems to me a lot of parents I meet have this guilt trip about 'Well, I didn't have the opportunity to go to university, but now

my circumstances are that I can afford to send my kids.' But is that the right reason? When they say to me: 'What are your kids going to do?' I say: 'Everybody knows I am not a university fan.' So to me there has got to be a rational or logical reason to . . . And I don't think further education has to be university. Hence I've been building this [vocational] academy. Or you can go to business school, you can do a year, you can do six months. I mean, Tina's son, my stepson, went to Millfield [the fee-paying school]. We got to 17 or 18. He took his O levels and A levels. And the headmaster is going on: 'Well, I think dee dah dee dah dee dah.' And I said: 'Do me a favour, go and ask him, "Why are you going to spend the next four years of your life doing something when you want to go into business?"' [ibid.]

In recent years, Green has worked to expand the provision of vocational training in the UK, putting £5m of Arcadia's cash into the creation of a Retail Academy in central London for 16-year-olds who want to learn about retailing rather than doing A levels. Green himself attended an expensive Jewish boarding school, Carmel College, which he didn't enjoy, though he baulks at the suggestion that he hated it ('I always tell my children not to use the word "hate",' he says). Now defunct, it was on the bank of the Thames near Oxford and aspired to be the Jewish Eton. For all his intrinsic cleverness, Green's academic performance was lamentable: he left school at 16 without a single O level.

His Jewishness matters to him. For the bar mitzvah of his son Brandon in 2005, he erected a synagogue in the grounds of one of Monaco's most lavish hotels. And much of his *pro bono* and charitable work has a Jewish flavour:

I took a group the other week from a school, the Jews' Free School, 88 sixth-form students. Ruth Robins [Dame Ruth Robins, JFS's head]. I went to see Ruth. I liked her. Largest Jewish school in the world, 2,000 students. She came to see me, chit-chat, chit-chat, chat. I said: 'Come on, Ruth, I'll take your 88 sixth-formers for the day.' Got them in. Did one-on-one with them. Saw them. Sent them all round the business, dah dee dah dee dah. Got them to write letters. Some are interested for holiday work. But it's just letting them see there's another world. I don't want to become a preacher, but we need a much broader business community to get engaged. And I think if we all as a business community got engaged at that sixth-form level, I think we could make a massive difference, massive. If there was one big push. [ibid.]

The president of JFS is Lord Levy, Labour's erstwhile chief fund-raiser – who was arrested by police in 2006 during their investigation into whether the Labour Party had illegally attempted to sell peerages (see Chapter 8). Levy, who was cleared of wrong-doing in 2007 and was never charged, is also president of Jewish Care, the leading health and social care charity for Jews in the UK (it was created in 1990 by the merger of the Jewish Welfare Board and the Jewish Blind Society). Green is friendly with Levy, but he steered clear of Levy's political activities, as he made clear to me.

I can only speak as I find . . . The answer is when I first met him, which was to do with Jewish Care, and we ironed out a little problem, a community issue, I said to him: 'I'm happy to be in that box, I don't want to be in that one [the political box].' He says: 'Do you want to meet anybody?' I say: 'I am basically relaxed either way.' End of the day I employ 40,000 people, I bump into these people [leading politicians] now and again. But I don't want to get myself caught up in something. And this is not after the event, it is way before.

I said: 'I don't want to be into something where there might be an embarrassment for either of us. Got it? That's all. So please don't ask me and we can be friends. You need help, charity, no problem. Jewish Care, no problem. But that other jungle, not for me.' [ibid.]

Green, who was knighted in June 2006 for services to the retail industry, appears to have it all. What is striking is that he collected his jackpot in a few short years from the late 1990s onwards.

Before that, his business career had been something of a struggle. He worked his way up in an unglamorous way after quitting formal education. Green's first job was a sign of things to come:

> I got a job at a shoe importer from a family friend. At 168 to 172 Old Street [on the periphery of the City of London], importing from all round the world, Hong Kong, China, Taiwan. They were the first people actually to be importing from China, Taiwan. I started off doing filing, warehouse, sampling. They taught me importing, they taught me letters of credit. I was there five years. Family business. I then decided shoes looked a bit narrow. That was the best training: I worked in the warehouse, humped the boxes, you know, did everything. Very good grounding, good training. [ibid.]

What is striking about his business debut is that he was learning about the potential of working with Chinese businesses decades before the City caught on to the massive potential of the Far East. It is characteristic of him to identify trends early.

> In 1973, I went to the Far East, spent six or nine months looking around, went to Hong Kong, China and so on. And then went to one of the agents we used to deal with. And I started off buying and selling late deliveries, cancelled orders, whatever. It was a mix of goods, a bit of footwear, a bit of clothing. And then I started importing clothing in 1976 on my own account. I was a wholesaler serving retailers. I used to buy stock, put it on the floor and then sell it. I learned how to manufacture, learned what it cost to make the garments. [ibid.]

His entrée into retailing came when a small-store business went bust. This, again, was prophetic, in that he picked up stock at well below its intrinsic value:

> I bought some stock in 1979, a retailer went broke, ten shops. I got the stock delivered, paid about 10p in the pound for it from the

liquidator. Had a look at it, it didn't look that bad, so I thought I would retail it myself. So I opened my first shop, 41 Conduit Street [in the West End]. That was designer discount. It was 1979. I then bought and sold a few shops. Opened one in Bond Street, bought another one in Bond Street, bought all their shops. [ibid.]

Green was in his late 20s and it was all still pretty small beer. It was not until he was well into his 30s in the mid-1980s that he did his first deals of any size, when he bought a financially stretched jeans wholesaler, Bonanza, and a troubled fashion chain, Jean Jeanie. He put them into a new company, Lunabond, and was rewarded with a swift profit when a public company, Lee Cooper, bought it:

Jean Jeanie was 65 shops and a concession business in depart-ment stores and a wholesale business called Bonanza Jeans that had gone bust. It was basically losing 60 or 70 grand a week . . . When I bought Jean Jeanie in 1985 it owed three-and-a-half million quid to Barclays Bank. They were skint. And I said [to Barclays] give me six months, freeze the interest, freeze the debt, let me see if I can fix it. We got to three days before the six months was up and we sold. It's all about the moment, seeing the opportunity, knowing how to take that opportunity. [ibid.]

What was important about the deal was that Green paid off substantial bank loans incurred by the businesses he had bought. This helped him develop a reputation among lending banks as someone who would get their money back for them when a business was looking stretched. That reputation was to be worth gold over the coming 20 years. And there was an important lesson, which was that it is important to sell assets when the right opportunity presents itself, even when an emotional attachment to a business has been formed:

Jean Jeanie was one of the few times in my business life when I all but cried when I sold it. Although I had turned 65 grand into three million quid, which was a lot of money, I didn't want to sell it. But in order to build your capital base you have to buy and sell. [ibid.]

Green then joined Lee Cooper, but did not enjoy working with its chief executive, Pierre Pouillot. In characteristic fashion, he sacrificed cash rather than stay and be unhappy:

> I worked for Lee Cooper for a year. I fell out with him . . . In the end, one of my funny moments, left there, forfeited six million quid – had a contract for an earn-out and I just thought: 'Fuck it.' In 1987, 20 years ago, that was like 60 million today. That went up in smoke.
>
> And then, a couple of years later, the whole group got into trouble, Lee Cooper . . . So I called up the bank and said: 'We're interested to buy it.' And then I got hold of their bank, I chartered a jet, and took the banker in the plane and landed in Paris, where their head office was. And then this bloke comes to get in the plane, the Frenchman. And he says: 'What are you doing here?' I said: 'I'm the buyer.' Just for a bit of sport. It really pissed them off. They got into serious trouble eventually. Anyway that was '87. He wouldn't sell it to me. He should have done. [ibid.]

The real making of Green was the episode widely seen in the unimaginative City as his nadir, the four years from 1988 to 1992 when he became chief executive of a publicly listed retailing company, Amber Day – because it was here that he decided to eschew working for stock-market listed companies and to concentrate on buying businesses for his own account. The long-term losers from Green's time at Amber Day were the very fund managers who decided that he wasn't the right kind of executive to run a public company. But the way the City mistrusted him – even though he put £3m of his own money into Amber Day – still rankles with Green:

> In 1988, I went into Amber Day, took a stake in there. I can genuinely say that I worked no less hard owning 10 per cent than

when I own 90 per cent. I didn't realize – and I don't use the word 'naive' very often – naively, I didn't realize that you don't put your own money in [to a publicly listed company]. I put in three million quid in 1988. I naively assumed that if you put your own money in people would believe you are grafting. I didn't realize it was a prison sentence, that it says on the back 'not for resale' – frightening. And you are spending half your time with analysts, institutions, managing your share price – all basically managing expectations. [ibid.]

Even so, Green is scathing about executives at substantial businesses who never risk their own capital on shares in their own companies:

If you went down the index in 2006, with all the crap and bullshit you read, £3m is more than the entire board of [big quoted retailers], all these hotshots. In 2006 they haven't got £3m [of their own money] invested in their company's stock. [ibid.]

At Amber Day, he started by building up a substantial presence in upmarket menswear retailing (it had two chains that were well known at the time, Review and Woodhouse). Then, as the economy headed for recession, he took the company into discount fashion retailing by buying What Everyone Wants, a retailer created by Gerald and Vera Weisfeld, whom he knew well. Amber Day's shares soared through 1990 and 1991 to a peak of 129p. But in 1992, Green faced a series of setbacks. He fell out with his finance director, Graham Coles, and with the only independent non-executive director on his board, Leslie Warman. They made complaints against him, the gist of which was that he was running the business as if it were his own private company rather than as a listed one with responsibilities to its outside shareholders. There was also a whispering campaign against him in the City fuelled in part by his friendships with two controversial business people: Tony Berry, the chief executive of Blue Arrow, the recruitment

company, and Roger Levitt, the creator of a boom-to-bust investment company. (In June 1991, a Department of Trade and
Industry enquiry found that Berry paid insufficient regard to
his statutory obligations as a director of Blue Arrow when he lent
£25m to Peter de Savary, a property developer; Levitt's company,
Levitt Group, collapsed in 1990 with debts of £34m and he was
subsequently banned for life from carrying out investment business in the UK.)

Amber Day's share price started to fall sharply. But what really
did for him was that the company's profits for the year 1991–92
were far less than Green himself had predicted. On 24 September
1992, Green resigned. He received £1.13m in compensation and
was asked to stay on until the end of the year as a consultant.

> I was four million quid under water with the stock. Went all
> night for a meeting to pay me off. And after that was sorted they
> said: 'By the way, will you stay three months as a consultant?' I
> go home. I sleep for three hours. I go back to the office. The only
> difference is I was not chief executive or chairman, but I was
> carrying on doing the same job. [ibid.]

His exit could have been a personal disaster because his shares in
Amber Day had collapsed in value:

> I nearly lost my house. When I came out of there at 30p, I was
> £4m below water. Could have been living in a caravan, would
> have been unpleasant. By default, I staked everything on that. As
> you are going along, hopefully you unpick. I would say that was
> the worst moment. [ibid.]

But then came what he describes as 'the best lesson of my whole
business career':

> I have nine or ten million shares. The stock is 30p . . . I leave in
> December. Still got nine or ten million shares. The stock price
> recovers to 85p . . . I get a call at 10 o'clock at night: 'Would you

like to sell the shares?' I said: 'No, actually. I thought they were made by McVitie's and I was going to eat them.'

I mean – and that summarized why to this day, other than that one misadventure with M&S stock [see Chapter 4], that's why I've never bought and sold a share, don't own a share. Because when I saw that nobody phones you between 30p and 85p, that's why I don't want to buy and sell stock. They wait five and a half million quid later. I'm underwater with my wellingtons on, the water's eight foot high, I'm drowning – and that summarized the whole episode for me. So I got out alive and got on with the next part of my life. But it was scary stuff, scary. [ibid.]

So there were two lessons from Amber Day for Green: he determined never again to run a publicly listed company and to largely avoid trading in shares. From now on, he would concentrate on buying whole companies, rather than small stakes in them. Although he could not have known it at the time, it meant he has accumulated much greater wealth than he would have done otherwise. And in generating unimaginable personal profits from his purchase of public companies such as Arcadia and Bhs, he deprived pension funds, unit trust and other investment funds of those profits. Green's later career was the emblematic example of how the success of private-equity and other private purchasers of businesses represents the distribution of wealth from the many – the millions of us who entrust our savings to pension funds and other institutions – to the few.

Green has a very clear view of how the City was the loser from the way it effectively blackballed him:

If they had left me alone, Amber Day would probably have been a FTSE company. If they had left me on my own, all the deals I have done would have been done in there. But I bought my own car – 'Oh, this guy's got his own Bentley.' I turned up with my own money. I didn't come and say: 'Give me a bucketful of options.' I didn't have an option, never had an option, never read my contract. As far as I was concerned I was working as hard as I could. And all these people beat me up. So I thought: 'How does this work?' It wasn't an arena I understood and I certainly didn't understand how it worked. And you have all these poncy people who can't even spell 'business' or 'retail' saying: 'Oh, we don't want to deal with people like him' – snooty, tooty people. Like I said, when I look back 18 years later and I go down today's FTSE, three million quid is 30 million quid. People [directors of public companies] don't buy shares. You read in the share column of a Sunday that somebody bought three quids' worth of shares – it's embarrassing. So-and-so bought 10,000 shares. What is it all about? [ibid.]

When Amber Day's annual report for the year 1991–92 was published, it said that the board and the company's auditors had reviewed transactions initiated by Green in the financial year, about which there had been complaints. The board said it was 'fully satisfied that all these transactions were undertaken in the commercial interests of the group'.

In his entire career, Green says he has made a loss on only one deal: the purchase in 1993 of Parker & Franks, a rival to Amber Day in discount retailing. He rebranded it as Xception and turned it into a 'value multi-store' selling fashion, toys, videos and dis-counted computer games. 'We lost 15 million quid. Just couldn't get it to work. Bad sites, wrong format. In the end, paid it and closed it, sold off the sites and got rid of it.' [ibid.] But Parker & Franks was an anomaly.

Prior to Bhs and Arcadia, two deals stand out for the profits they generated and the way in which they made a well-known and long-established public company, Sears, look amateurish in the ex-treme. They were the purchase of Olympus Sports from Sears and then the takeover of Sears itself. Olympus was bought in Novem-ber 1995 for £20m. Green's partner in the deal was a Scottish sports entrepreneur, Tom Hunter – who has since become a leading philanthropist and has been knighted. (In 2007, Hunter, the son of a fourth-generation baker and grocer from the former mining village of New Cumnock in Scotland, pledged to give away more than £1bn to charity.) Green secured an option to acquire Olympus from Sears but then did not buy it on his own because he was in hospital having a heart-related operation:

> The only reason I didn't do it myself was that I was in Wellington Hospital in the intensive-care unit when I got the call. When I was offered it I was in the hospital. So I said: 'Can't do it this week: can we do it next week?' I had other things on. Couldn't do it. But it worked out well. Tom did it. Worked well. Everybody won. [ibid.]

That is an understatement. Olympus's stores were combined with Hunter's smaller existing chain. Less than three years later, in July 1998, the whole thing – which was called Sports Division – was sold on to a rival, JJB. Green received £37.7m in cash while Hunter received £250m in cash and shares.

Sears had sold Olympus for a fraction of what it was worth. But this was not a case of once bitten, twice shy. In January 1999, Green secured the agreement of Sears's board for his offer to buy the entire company – which had been created as a retailing conglomerate by a Green-like mogul from an earlier era, Sir Charles Clore. With financial support this time from Sir David and Sir Frederick Barclay, the magnates who have bought and sold countless well-known businesses since the 1960s (and these days own the Ritz, the Telegraph Group and Littlewoods, *inter alia*), he paid £549m.

Sears had lost its direction years earlier and had been on the market for many months. So if the stock market was an effective pricing mechanism – and if the directors of Sears really understood what their company owned – Green should not have been able to break up the business rapidly to generate a vast profit. But this is precisely what he did. In April 1999, he sold Sears's mail-order business, Freemans, to Germany's Otto Versand for £150m. In July, he sold Wallis, Warehouse, Miss Selfridge, Richards and Outfit to Arcadia for £151m (and, of course, got most of these stores back again when he bought Arcadia). The following week, he sold Adams, the children's clothing chain, to its management for £87m. With other deals, he had raised £530m, and he still owned Sears's property assets, which were worth about £200m.

At the time, he told the *Financial Times*: 'I have a clear conscience. I bought businesses with 26,000 employees and I've sold businesses with 26,000 employees. I haven't made any profit out of someone else's misfortune.' Except, perhaps, for the members of Sears's board – and their financial advisers – who sold the company to him:

> We got our money back in 11 weeks. That was a record. They had spent £16m on consultants, there was a cupboard full of books telling them what to do. We were hostile, we were outside the door, they wouldn't meet with us [in other words, he did not have the detailed financial information available to the board]. But we did it in 11 weeks. [ibid.]

The Sears transaction was a breakthrough deal. It demonstrated to the financial world that Green was a brilliant money-maker and – perhaps more importantly – that he was happy to see a disproportionate share of the profits go to his backers, in this case the Barclay brothers. Green understands the power of the media to make or break reputations and he made sure that his financial success in this deal was widely disseminated. The Sears episode also cemented his relationship with Peter Cummings, the banker at Bank of Scotland who has been his most important financial supporter:

> It was the night of the deal, Sears. The Barclays were funding. I put in X, they put in Y. We borrowed Z. At five o'clock, the night before, £150m of the financing falls out of bed. Bank finance. They couldn't get it done. I called Peter Cummings. I had a relationship with him from Sports Division. I said: 'Peter, I need a favour.' 'What do you need?' I said: 'I need 150 million quid.' 'When?' I said: 'Tonight.' He said: 'Is it for what I think it's for?' [A potential embarrassment for Cummings was that Bob Reid,

Sears's chairman, was the deputy governor of Bank of Scotland and therefore, by extension, Cummings's superior.] I said: 'Yes.' He said: 'Bit tricky, give me twenty minutes.' Called back. He said: 'All right, I'm on, on the following basis: boom, boom, boom.' I said: 'Right, let's go.' We did it through the night. So I brought more than my Y. To get it over the line, I got it over the line myself. But it was on a handshake. [ibid. (and see Chapter 4)]

Having seen Cummings and Green together, it is clear they have an unusual understanding. They are each other's biggest fans:

Look, I've always said to Peter – hopefully I won't rue these words – I have always under-promised him, and over-delivered. I've said we'll do this, this and this. [ibid.]

His relationship with Cummings and other banks became the envy of private-equity houses. The senior partner of one told me in 2006 that his firm was desperately trying to emulate Green by persuading banks to lend more for its purchases of companies and on less onerous terms. This private-equity superstar and his competitors eventually got what they wanted from banks with more money than sense. Green's astounding record may therefore have played a role in creating the conditions for the private-equity banking crisis of 2007. A collapse in lending standards for private-equity purchases in 2006 and 2007 coupled with a great increase in such lending was a dangerous combination. And in the summer of 2007, banks found they were unable to do what they normally do, which is to repackage most of this debt for sale to other investors. These investors simply did not want to buy the debt, because they began to see that it was a much riskier proposition than they had thought. So the big international lending banks were stuck with more than $300bn of loans to private-equity-financed companies. The banks were deeply unhappy that they could not offload this debt from their balance sheets and were even more unhappy that they had to write down its value – thereby incurring losses – because the terms had been too generous to borrowers.

Predictably, they put a freeze of uncertain duration on further lending for private-equity transactions.

But Cummings has never been proved wrong to back Green. And his employer, HBOS, has made a great return from the relationship, because it has tended to take equity stakes in his deals. In this context, it is also relevant that Green is more conservative in his financial engineering than most private-equity firms – which provides reassurance to lenders. When he buys a substantial company, his motivation is never simply to strip out the assets and sell them rapidly for a profit. 'I can get into every area of the business,' he says. 'I'm not afraid to get underneath any of the detail, I won't pass it to somebody else.' His primary aim is to improve the trading performance and he regards the properties in a business primarily as insurance against the possibility that it might all go horribly wrong. He says:

> Each business I have looked at, bought, went into, I think I can see, understand the component pieces, you know the value; I am never looking at the assets other than as a comfort – never sold from Bhs or Arcadia one asset, not sold nor leased back any-thing. [ibid.]

Unlike private equity, which tends to flog off property and assets as quickly as possible after a takeover has been consummated, Green prefers to retain prime properties. Instead, he takes out mortgages against properties to secure cheaper funding.

He may be less aggressive in selling assets than private-equity firms, but he is critical of public companies with low borrowings and fat property assets, because he believes they tend to become lazy without the discipline of servicing debt. Strikingly, he told me years ago that he thought Tesco should find ways to return cash to shareholders from its freeholds, worth at least £20bn – and the supermarket chain has now started to sell and lease back a minority of its stores to hand £3bn to investors.

In general, Green is not a fan of the way that listed businesses are managed:

So the answer is, if you look at a study of UK PLC and ask me what do I see, I say: 'They are not traders, they are not operators, they are not driving the business hard, they don't want to outperform, they don't want to overperform . . . Now, of course, as a private operator, are you going to get years when you go up and down because you are not manipulating the profit? Of course you can. You are trying to do your best. But you are driving the business off a different momentum. [ibid.]

These days, Green seems restless in his Monday-to-Friday routine – in which the first half of the week is spent in Arcadia's head office off Oxford Street and the back end is at Bhs in the Marylebone Road. He has not done a big takeover deal for years, largely because he thinks that the private-equity boom drove up the price of companies to a level where he finds it difficult to see the potential for profit. So if the current crisis in financial markets leads to a substantial fall in share prices, he will be in his element – and would be tempted to start buying businesses again. Almost no weekends are spent in the UK. At lunchtime every Friday, he is driven to his £27m private jet, which he will typically fly to his Monaco home, where his mega-yacht is anchored. Every few years he holds a lavish family party, where superstars such as Jennifer Lopez and Destiny's Child are hired to entertain his megabucks guests. A Gulfstream G550 flies him to the Far East on business and to Barbados for an annual Christmas holiday at Sandy Lane, the hotel that charges up to $25,000 a night and is owned by the Irish plutocrats Dermot Desmond and JP McManus. When at Sandy Lane, Green plays tennis with Roger Federer:

He said: 'Do you want a game?' I said: 'If you are prepared to serve from 100 yards behind the baseline, we'll play.' I beat him. By game five, when he was serving at the baseline, I never saw the ball. [ibid.]

His connections and money have also made him a great secret power in Premier League football. A Tottenham Hotspur supporter, one of his close friends is the consummate football agent, the Israeli Pini Zahavi. In the summer of 2006, he played an important role in the fraught transfer of the England defender Ashley Cole from Arsenal to Chelsea. However, he has always told me he sees football clubs as lousy businesses, sources of aggro, consumers of cash that rarely yield a profit – so he would never put his own money into a club. That said, he enjoys more conventional gambling and his exploits at casinos are the stuff of legend.

With his wealth, Green has the ability to influence the climate of opinion on issues of personal concern – such as the availability of vocational training for youngsters (which he favours) as opposed to academic education. But he says that politics is not for him. Whenever I have talked to him about politics and politicians, he has evinced precious little interest – and what he does say about the Government and the Opposition is rarely flattering to either.

I asked him about some public remarks made in May 2006 by David Cameron, the leader of the Tories, attacking Bhs for selling padded bras to young girls (which Cameron said was an example of the 'increasingly aggressive interface of commercialization and sexualization'). Green was unamused because the bras had been withdrawn in March 2003 and were a small line:

> I called one of his treasurers and said: 'You need to get him to call me.' I said: 'David, that's a silly place to go, why would you go there?' I said: 'I'm not even sure what the point is.' I said: 'If you want retailers to get involved in not selling boom boom boom, I'm there. But that was just silly.' I said: 'Let's make sure we don't have any of those kinds of accidents.'
>
> You see, I'd seen him previously to that. He came round to see me. To be introduced. And I just said: 'I don't do politics, just as a rule. But it's interesting to chit-chat, need to know, don't want to be rude.' And they've tried to get me to all these lunches and dinners. I've said I don't want to know about it. It is not a place to be, is it? [ibid.]

Politics is not a place to which Sir Philip Green wants to go just now. But he has created a new dynasty. And he hopes that he has fashioned a family business empire in a twenty-first-century way that might stand comparison with the achievements seventy years earlier of the Markses and Sieffs at Marks & Spencer. Whether he eventually gives his money to his children or to charity, the beneficiaries will have clout. He has no doubt about his place in history – it's the harvesting of the Arcadia dividend. I asked him what he would do with all that cash: 'Who knows? It is unusual. Not been done. This isn't make-believe. It is real cash.'

CHAPTER 4

MARKS & SPENCER AND THE NEW ESTABLISHMENT

It was a collision of old City and new megabucks. On Wednesday, 14 July 2004, David Mayhew was in Scotland trying to woo salmon on to his fishing line when he took the call on his mobile phone. The chain-smoking, wiry and wily Old Etonian stockbroker had for years been the trusted adviser to the directors of Britain's biggest companies. Marks & Spencer was one of his more important clients, in terms of prestige and profile. Which is why Philip Green was on the line, barking an ultimatum to the chairman of Cazenove.

The retailing billionaire with a voracious appetite for deals had raised almost £12bn from the world's most powerful banks to buy Marks & Spencer – 'never been done before, never been done before' was Green's typical incantation about his prowess in raising unimaginable sums by ringing up a few banking chums. But after weeks of sparring with M&S, he was fed up with the board's reluctance to agree to take his money. It was now or never, he roared at Mayhew – who privately believed that Green was close to winning enough support from shareholders and hedge funds to carry off the greatest name on the British high street.

Back in London, Paul Myners, M&S's chairman, had that morning been urging his company's army of small shareholders to keep the faith at a packed and raucous annual general meeting. He was still fighting the good fight, convinced that Green was not offering enough for the business – although he too could not help but notice that the mood of investors was swinging Green's way.

There was one last possible manoeuvre for M&S. Myners told his fellow directors at a board meeting later the same day about his planned whirlwind global tour of the investment institutions that were the company's largest shareholders. He would go to Edinburgh, Boston, Zurich, New York and San Diego. That last planned stop-off – in a world where capital knows no national boundaries – was home to the most important M&S investor, Brandes.

If a majority of these shareholders had told Myners and his chief executive, Stuart Rose, that they liked the colour of Green's money, then the game would have been up. It was the last roll of the dice – and neither Myners nor Rose was confident how the numbers would fall. But, as it turned out, all this anxiety was misplaced because Green was becoming exasperated at what he perceived as Myners refusal to talk to him. Green was tired of the fight, which was conducted under the bright lights of intense media interest. There was a strain on his young family. There were also enormous financial risks, not least from the demands from M&S's pension fund for a substantial cash injection. So, for reasons that have never made total sense, just at the moment when victory was probably at hand, Green walked off the field of battle. At around 8.30 p.m. a message came through on the BlackBerry of Robert Swannell, a banker from Citigroup who is close to Rose, that Green had abandoned his attempt to buy M&S.

The M&S directors could not believe it. 'We made Swannell read it twice,' says Myners [interview, 8 December 2006]. But for Rose and Myners it was really only the beginning of their ordeal. They had made the bold claim that Marks & Spencer could once again thrive as a public company, and had repudiated the City trend of selling out to private equity or – in this case – the supercharged, one-man-band version of private equity: Green. But Marks's recent history of a recovery that had slid into reverse suggested that reviving the company would not be easy. And what if they could not get Marks's share price above the £4-a-share which Green wanted to pay? Well, Myners and Rose would have suffered the opprobrium of shareholders for ever. Their victory over Green could have been severely career-limiting:

> Fifty per cent of me felt absolutely confident, that I instinctively knew what I had to do. The other 50 per cent was absolutely genuine 'fucking hell, this is such a mess, I'm not sure I am going to be able to do this'. [Stuart Rose interview, 4 July 2006]

For much of the late twentieth century, Marks & Spencer was Britain's most admired company. Harvard Business School produced weighty reports on why it was such a successful retailer. In an era of industrial malaise in the UK, M&S was a rare company in which we could all take pride; but when the rot set in during the late 1990s, its decline was swift and humiliating. The story of that decline is a parable of the waning powers of old corporate Britain and the etiolated aristocracy of the old City of London. But it was the events of the summer of 2004, when Marks & Spencer was under siege from Philip Green – the self-made billionaire who left school without a qualification and is revered and loathed in equal measure in the City – that really tell of a revolution in the boardrooms of Britain and a new rawness in global capitalism. They also demonstrate that despite the seemingly unstoppable impersonal forces of globalization, charismatic individuals can still make a difference. In the end, M&S fell under the sway of a duo whose respective backgrounds appear to show that Great Britain is a meritocracy: Myners, a man who never knew his parents and was raised by a Truro butcher; and Rose, the son of an émigré from China whose grandfather fled communism in Russia and then the communism of Mao.

The chaos of 2004 would have been the stuff of fantasy back in 1985 when I was first granted an audience with M&S's management as a cub reporter. On arrival, I was left in no doubt of the privilege being bestowed on me. The walk to the office of the then joint managing director, Richard [Rick] Greenbury, seemed to go on for mile after Kafkaesque mile of darkling corridor in the firm's Marylebone Road headquarters in central London. Everything about the place was sombre and serious, including the traffic lights above the doors of the more important executives that told minions whether or not they had the right to knock on a door. Greenbury sat across from me at the largest desk I had ever seen. 'I hate journalists' was his opening line. Not for him the fawning and flattering employed by so many business people these days to obtain kind reviews of their prowess.

Greenbury had an almost religious conviction that M&S simply was the nonpareil, whatever oiks such as me might think. Founded in 1884, it was the product of an earlier age of flux and opportunity in the UK. Created by a Polish-Jewish immigrant, Michael Marks, and his son, Simon, it had become the most successful retailer in the UK, arguably the most successful in the whole world. It planted itself firmly in the middle-price section of every part of the clothing market in Britain, and dominated it. In food retailing, it was the great innovator. The scions of the founding families became knights and peers. They played an influential role in the creation of the state of Israel. M&S was a world unto itself, beholden to no one, contemptuous in equal measure of bankers, of the City and of the media (although Greenbury's complaints to editors and journalists were legendary in their tenacity and ferocity, as and when anyone deigned to criticize the business or its representative on earth, him).

By the mid-1980s, however, it was all change at M&S. The descendants of those founders – the Markses, Sieffs and Sachers – were on their way out. They no longer filled the important executive positions or even owned many shares. A generation of professional managers, trained by M&S, was taking over. First Derek Rayner served as chairman and chief executive from 1984; then Greenbury, who joined the company as a management trainee in 1952 straight from Ealing County Grammar School, took the reins as chief executive in 1988 and became chairman as well in 1991. Although not of the blood-line, they stuck with the M&S management tradition set by Michael and Simon Marks. Which means they were both autocrats. In fact, it was a characteristic manifestation of Rayner's capricious dictatorial style that led the current chief executive, Stuart Rose, to quit M&S in 1989 after 18 years of progression from trainee to middle manager. Rose was working in food and had a disagreement with Rayner.

> The fall-out was about something ridiculous; it was about mangoes. It was about 'you should be buying mangoes from X' and I was buying them from Y. He [Rayner] thought he knew more about mangoes than I did and he wanted to show that I was nothing but a jumped-up boy. So I was sent to Coventry. The chairman didn't speak to me for six months. [Stuart Rose interview, 22 June 2006]

Part of Rose's punishment was to be given a job in Paris, well away from the seat of power.

> They used to beat you up. I was told to keep out of the chairman's way. But when the chairman came to Paris, I had nearly got myself rejuvenated. I did all the presentations that afternoon for all the textiles and foods, for two days. There was a dinner for 12 of us, the senior management team, at the Crillon [the lavish Parisian hotel] that night. But I was discreetly taken aside by another director just before dinner, who said: 'The chairman has asked that you don't attend dinner this evening.' It was a huge blow to my ego. Huge blow. [ibid.]

Soon afterwards, Rose was approached by Burton Group – the retailing conglomerate that Sir Ralph Halpern had been expanding rapidly through a series of acquisitions – with an offer to help run its Debenhams department-store business. 'I was 39 and I was deeply pissed off about this incident,' Rose says. 'I was on 50 grand a year and Ralph offered me 100 grand a year to go to Debenhams. I went, and I was the first senior bloke to leave the business.'

At the time, Rose's departure was seen by M&S as no more than a minor annoyance. In the 1980s, Rayner and his anointed successor, Greenbury, were continuing to grow M&S by stressing the quality of its goods and its reputation for value. But, under its long shadow, other retailers were springing up that were more in tune with the mood of individualism fostered by the Thatcher Government than with utilitarian M&S. The most significant of these was Next, a chain of womenswear shops aimed at M&S's core market but offering more of a fashionable edge. Next was the creation of George Davies, a slightly manic, unpredictable Liverpudlian with a genius for identifying and exploiting fashion trends in the mass market. Over the coming years, Davies would first batter Marks as a competitor and then help to redeem it – and along the way make a fortune for himself.

Although Rayner and Greenbury did not ignore Next and Burton, they were irked when anyone suggested they should be seriously worried by them. More resonant for M&S was a contest of an altogether different magnitude – to be the biggest, most profitable, most respected retailer in the UK. There were only two contestants in this race. The other was J Sainsbury, another family business, which dominated the grocery trade and supermarket sector. In 1992, Sainsbury made pre-tax profits of £632.2m, just ahead of Marks's £623.5m. Lord Sainsbury, the chairman and descendant of the grocer's nineteenth-century founder, did not hide his glee: 'I never imagined when I took over as chairman that by the time I left Sainsbury would be earning more than Marks & Spencer. In 1969, their profits were nine times higher than ours, and since I have the highest regard for Marks & Spencer, I could not be more delighted.' [*The Times*, 14 May 1992]

Such rivalry over profits may seem understandable and harm-less, or possibly even good for their shareholders. But in fact the reverse was true. Sainsbury and M&S were creating the conditions that would generate serious reversals at both companies. Their obsession with maintaining and widening – where possible – their profit margins gave Tesco and Asda a golden opportunity. In the early 1990s, Tesco and Asda reacted by adopting a strategy of cutting prices to gain customers. They deliberately reduced their profit margins to win extra sales. As a result, Tesco not only succeeded in toppling Sainsbury from the position of Britain's leading supermarket group, but along with Asda it also started to challenge M&S directly by selling clothes at stunningly low prices, causing havoc at M&S itself. The designer who created the 'George' range of clothes for Asda that hurt M&S was none other than George Davies.

In the mid-1990s, however, M&S under Greenbury seemed impregnable. Knighted in 1992, the grammar-school boy was now a grandee, one of the UK's most influential and respected business people. In 1995 he sat in judgement on his fellow business leaders by chairing a review initiated by the Confederation of British Industry about how boardroom pay was set, the Greenbury Re-view – which was precipitated by a public outcry at the pay awards for the bosses of the privatized gas, water and electricity companies (remuneration in six figures which today would be regarded as paltry). His apotheosis came in 1997, when Marks's annual profits soared past £1bn for the first time: it made £1.1bn in the year to 31 March. Sainsbury was left in the dust, generating £651m for the same period.

In this moment of triumph, Greenbury pushed it all a bit too far. The company's 1997 annual report set out a bold plan to become 'the world's leading volume retailer, with a global brand and global recognition'. Around the world, it was trading from 651 different locations, including 286 in the UK, 20 in France, 44 in Canada and 8 in Hong Kong. In the US, it owned Brooks Brothers, the fusty, preppy outfitter and purveyor of renowned button-down shirts. M&S's turnover was almost £8bn and it employed 68,000 people, including 11,000 outside the UK. It was big but Greenbury wanted it to be bigger still: he announced a programme to spend £2.2bn on adding three million square feet of new selling space by March 2000.

This was more than a doubling of Marks's annual rate of investment. The target was to increase store space in the UK, where it was already the market leader, by 18 per cent and in the rest of the world by a staggering 41 per cent. As Greenbury himself now acknowledges, it was too ambitious and it was badly timed. Managers would be stretched to the limit and the new stores would be a drag on group profits until they reached maturity. All of this could have been foreseen by the group's seven non-executive directors, who should have scaled back Greenbury's proposals. But the board was big and unwieldy: the non-executives were massively outnumbered by the 18 executive directors, which was typical of companies at the time. Like his predecessors, Greenbury was the supreme being. Unless the entire board ganged up against him, he could more or less do what he liked.

There had been an apparent strengthening of the quality of the non-executive contingent. In October 1996, Sir Michael Perry, erstwhile chairman of the giant food manufacturer Unilever, joined the board, along with Brian Baldock, the former deputy chairman of Guinness. Then in January 1997, Dame Stella Rimington, who had been director general of MI5, Britain's secret service, became a non-executive director. In their non-executive colleague, Sir Martin Jacomb, a former merchant banker and chairman of the British Council, they had a genuine City eminence. An Old Etonian, Jacomb was the paradigm of the well-connected banker, having played an important role in the Tories' privatization programme of the 1980s. On paper, the M&S board was a microcosm of Britain's elite, but the non-executives turned out to be a bit of a fig leaf. For non-executives it is always tricky to strike the right balance between on the one hand motivating and empowering executives, and on the other making sure that the executives do not get carried away with their own enthusiasm, to the detriment of shareholders. In M&S's case, it is difficult to argue that the non-executives got it right, because it was about to embark on seven manic years of lurching from crisis to crisis.

That said, the big City institutions that controlled M&S's shares proved equally ineffective at exerting the right kind of pressure at the right time. The largest shareholder, with 4.7 per cent of the company, was the Prudential, which had been an investor in M&S since it was listed on the Stock Exchange in 1926 and was regarded as a symbolically important supporter. The link was reinforced by the presence on the board of Jacomb, who was also chairman of the Pru. But the Pru was probably the last shareholder capable of seeing the mess at M&S because it was in a strikingly similar one itself. The Pru's decline from an awesome position of power both in the City and over the financial prospects of millions of savers corresponds in an unnerving way with M&S's decline. Marks and the Pru were both twentieth-century powerhouses that had grown arrogant on decades of success. And as paternalistic vendors of mass-market, utilitarian products they were both slow to notice that consumers were increasingly demanding to be treated as individuals with differing tastes and needs.

A symbolic manifestation of M&S's arrogance and distance from commercial reality was that in 1996–97, it made a contribution – of £40,000 – to the Conservative Party. Such political contributions were increasingly frowned on by big shareholders in listed companies. It was money that would yield no return: what precisely could any Government actually do for M&S that would allow it to pay a bigger dividend? Also, by then every British pundit was anticipating that Labour would romp home under its young leader, Tony Blair, in an election that was only months away. Giving money to the Tories was not just a waste; it risked irking the new powers in the land.

The devastating failure of the M&S board, however, was the mishandling of the process of finding a successor to Greenbury. He turned 59 in 1995, yet there was no consensus on who would succeed him. At the time, the world's most admired businessman was probably 'Neutron' Jack Welch, the chief executive officer of General Electric, the enormous US industrial conglomerate. In 1991, Welch said: 'From now on, [choosing my successor] is the most important decision I'll make. It occupies a considerable amount of thought almost every day.' In 1991, Welch was 10 years away from retirement, so this was impressive forward planning – and the man to whom he eventually handed the baton, Jeff Immelt, has performed better than could have been expected. Within M&S, however, preparations for a handover from Greenbury were rather less successful.

According to board minutes I have seen, M&S's directors resolved at a board meeting on 2 August 1995, shortly after Greenbury turned 59, that he should 'continue to hold office as chairman and chief executive until 31 July 1998'. They agreed that 'for any period thereafter his position would be reviewed by the board on an annual basis' and that the 'initiation' of such a review would be 'delegated to the non-executive directors'. Greenbury's tenure was extended at another board meeting on 3 September 1997, when the non-executives – led by Jacomb and Baldock, who had drafted a paper – proposed that Greenbury continue as chairman and chief executive until the conclusion of the company's annual meeting (AGM) in 2000, shortly before his 64th birthday or, 'if otherwise determined by the board, until the conclusion of the AGM in 1999'. Even after ceasing to be chief executive, Greenbury would remain as non-executive chairman until 'the conclusion of the AGM in 2001 [shortly before his 65th birthday]'. The board, minus Greenbury – who was not present for this discussion – gave 'unanimous support' to the proposal, and when Greenbury entered the boardroom, he said that he was pleased to accept the offer. The minutes record him as saying that 'considerable challenges lay ahead for the board but the chairman expressed his expectation in these being met with confidence and with continued reliance on the founding principles of the business'. The implication appeared to be that

Greenbury would simply go on and on, as M&S became bigger and bigger.

But if the non-executives regarded him as the immaculate chief executive, the City was beginning to be concerned that his sell-by date might not be far off. Marks's profits only inched forward in 1997–98, to a new record of £1.17bn: the impact of strong sales growth in the UK was limited by a weaker performance overseas. Investors and journalists began to fixate on when Greenbury might retire. Greenbury was also vulnerable to criticism for holding the offices of both chairman and chief executive, against what had become best boardroom practice (investors increasingly wanted companies to appoint independent, part-time chairmen, who were capable of standing up to a chief executive, as and when that chief executive's judgement went awry). With his history of berating hacks, Greenbury could not count on deep reserves of goodwill in the media to suppress a whispering campaign against him.

M&S tried to stem the speculation about Greenbury's future by announcing on 20 May 1998 that 'the board plan is for the company's chairman, Sir Richard Greenbury, to retire at 65' and that it was 'the unanimous wish of the board that Sir Richard stay until he is 65 and he agreed'. It added:

> The board discusses the issues relating to organization and succession on an ongoing basis, including the roles of chairman and chief executive. When any formal decisions are made they are announced. No such announcement is imminent.

The statement seemed naive. It implicitly acknowledged the contentiousness of vesting the powers of chairman and chief executive in a single person: it fuelled gossip and rumour rather than knocking them on the head.

Within the executive cadre, the uncertainty about the succession was fomenting disunity. For years, the leading candidate to take over from Greenbury was Keith Oates, a joint managing director and deputy chairman. He was rated by analysts and fund managers for having built a financial services operation for M&S that offered store cards, loans and unit trusts. But it counted against him within M&S that – unlike Greenbury and Rayner – he was not a lifer. He had been with the group for 'only' 14 years, having joined in 1984 after working for IBM, Rolls-Royce, Black & Decker and Thyssen Bornemisza. Nor had he ever worked on the shop floor or been a retailer. Worse still, he was pushing 56. If Greenbury stayed as long as he wanted, Oates might well become too old to enjoy a proper stint at the top.

It became clear to journalists and analysts that Oates was no longer a shoo-in, and a new name began to be whispered as a potential chief executive – Peter Salsbury, a reserved individual who joined M&S in 1970 (14 years before Oates) when he was just 21. Like Greenbury, Salsbury had been a management trainee. Unlike Greenbury, he went to university (both Oates and Salsbury were graduates of the London School of Economics). At various times, he had been in charge of footwear, home furnishings, womenswear, personnel and store operations. Since March 1998, he had been the managing director in charge of clothing, home furnishings, mail order, European retail and international franchises.

Suddenly, in the autumn of 1998, the absence of proper succession planning became incendiary after M&S's first-half results were significantly worse than expected. Pre-tax profits for the six months to the end of September fell for the first time in seven years, by 23 per cent to £348m. The causes, according to the company, were the costs of Greenbury's expansion plan at a time of shaky confidence in the UK and a strong pound that undermined the profitability of the overseas operations. The shares plunged 10 per cent, wiping £1bn off the company's market value. Greenbury was typically resolute. 'We are better in tough times,' he said. 'We have a 16 per cent market share, the lowest cost base of any UK retailer and the biggest single brand in the world. We will leverage that in a big way in the next year or two. We may be an oil tanker which takes five miles to turn, but oil tankers are rather efficient.' Nevertheless, investment had to

be cut and £300m was shaved from the capital spending programme.

Although there was frenzied coverage in the press of M&S's
problems, Greenbury flew to Bombay two days after the results for
a spot of holiday and a bit of business. What happened next was
reminiscent of an attempted coup in a tinpot state ruled by
dictatorship. With the autocrat safely out of the country, Oates
wrote to each of the non-executive directors, laying out his analysis
of what was wrong at M&S and his claim to take over as chief
executive. One director told M&S's chronicler, the journalist Judi
Bevan, that 'the form of the letter was not inflammatory but the
substance was explosive' [*The Rise and Fall of Marks & Spencer*,
Judi Bevan, 2001].

What were perhaps even more incendiary for this proud
company were leaks to Sunday newspapers about the tension
between Oates and Greenbury. In the *Sunday Times* John Jay
wrote:

> Open warfare is about to break out in the boardroom of Marks &
> Spencer . . . Hostilities will be triggered by the decision of Keith
> Oates, the deputy chairman, to start lobbying the company's
> non-executive directors to pick him as chief executive when Sir
> Richard Greenbury splits his roles, probably next year. Oates,
> 56, is thought to have made plain his ambitions to two non-
> executives, Sir Martin Jacomb and Brian Baldock, last week . . .
>
> Oates's desire to be chief executive will bring him into open
> conflict with Greenbury, who is said to favour Peter Salsbury,
> 49, currently managing director in charge of general merchan-
> dise. The M&S deputy chairman will attempt to improve his
> relations with Greenbury but some observers believe the rift is
> irreparable and that one of the two men eventually will have to
> leave the company. Last week one friend said: 'Oates is loyal. He
> is not trying to rock the boat – the boat is already rocking. He just
> wants to be part of the changes M&S needs to make. He will be
> happy to work with Greenbury as his chairman although some
> people have suggested the best team would be Oates as chair-

man and Salsbury as chief executive.' [*Sunday Times,* 8 November 1998]

When Greenbury discovered what had gone on, he was incandescent. From India, he spoke to all the directors on the phone. According to Tony Good, a public-relations executive with strong links to Indian business who had accompanied him on the trip, Greenbury flew back early to the UK wanting to dismiss Oates. But the non-executives insisted that due process should be followed.

An emergency board meeting was held at M&S's Baker Street headquarters at 11 a.m. on 9 November. The panic at the company is reflected in the minutes: 'The Secretary advised the Board that as the meeting had been called at such short notice, certain directors had not been notified of the meeting.' In fact, eight directors were missing. Those that did attend agreed that the uncertainty about Greenbury's successor was no longer sustainable, as the minutes reveal:

> Against a background of regrettable and extensive continued media speculation, Sir Martin Jacomb proposed that as a matter of urgency the board establish a special nominations committee consisting of all the non-executive directors. This committee would be delegated the single purpose of making a recommendation to the chairman and the board as to the appointment of a chief executive officer for the company . . . The process would commence immediately with a view to the committee reaching a conclusion by the end of this week.
>
> Sir Martin added that it was imperative that there now be a total embargo on any press contact by any member of the board during this process in view of the damaging leaks which have occurred recently.

But it took rather longer than a week to finalize the appointment. A director from that time explains: 'After discussions with each member of the board (privately), Salsbury was chosen almost unanimously as Oates's supporters largely deserted him because of his behaviour.' The changes were ratified at a board meeting on 25 November. The following day, M&S put out a statement saying that, as of 1 February 1999, Greenbury would become a 'non-executive' chairman and Salsbury would take the role of chief executive. Greenbury would stay at the company until the annual meeting in July 2000, but Oates would resign from the board and take early retirement on 31 January 1999.

In a written corporate statement that attempted to restore dignity to the chaos, Greenbury said: 'I would like to thank Keith Oates for his most valuable contribution over the last 14 years, especially to our Financial Services and overseas businesses. It is very sad that as part of the modernizing of our top management structure there is no longer a full-time role for Keith and he is therefore taking early retirement.' As it turned out – and as Greenbury now concedes – the board picked the wrong man. Oates would almost certainly have been a better chief executive than Salsbury proved to be.

Greenbury himself was still firmly implanted at M&S, having remained as chairman on the substantial salary of £450,000 per annum, considerably more than most chairmen of the time were paid. He was expected to work a five-day week 'holding Salsbury's hand', according to an M&S director. Within months Greenbury became convinced that Salsbury was 'not up to the job' and was 'already damaging the business with his people and product policies'. He expressed these views to Jacomb and the other non-executives, who urged him to be patient and give Salsbury more time to settle in. When the full-year results were announced, however, they were dreadful. Pre-tax profits fell by almost half to £635m on flat sales of £8.22bn. The company conceded that for the first time in years it had lost market share in its most important business, selling clothes in the UK, where there was a fall from 15.1 per cent to 14.3 per cent. To make matters worse, sales per unit of selling space – or like-for-like sales, the measure of choice for City analysts – collapsed in the first four weeks of the new trading period. They dropped a staggering 10 per cent (though the decline narrowed to 6 per cent in the opening weeks of May).

It was a mess. And Greenbury – who did not attend Salsbury's public presentation of the results – feared that Salsbury was using him as a scapegoat by failing to explain that about half the fall in profits was due to the strong pound (which was beyond the company's control) and one-off costs associated with the expansion programme. Greenbury felt humiliated. His working relationship with Salsbury had become intolerable.

In June, Greenbury took a holiday in Venice with his wife. On his return, he arranged to see Jacomb and told him that he was determined to retire a year early, at the annual meeting in July. Jacomb did not attempt to dissuade him. In fact, he suggested that Greenbury should quit immediately. On 22 June, M&S announced that Greenbury was resigning. Salsbury described Greenbury's departure as 'a genuinely joint decision'. Greenbury said:

> Having been chief executive, it is difficult to step into the role of non-executive chairman. I feel that my contribution is complete and that now is the right time for me to retire as the business is clearly entering a new era. [*Guardian*, 23 June 1999]

Greenbury also said that a forthcoming strategy review contained 'some radical new thoughts . . . and I decided that I wasn't the right person to be influencing those judgements'. Years later, according to a director, Greenbury characterized the document prepared for the review as '700 pages of garbage produced by 10 management consultancies.'

Greenbury was replaced as chairman, on a temporary basis, by Brian Baldock, the former deputy chairman of Guinness. He was the first outsider to chair M&S in its 115-year history and, in a further remarkable break with precedent, headhunters were appointed to find a new permanent chairman. The successful candidate would eventually be found – many months later – by Anna Mann, of the headhunting firm Whitehead Mann, and then the doyenne of that rarefied branch of the job-search industry called 'boardroom practice'. She was held in great esteem by directors of the UK's biggest companies, although her reputation took quite a knock in early 2004 when she badly misread the mood of the City by recommending the appointment of Sir Ian Prosser as Sainsbury's chairman. After Prosser's selection for the job was announced, Sainsbury's shareholders signalled that they were unhappy, which meant that Prosser had to relinquish the job even before he had started it. The Prosser incident demonstrated that boards were powerful only so long as they retained the confidence of investors. That was a lesson the M&S directors also took some time to learn.

If Marks & Spencer had been following best corporate governance practice or doing what its shareholders would have preferred, it would have recruited a part-time, non-executive chairman. However, a director says that the board was already losing confidence in Salsbury by the autumn of 1999 and wanted to appoint someone above him who would effectively run the business. So it gave executive powers to the new chairman. He would be Luc Vandevelde, a suave, 48-year-old Belgian who had chaired the successful French superstore group, Promodes. Having merged Promodes with Carrefour to create a retailing giant, Vandevelde was ready for a new challenge. Rumours of his arrival at M&S were circulating in December 1999, but negotiations dragged on and his appointment was not announced until 24 January 2000. He started a month later.

M&S was still in trouble. At the annual meeting in July 1999, Baldock had told shareholders that sales of clothing continued to fall sharply and even food sales – which had seemed more resilient – were in decline. The company's value on the stock market was down to £7bn, considerably less than half what it had been 21 months previously. In the six months to the end of September 1999, pre-tax profits fell to £192.8m from £337.4m – and the share price remained weak.

Salsbury took what he hoped would be remedial action, having recognized that M&S was no longer so powerful that it could ignore how its rivals managed their businesses. For the first time M&S would accept credit cards in its stores. Salsbury also announced plans to save £450m per year in costs by 2002 by changing the way in which the company bought clothes and distributed them to its shops. In what was seen as a hammer blow to the British garment industry, it reduced its commitment to purchasing clothes from domestic manufacturers, because they were simply too pricey compared with the overseas competition. The forces of globalization could not be ignored even by the mighty Marks. Its historic and totemic role as the prop and support of UK textile makers had become too expensive.

M&S's survival instincts were not, in fact, so out of step with its history. When it started to buy clothing direct from British makers in the mid-1920s, M&S was not acting out of any philanthropic motive but simply because doing so gave it better control of price and quality. It was only after the Second World War – and especially under the chairmanship of Lord Sieff – that Marks's 'buy British' policy took on more of a social and political tinge. By the 1990s, however, British manufacturers were being undercut savagely by factories in the Far East. M&S's slowness to take advantage of those lower prices put it at a dire competitive disadvantage. Salsbury was doing the right thing for the rehabilitation of his business. But he caused a massive furore, not least when in October 1999 he announced that he would no longer buy from one of its four largest suppliers, William Baird, a Scottish textile firm that had been selling to M&S for 30 years. Baird was forced to lay off 4,500 staff. And over the succeeding two years other British suppliers relocated their operations to lower-cost factories in China, other parts of Asia and North Africa. What Salsbury started has been pursued by his successors to the extent that today a negligible quantity of M&S's clothes, just between 1 and 2 per cent of the total, are made in the UK. It takes about 45 per cent from the Far East, 20 per cent from India and the Indian sub-continent, and 35 per cent from Eastern Europe, Turkey, the Middle East and North Africa. Under Stuart Rose, its latest chief executive, M&S has set up buying offices in Istanbul, Bangalore, Bangladesh and Hong Kong.

But if much of Salsbury's strategy made sense, he was a poor motivator. Morale at the company slumped. And the pace of reorganization played havoc with the most basic element of any retailer's business – making sure the right stock was actually on the shelves. Customers lost faith in the business and the share price wilted. Rarely, if ever, had Marks seemed so unloved. It might well have been a once-in-a-generation opportunity for an ambitious company or wealthy individual to launch a takeover attempt and seize control of a business with a great name and fabulous property assets. Or at least that was the calculation of Philip Green, the retailing entrepreneur who had already accumulated a tidy fortune from buying and selling substantial chains of shops but whose most triumphant days were still ahead of him.

Green sees himself as constructing an empire – a dynastic one, no less – to rival those of the great Jewish entrepreneurs of the twentieth century such as the Wolfsons, the creators of Great Universal Stores, or Sir Charles Clore, who built Sears, the retailing conglomerate. If Green really wanted to join their ranks, there was only one business to buy: the most successful retailer ever constructed by an Anglo-Jewish dynasty, Marks & Spencer. He put together a team of City firms to help him with an attempt to acquire M&S. Green tried to recruit Warburg, the leading investment bank, but was rebuffed because Warburg did not believe that Green would be able to succeed (Green is not easily put off, however, and he rang a Warburg director every day for five successive days; he harangued the director, telling him that he was making the biggest business error of his career, but to no avail). In the event, Green's bidding team was led by a US investment bank, Donaldson Lufkin & Jenrette (DLJ), which was later acquired by Credit Suisse First Boston. DLJ was not an absolutely top-flight firm, or what is known on Wall Street as part of the 'Bulge Bracket', but it was well regarded, imaginative and highly profitable.

By December 1999, M&S was in such a conspicuous mess that rumours started to swirl that a takeover was in the offing. Most gossip was about a possible offer from Tesco, which kept its options open by refusing to make any formal statement. The press highlighted David and Frederick Barclay, the intensely private and immensely wealthy dealers in whole companies, as potential bidders. They had backed Green's £549m purchase and break-up of Sears in early 1999, and newspapers also mentioned Green as thinking about making a bid for M&S. On 13 December, Green issued a statement confirming that he had hired advisers to help with a possible tilt at M&S. The Takeover Panel, the City watchdog on mergers and acquisitions, had forced him to make the announcement, following a surge in the M&S share price.

At the time, few investors believed Green could do it. M&S had a market value of almost £8bn, far more than any company that Green had bought previously. In addition, Green's interest in buying M&S had been exposed earlier than suited him. In the full glare of media attention it became much harder to raise the finance for what he and his bankers had called 'Project Mushroom'. In fact, the price of M&S's shares actually fell after the formal disclosure that it was Green who was contemplating making a bid – which indicated that the City did not believe he could pull it off. However, Green is nothing if not irrepressible and tenacious:

> It looked brave the first time, the first attempt in 2000. I thought we weren't going to get up the hill, then suddenly all the pieces started to fit. [Philip Green interview, 31 May 2006]

Green made considerable progress in raising billions in loans from banks to finance the deal. He was close to making a credible offer when he was undermined by M&S's public-relations advisers, Brunswick, which briefed newspapers that Green's wife, Tina, had bought 9.5m shares for £23m a few days before his interest in acquiring M&S had been made public. There was nothing illegal about this; Green had in-formed the Takeover Panel about the purchase and been given approval for it. But it looked fishy because Tina Green's ownership had not been described initially by Green's lawyers as being 'in concert' with Green's plan to buy M&S. It could therefore be interpreted – wrongly – as an attempt to profit personally from the rise in M&S's share price prompted by the takeover attempt. The *Sunday Times* in particular put a dama-ging spin on the affair in an article on 6 February 2000, under the headline: 'Tycoon faces insider deal row over M&S shares'. The report quoted an M&S adviser as saying it was considering asking the Department of Trade and Industry and the London Stock Exchange to investigate.

Green says that article blew up his attempt to buy M&S, even though he had done nothing wrong, because it undermined the confidence of City firms. He remains livid with John Jay, who was business editor of the *Sunday Times* at the time.

> Whether you like it or not, people [banks] get spooked. They've all got committees. Now I'm dealing with you. But you're not the decision maker. It's some guy on a credit committee. He says: 'What's this, insider dealing?' Now all the people who were involved in the deal knew it was bollocks. But it spooks them. I don't think journalists realize the danger of the wrong article on the wrong day. [ibid.]

On 10 February, within four days of the *Sunday Times* article, Green announced that he was abandoning his attempt to buy M&S – for a while, at least. He was intent on clearing his name, however, and just a few weeks later, on 23 April, the *Sunday Times* printed an apology to the Greens, saying that the references in its earlier piece to insider dealing were unwarranted.

Freed, for now, from the threat of takeover, Marks could get on with the task of trying to rejuvenate itself. Vandevelde's first day as executive chairman was 28 February. The tussle with Green had further undermined the authority of Salsbury: advisers to the company were now describing his role as being a lieutenant to Vandevelde rather than a general in his own right. On 18 September 2000, Salsbury – and two other directors – left the company. Vandevelde added the title of chief executive to his existing role of chairman and he announced that Roger Holmes would be joining as head of UK retailing operations. Holmes came from Kingfisher, where he had run its electricals business. Significantly, neither Holmes, a former management consultant at McKinsey, nor Vandevelde had any meaningful experience of running a fashion clothing business.

Even so, for a period they appeared to have engineered a revival at M&S. They closed or sold most of the company's overseas stores (much to the chagrin of Stuart Rose, who wants to beef up the international business) and tried to modernize the look of the shops. In 2001, M&S's shares were the best performers in the FTSE 100 list of Britain's biggest companies. Probably the most positive initiative taken at this time came in February of that year when George Davies was persuaded to create a new range of more fashionable women's clothing to be sold under a new brand name, Per Una. Davies created a renewed buzz around M&S and the range did well. But the deal with Davies also showed how weak M&S had become. Davies retained ownership of the Per Una brand, which was without precedent: the notion that someone else's brand should be allowed space in M&S stores would have been unthinkable to Greenbury or the Sieffs. However, the Christmas of 2001 – the most important season for most retailers – was the best at M&S for years: sales rose almost 9 per cent in the seven weeks to January 2002. Pre-tax profits in the year to March 2002 exceeded City expectations, rising from £384m to £688m.

Such was Vandevelde's conviction that the recovery was real that in July 2002 he decided to become part-time chairman and hand over the chief executive's role to Holmes. One non-executive director, Tony Ball, had serious doubts about whether Vandevelde should have been allowed to scale back his commitment to M&S while retaining the substantial remuneration of £450,000 a year.

Ball, who at the time was chief executive of British Sky Broadcasting, resigned from the M&S board in September – yet in the great diplomatic tradition of British directors, he did not give a public explanation of his concerns. Shareholders were none the wiser, which is a shame.

As 2003 progressed, it became clear that the recovery in M&S's clothing business had stalled. The company tried to put a positive gloss on it by saying that future growth would come from homewares, financial services and food, but with children's clothing in a terrible mess and womenswear sales flat, investors were increasingly unimpressed. M&S is so big in garments that unless it has a convincing competitive strategy for clothing it will always look like a declining business.

If M&S's revitalization turned out to be less firmly based than had been widely thought, the reputation and financial strength of Philip Green had been transformed since his previous encounter with the retailer. Since early 2001, he had bought two substantial store groups, Bhs and Arcadia. He had become a billionaire in record time and had become the second largest retailer of ladies' fashions in the UK – after M&S. A hyperactive deal-maker, he had been toying with the idea of making a formal bid for Safeway, the supermarket group that was eventually sold to Wm Morrison. But he was now evaluating whether M&S was once again in enough trouble for its shareholders to sell out to him.

> I walked into the business. I walked into Oxford Street [M&S's flagship branch] in October 2003. I walked round the store. I took a look at it. I came out. I called my guys and said: 'You've got to come and have a walk with me.' I got them to come over.
>
> We walked the store. I said: 'Have you ever seen anything more appalling than this?' I said: 'We've got to buy this company; anybody could do better than this.'
>
> I met Roger Holmes then at a trade dinner, walking down the stairs at the Grosvenor House [the hotel on Park Lane]. He couldn't run away too fast. But as we were walking down the

stairs, I said: 'I was in your Oxford Street store yesterday.' He said: 'What do you think?' I said: 'I've never seen a bigger pile of shit in my life.' He was this colour. He wanted to run away. [ibid.]

By this time, one member of the M&S board was also becoming concerned about how the business was being managed. He was Paul Myners, a businessman who had made his reputation through running, expanding and then selling (several times) a fund-man-agement group, Gartmore. Myners, who is now 59, was as much a self-made success as Green, as he explains:

I grew up in Truro in Cornwall and went to a local grammar school there. I had been adopted at the age of four by my father, a Truro pork butcher. I've never wanted to know who my real parents are and have never tried to find out. I'm perfectly comfortable being who I am.

I trained to be a teacher at the Institute of Education in London. It wasn't a proper degree. Then in 1971 I taught economics and business studies for a year at a state compre-hensive in Wandsworth [London] and didn't really enjoy it. I wanted to work in the financial community, thought that would be exciting. I read the business pages and a book about Bernie Cornfeld [the legendary and ultimately disgraced 1960s finan-cier]. Cornfeld said if you want to make money, work with money. And that's what I did. [Paul Myners interview, 2 May 2006]

Gartmore made Myners wealthy, though it did not put him in the same league as Green. Then, in the late 1990s, Myners decided he wanted variety in his business life, so he took on a dizzying number of responsibilities, many of them with a leftish-leaning bent – though he describes himself as a 'progressive liberal' and says he has never been a member of the Labour Party. For Gordon Brown he wrote a weighty analysis of the shortcomings of the way British pension funds invest their money, which was published in 2001 – and which, as he

admits, was extremely unhelpful to fund-management businesses such as the one he had built up over many years,
Gartmore. He also chairs the Low Pay Commission, which
sets the minimum wage in the UK, and is chairman of Guardian Media Group, the company that owns the *Guardian*
newspaper. He is a member of the court of the Bank of
England (its board) and chairs the trustees of the Tate Gallery.
Myners has been a non-executive director of two mobile-phone
groups, Orange and O_2, and PowerGen, the energy company.
And he is chairman of the UK's largest property company,
Land Securities. He is a great supporter of the Smith Institute,
the think tank which has been an unofficial source of policy
ideas for Gordon Brown, and he is a regular attendee of its
seminars in 11 Downing Street. In July 2007, Myners became
chairman-designate of the Government body which will construct possibly the most important institution to emanate from
the Blair/Brown years, the National Pensions Savings Scheme –
which is intended to deliver cheap private pensions for millions
of relatively low-paid employees (see Chapter 7). And at the
time of writing he is involved in an attempt by a private-equity
group, JC Flowers, to rescue Northern Rock, the bank which
suffered a humiliating run in September 2007. So if there is
such a thing as a Brownite establishment class, Myners would
be one of its elders.

Unlike most members of public-company boards, Myners almost always speaks his mind, even if that means offending or
upsetting colleagues. Based on his track record, his judgement is
good. More conventional non-executives, however, feel threatened
by him and regard him as irksome. He is not a typical, clubbable
corporate grandee, as M&S found out pretty quickly after he
joined its board in 2002. In November 2003, Myners sent an e-
mail to his fellow non-executives – although not to the chairman,
Vandevelde – saying that Roger Holmes did not have the necessary
qualities to be a successful chief executive of M&S. At the time, he
was a lone voice; the other board members were hopeful that
Holmes's strategy would come good.

Holmes himself is an intelligent business analyst and did not try to delude himself that all was well at M&S. By early 2005, it became clear to him that the recovery had run out of steam and that much more radical change was required. At the time, one of his colleagues said to me: 'The quick fixes have been done.' During the Christmas season there had been a 2.3 per cent fall in underlying trading, the like-for-like sales figures regarded in the City as the crucial measure of a retailer's performance. M&S's rivals were performing much better. 'Vandevelde talked a very good talk, he sold some assets and added a coat of paint,' says an M&S director, 'but the structural problems remained.'

Holmes was also increasingly isolated because Vandevelde was spending less and less time at the business. This was causing particular concern to Myners, who noted that Vandevelde had not scheduled a single appearance at M&S's Baker Street headquarters for the first three weeks of April, when there were important strategic decisions to be considered. Myners was convinced that it was time for Vandevelde to leave. On 10 May, M&S announced that Vandevelde had 'indicated that he wishes to leave the company's board of directors'. M&S appointed Russell Reynolds, the headhunters, to begin looking for a new chairman with a view to having him or her in place by the time of the annual meeting in July.

Just days earlier, on 6 May 2005, in a private dining room in the Holborn offices of Brunswick, a leading financial public-relations firm, Holmes shared with me his gloomy assessment of what needed to be done at M&S. The dinner was hosted by Alan Parker, the founder and major shareholder in Brunswick. For the past 20 years Parker has exercised significant influence on the British corporate scene. He has a network of close contacts at the top of British companies and a similar network within the financial press. As an intermediary between these two networks, he tries to shape perceptions of companies or business people. He is loyal to clients, even when they are on the ropes – as Holmes plainly was. Parker is much more the showman than Holmes, who is polite, reserved and brainy in a way that is typical of a former McKinsey consultant. Anyone meeting these two with no prior knowledge would have assumed that it was Parker, not Holmes, who headed one of the UK's more important businesses. But in his understated way, Holmes pointed out that deflation and intense competition were powerful forces from which there was no shelter for any retailer; official statistics at the time showed that garments in general in the UK were 36 per cent cheaper than in 1996. What was his conclusion? Broadly, that M&S's costs of doing business – from the pay and inflexible working conditions of staff through to the way it bought and distributed its goods – were still way too high. He was right and he had a plan to restore the competitiveness of the business. But it was too late.

For the media, the M&S story was once again one of crisis and Holmes was already a member of the walking corporate dead. Meanwhile, in the shadows, a prominent retailer, Stuart Rose, was ruthlessly exploiting his own media contacts to promote his prospects of taking over from Holmes. Rose had been out of a job since standing down as chief executive of Arcadia, the owner of the Topshop and Burton chains, in the autumn of 2002. That was when Green acquired Arcadia for £775m and in the process enriched Rose to the tune of £25m by buying out Rose's shares and share options. Rose did not need to work, but he wanted to – and the business he most wanted to run was the one that trained him and employed him until he was 40: Marks & Spencer.

Rose's full name is Stuart Alan Ransom Rose. The 'Ransom' commemorates a remarkable woman, Nona Ransom, who was governess to the last emperor of China, Pu Yi. She came across Rose's father, Harry Ransom Rose, in the 1930s, when he was a boy living in Tientsin, which is now called Tianjin, an ancient walled city in northern China. At the time, the family name was Brianzeff. They were White Russians and were in China because Stuart Rose's grandfather had been sent there as a Cossack colonel by Admiral Kolchak, the leader of the anti-Bolshevik forces. The Cossack colonel could not go home to Russia after Lenin took power.

He [Rose's grandfather] only had two skills. He was a draughts-man and a soldier. There was fuck-all call for soldiering. So he then became a teacher of draughtsmanship and woodwork in Tientsin grammar school. And in Tientsin grammar school he met Nona Ransom, a spinster lady of Quaker origins who was a teacher of English at the school. Now my dad was living between his parents, who had then split up and were pretty impoverished. Nona Ransom took a shine to my dad. So he used to spend a couple of days a week with Nona, a couple of days a week with his dad and three days a week with his mother. In 1937 or '38, she knew that war was coming and the Japanese were going to invade China, so Nona Ransom said: 'I'll take your son and educate him.' [Stuart Rose interview, 22 June 2006]

Nona Ransom and Rose's father emigrated to England, where she adopted him and paid for his education at Bootham, the Quaker school in York. He changed his name from Igor Brianzeff to Harry Ransom Rose, reverting to the 'Rose' name of his seventeenth-century forebears in the German town of Eisenach in Thuringia. Harry Ransom Rose never saw his father again and he met his mother just once more, in the 1970s. Both his parents were interned by the Japanese during the Second World War and then moved to South America, having been made stateless.

Harry Rose served in the RAF during the war and then went to the London School of Economics.

My mother was born and brought up in Egypt and she was evacuated when she was about 16 from Egypt, when they thought the Germans were going to overrun it. She came back to England and she met my dad when they were about 17. And they got married in 1945. So they were two 18-year-olds, very young. My dad was a foreign bloke in a foreign land. My mum was a very young girl and was also in a foreign land. She hated England.

I was born in 1949, when my dad was still at university. With my sister, who was two years older than me, already born. And he was studying at the LSE [London School of Economics] and working on the railways at night to earn some money. It was a tough time. We lived in a prefab. We lived in a caravan when I was two, not a holiday caravan, a caravan in a field. My dad dug the fucking lavatory in a field out the back. I remember it. [ibid.]

Rose's father did a variety of middle-management jobs, including a stint at the BBC. His great love, however, was painting. He also worked for the British Colonial Service from 1955 to 1962, supervising the building of roads in what was then Tanganyika, now part of Tanzania, which was then under British rule. Stuart Rose describes his African childhood as an idyll.

On return from Africa, Stuart Rose followed his father to Bootham, the York Quaker school with a distinguished roll-call of alumni, including the Nobel Peace laureate, Philip Noel-Baker.

It taught you about humanity. It taught you about people and about being honest and straightforward and whatever else, but it didn't drive you academically. And I do regret that because I was probably nine months behind my set because I had a local education in Africa. I struggled a bit, and if I had been give a bit of a push I would probably have been all right. But, you know, I got my O levels, I got my A levels.

And then I basically bummed around. I didn't go to university. I did a whole pile of jobs, worked in a hospital for a while. When I was 21 or 22 – I was late leaving school – my father collared me one morning and said: 'Where's the front-door key? I want it back.' He said: 'You can't live at home any longer, bye, bye.' So I wrote to a whole pile of companies, 25 or something, and literally the first one to write back was Marks & Spencer. And they offered me three interviews. And I got put, without a degree, on to their management training scheme. [ibid.]

Shortly after his arrival at M&S, there was a cataclysmic event in Rose's life. His mother committed suicide. She was of British-Greek descent, but he says she behaved like an archetypal Jewish mother who had tremendous confidence in him and wanted him to be a doctor. Her death shaped him.

> I was angry, probably. She'd said: 'I believe in you', and I wanted to prove to her that she was right. I probably became overly pushy. It made me think: 'I'll have to do everything myself, only I can make it.' And it made me think you can't trust anyone emotionally, you can't count on them. [Stuart Rose, interviewed in the *Sunday Telegraph*, 21 April 2002]

Rose's rise at M&S was not seamless, but he sufficiently impressed a manager in Llandudno, north Wales, to be made a departmental manager at Wood Green in north London, from where he was sent to the flagship store in Marble Arch. That promotion put him on the fast track.

> I had only been there a couple of years when serendipity played a part. I won a wine competition run by the *Evening Standard*. I came in after I had my free holiday and the managing director of foods – he was called Henry Lewis – asked to see me. And he said: 'Ee oop, lad. It seems you know something about wine; well, we're going to start a wine department and you're doing it.' And I always said if I had won a driving competition, I would have been the chairman's chauffeur. It was that close-run – I got lucky. [Stuart Rose interview, 22 June 2006]

So Rose moved to M&S's food division, initially travelling around Europe selecting wines for the company. He stayed in foods till his great falling-out with the chairman, which prompted him to do that unthinkable thing for a member of the M&S management class – he left.

Quitting M&S was the making of Stuart Rose even though the timing of his arrival at Burton Group, in 1989, was not brilliant. In 1990, Burton's profits slumped and its flamboyant chairman and chief executive, Sir Ralph Halpern, quit. However, Rose helped to turn around Burton's department-store chain, Debenhams, and he eventually became chief executive of its 'multiples', which included the Topshop and Burton chains. In his time there he worked with retailers who – in their different ways – would help to remake the British high street over the following decade. Among his colleagues were John Hoerner, who became chief executive of the group, Terry Green and Andy Higginson. All of this trio now work for the UK's most powerful retailer, Tesco. But for Rose it turned a bit sticky in 1997, when his relationship with Hoerner soured:

> I have never quite found out the truth, but I went downstairs to find John's outer door was closed – and that was never the case. As I went down the staircase, out came Karen Cook, who is now at Goldman [the investment bank] but was then at Schroders. And being reasonably smart, I thought: 'Hello, what's she doing here?' I had had a few difficult times with John about what we should be doing to the direction of the business and how well or not the business was doing. And I smelled a rat.
>
> Anyway, I found out by leaning very hard on a few people and taking the personnel director round the back and sticking a poker up his arse that a plot had been hatched to split the business into two. I realized I was going to be sidelined, it wasn't going to do me any good. So John and I had an enormous row and I left within a week of me finding this out – and then the demerger was announced the following day. [ibid.]

Rose pocketed compensation of £600,000 from Burton and then went to Argos, the catalogue retailer, where he had his first taste of defending a company against a takeover attempt. In his few months as chief executive, he forced Great Universal Stores (GUS), the mail-order business with a history almost as distinguished as Marks & Spencer's, to pay a much higher price for Argos than it wanted to do.

> Lord Wolfson [GUS's chairman] created a huge stink about the fact he thought the fees we were paying Schroders [Argos's

advisers] were too high. But, more importantly, he claimed that in the defence document, I had – or we had – said something that was misleading. And he took me and Schroders to the Takeover Panel [the City watchdog] and it was thrown out. But he got very angry . . . He never spoke to me again. [ibid.]

Rose's short stint at Argos earned him £500,000, but once again he was unemployed.

Wherever he went at this stage of his career, Rose seemed to make waves. His next career stop was at the food wholesaler, Booker.

The short answer is I went into Booker, a complete shithole. We turned that round and we merged it with Iceland [the chain of frozen-food supermarkets] . . . And when I got in there after three months, first of all I discovered I was working for a maverick, Malcolm Walker . . . Anyway, within two months of the merger I then got a phone call from the chairman of Arcadia, where John Hoerner – whom I'd had the row with – was the chief executive. The chairman was a guy called Adam Broadbent. And he said: 'Can I have a cup of tea with you?' He said: 'Arcadia is going down the toilet. Would you like to come and run it?' [ibid.]

Arcadia was half of Burton Group. So in an extraordinary twist of fate, Rose was being invited back to the company he had left in 1997 after Hoerner decided to reorganize the business in a way that made Rose surplus to requirements.

I had a dilemma. I had just done the Booker-Iceland merger. I had given a sort of verbal agreement that I'd stay. The short answer is I made a big decision overnight, went to see Malcolm Walker and said: 'Malcolm, I am leaving.' He went absolutely fucking ape and never spoke to me for two years after that. [ibid.]

Restoring the fortunes of Arcadia occupied Rose until the autumn of 2002. During his tenure he became increasingly close to Philip Green, who was limbering up to buy the company. After he did just that, Rose and Green remained in close contact.

Rose then had an extended period of unemployment. In 2003, he teamed up with the private-equity house Permira, in an attempt to buy Debenhams, the department-store group for which he had worked more than 10 years earlier when it was part of Burton. Ultimately, it was sold to a rival consortium of private-equity bidders. So as Marks & Spencer's recovery was increasingly perceived to have been over-hyped, Rose wondered whether there might be a role for him at his alma mater. In early 2004, he pursued a dual strategy: to put pressure on the M&S board to appoint him to run the company; and, if the board could not be moved, to examine whether he could take matters into his own hands by buying the business in collaboration with a private-equity fund. He had preliminary discussions about a possible takeover with Blackstone Partners, the US private-equity house.

> A number of people were calling me early in the year [of 2004] who obviously knew that I was out of work, and they would ask: 'What do you think is happening at Marks & Spencer?' It was that sort of cursory conversation.
>
> In the case of Blackstone I had a more substantive conversation along the lines of 'what if?' But there was nothing formal. And in the end it got overtaken by events. [Stuart Rose interview, 26 July 2006]

As for Rose being invited by the M&S board to join the company, that was looking increasingly unlikely:

> In February 2004, I was alerted to the possibility that something might happen at M&S but I could not see how that might involve me because I knew from all the spinning that was going

on that the board was incredibly hostile to my candidature. At the time, the only job available there was the chair and they thought I would be completely the wrong bloke, probably because they thought I would sack Roger [Holmes] in five minutes. You were in that sort of phoney war. The board was briefing through Brunswick that I was unsuitable all the way through January, February, March. [Stuart Rose interview, 4 July 2006]

Rose believes that one non-executive, Kevin Lomax, was 'particularly hostile' to him – and later the uneasiness of his relationship with Lomax was to become more significant. But Rose was not prepared simply to give up on M&S. He set about trying to persuade newspapers to campaign on his behalf, and largely succeeded, thanks in part to the strong relationships he had established with a number of business correspondents at leading national newspapers.

I won't deny that I was promoting my own cause. Of course I was. I was using them [the journalists] diligently. Steve Sharp [a long-standing colleague of Rose who is now marketing director at M&S] was sharing an office with me and he said: 'I've never seen one bloke work a phone as hard as you did. You were fucking sitting there and I could see the look on your face. You thought: "I am not going to go down dying here without a chance."' [ibid.]

But there were no overtures to Rose from the M&S board.

At precisely the same time, Green was laying careful plans for a renewed attempt at purchasing M&S.

Come the turn of the year, it looked to me that they had nowhere to go. Probably my single biggest mistake is I should have waited another three months. There would have been a profit warning, crash. I was probably a bit too early. But the reason I did it then was I wanted to affect the inventory for Christmas. But everything about it [the deal] looked right. [Philip Green interview, 31 May 2006]

Green's ally in the takeover attempt would be Goldman Sachs, the world's most powerful investment bank. It is hard to exaggerate Goldman's fearsome ability to determine the fate of the world's biggest companies and to generate profits for itself along the way. Its senior directors are each worth tens of millions of pounds and they exude confidence bordering on arrogance. If ever there was a symbol of Green's astonishing reputation as a money-maker it was that Goldman was prepared to be his junior partner and invest many hundreds of millions of pounds from its own resources in the attempt to buy M&S. In addition, two of Goldman's European superstars were working with Green: Richard Sharp, then head of its European private-equity business (he stepped down at the end of 2006), and Mike Sherwood, a former bond trader who was shortly to become joint chief executive of Goldman's entire European operation. Sharp and Sherwood are contrasting European characters: Sharp is Oxford-educated, soft-spoken and cerebral, the son of the late Lord Sharp, a 1980s business eminence as chairman and chief executive of the international telecoms group, Cable & Wireless; Sherwood, who went to Manchester University, is Estuary-accented and brash. It was striking that they both deferred to Green throughout the attempt to buy M&S. 'It was unconditional money,' Green said to me at the time.

Nor was it just Goldman that was prepared to put its money and reputation on the line for Green. On 16 June, Green sent M&S a letter saying that he had raised an astonishing £11.9bn in finance for the takeover attempt. He provided £1.1bn of equity financing from his own resources. An additional £1.4bn of equity was made available by three banks, HBOS (which owns Halifax), Goldman and Barclays Capital, the investment banking arm of Barclays. Meanwhile, debt of £9.4bn was promised by Barclays, Goldman, Halifax, Royal Bank of Scotland and Merrill Lynch. With no exaggeration, Green describes their support as 'unique'. For a single individual to raise so much money – at great speed and at very low cost – was unprecedented and has not yet been matched. How does he think he pulled it off?

Partly, it stems from Green's ability to forge strong relationships with bankers – and the most important of these relationships is with Peter Cummings at Bank of Scotland (part of HBOS).

> Goldman Sachs said there's no relationship on the planet that anybody's got [like the one between Green and Cummings]. What flipped Goldman Sachs's lid was that in the middle of the night – in the middle of the night – we were 900 million quid short. They thought we could not do it. I said: 'Why not?' They said: 'Look, we'll do half.' I said: 'Okay, I'll do the other half. Give me ten minutes.' I called him [Cummings] up. He said: 'Right, let's go.' We got a fax inside seven minutes, while they were having meetings, conference calls, meetings of compliance committees [for their £450m]. [Philip Green interview, 31 May 2006]

But it was Green's basic grasp of how to run a retailing business that particularly impressed the lending bankers.

> The turning point in funding £12bn for M&S is that I had two rails of garments in this room. One was 80 garments out of their stores, which I had bought across a wide range; one was a reproduction of those 80 garments, which I had reproduced in my factories. And the banks, I got them in one by one, I showed them the rail. And I said: 'This is how it works.' I said: 'This is the engine room of the business. Go and get that bit right. All the other jigsaw-puzzle pieces fit.' What we showed the banks is what we could produce [M&S clothes] quicker, at better quality, and at better value. It was clear to me that their supply chain, I believed, was totally, totally fucked. [ibid.]

However, if he wanted to own M&S, there was one obstacle Green needed to remove. He was aware that Rose had his own ambitions to run M&S and wanted him out of the game. So on 7 May, at 1.47 p.m., he rang Rose on his mobile and invited him to his West End office for a chat. Rose says that he did not read anything much into Green's request for a meeting because they talked all the time.

> The innuendo at the time was that it was unusual for him to ring me and therefore there must be something up. But in fact he was ringing me every other day. It was what we used to call: 'come round and have a chitty-chatty bollocks'. And because at that time I was doing nothing, I used to go round and see him fairly regularly . . .

> He used to ring me up and say: 'You're never going to get a fucking job, son.' And so I used to regularly go round and say: 'Chitty-chatty bollocks,' except this time when I went round and said: 'Chitty-chatty bollocks,' he said: 'Sit down, I've got something to talk to you about.' [Stuart Rose interview, 4 July 2006]

However, what Rose did only shortly after the telephone conversation on 7 May was later to cause him embarrassment: he bought 100,000 M&S shares through his broker, Brewin Dolphin. When details of this purchase became known in June, Rose was adamant that in the phone call he was given no inkling of Green's desire to buy M&S so as to squash any suggestion that he was profiting illegally from inside information.

Rose went to Green's office at 11.30 a.m. on 12 May, and the first thing Green did, before saying anything, was to insist that Rose sign a confidentiality agreement.

> He said: 'I can't talk to you about it, son, unless you sign this piece of paper.' I had nothing to lose – because I knew it was just a confidentiality agreement, which simply means I won't tell anybody. So I signed the piece of paper and then he said to me that he was looking at M&S. But he never came out with a

specific offer of what he wanted me to do, but, broadly speaking, I got the feeling it was to run foods. But I didn't give him a yea or a nay. I said: 'What's the timescale?' and he said: 'I dunno.' He said: 'What do you think?' And I said: 'I'll let you know in a few days.' [Stuart Rose interview, 4 July 2006]

The one person Rose wanted to consult about Green's plans was Charles Wilson, a businessman with whom he works closely. Green gave him permission to talk to Wilson. Rose also sought legal advice about the implications of signing the confidentiality agreement.

I then consulted a lawyer, David Cheyne [from Linklaters, the leading firm of solicitors], and I said: 'David, I want to be absolutely fucking clear, what does this piece mean I can and can't do?' He said: 'Don't tell anybody [about Green's plans]. Who have you told?' I said: 'I have told the one person I was allowed to tell and you.' And he said: 'Don't tell anybody else.' [ibid.]

Rose also says he made clear to Green that he did not want to work with him on the bid.

I then rang Philip the following Wednesday – though Philip disputes this – and said: 'Philip, this is not for me.' [ibid.]

At the time, Britain was in the grips of a consumer boom – although the boom appeared to be happening everywhere apart from in M&S stores. On 25 May, M&S announced annual results which showed that sales of 'general merchandise' (which is mostly clothing) had fallen by 3.7 per cent in the second half of the year to the end of March (they had grown 2.6 per cent in the first half). The drop was much worse at 4.7 per cent on a like-for-like basis (taking out the effect of new selling space) in those six months. Vandevelde tried to put a positive interpretation on this disappointing performance. 'We have delivered financial performance which I would describe as "solid" but clearly we are not satisfied with our sales progress,' he said. 'The market-share gains that we had hoped to achieve were not delivered.' Holmes was more clinical, saying: 'Our clothing share declined by 0.2 per cent, reflecting underperformance in womenswear, particularly knitwear, and childrenswear.' With womenswear in decline, the engine of the business was breaking. 'In summary, we still have a lot to do,' Holmes said, 'but I am confident that we can succeed.'

Holmes's words were barely audible in the storm that was raging. Speculation was running wild that a bid was looming for the company. Hedge funds and traders were piling into the shares and also taking positions in contracts for differences (CFDs). These are tradeable contracts that deliver an interest in a company's shares but for a fraction of the market price. (CFDs have two other advantages over ordinary shares: stamp duty is not payable on a CFD transaction, which represents a significant tax saving compared with dealing in shares; and it is possible to take a 'short' position in CFDs, or to profit from a fall in the underlying share price.) The securities firms that sell the CFDs to the hedge funds and speculators have to borrow the stock. Consequently, the scale of speculative trading activity in M&S can be gauged from a dramatic rise in stock lending, from less than 2 per cent of the retailer's share capital on 20 May to 5.9 per cent on 26 May. Stock with a value of £330m was borrowed as security against assorted transactions in just four trading days. The unmissable implication was that some astute investors had a whiff that a takeover bid was coming.

Hedge funds and US investors, with no emotional links to M&S, had gradually and stealthily become the influential owners of M&S shares – and if any bidder offered them the right price, they would have no hesitation in handing over control of the company. Conventional British investment institutions – the giant insurance companies such as the Pru or Legal & General, or the famous names of the fund-management industry which managed the pension funds of Britain's great companies – had been almost emasculated when it came to determining the fate of businesses, even one so quintessentially British as M&S. Of M&S's shareholders, none was as powerful as Brandes, an investment institution based in San Diego, California, which had a fearsome reputation for taking substantial stakes in ailing companies and precipitating wholesale change at those companies.

On 26 May, the day after Marks & Spencer's lousy results, the company's share price rose by 3.6 per cent to 290.5p. That made the Takeover Panel, the City watchdog, sit up and take notice. It became concerned that there could be an unfair and unequal distribution of important information among M&S's shareholders, that some investors seemed to believe that there was good news looming for the company. Perhaps there had been a leak that a bid was on its way. So the Panel forced Philip Green to put out a statement on his intentions. At 4.01 p.m. on 27 May, this terse announcement was made to the Stock Exchange:

> Revival, a company owned by Philip Green and members of his family, confirms that Revival is considering a possible offer for Marks & Spencer. Revival intends to approach the board of Marks & Spencer in the next few days with its proposal and to seek a recommendation. Any proposal would involve a mixture of cash and shares in a new company which would seek a listing. There can be no assurance that any offer will be made. A further announcement will be made when appropriate.

That was it; there was no other detail. But it broke like thunder. M&S's share price immediately jumped by almost 19 per cent to 345p and 105m shares changed hands.

Just over four years had passed since Green had last signalled his interest in buying M&S but the whole shape of the retailing universe had changed since then. Green was now the most powerful force on the high street after M&S – and his businesses were growing, unlike M&S's. What is more, he was owner and manager, which gave him the power and independence that a Holmes or a Vandevelde – as the servants of shareholders – could never enjoy. While at the end of 1999 M&S's then acting chairman, Brian Baldock, could more or less dismiss Green as not a real threat –

and therefore refuse to meet him – in 2004 the M&S board did not dare be so aloof, especially since the company had failed to mend itself in the intervening years. M&S's survival as an independent, publicly owned business was in the balance.

It was crystal clear to Myners that M&S would not be able to see off Green unless the top management was changed immediately.

> My finest hour was after Philip made his announcement. On the Thursday night there was an emergency board meeting in Baker Street. Luc [Vandevelde] wasn't there. He stayed on holiday at his home in France. I insisted he come back for the following morning, which he did. After the board meeting, I insisted the non-execs meet separately from the executives, so Holmes and the others withdrew. I said that we would be dead within a week if we kept Holmes and Vandevelde, Philip would have us for less than £3.50. I had never met Rose, but I had heard good things of him. So I told the board meeting that we should speak to him. I believe if it wasn't for me, Philip would have had the company for less than £3.50. [Paul Myners interview, 2 May 2006]

By this stage there had been cursory contact between M&S and Stuart Rose; he had been approached by a headhunter acting on M&S's behalf. Rose believes, however, the only reason for this was to demonstrate to anyone who might ask, especially journalists, that he had not been dismissed out of hand as a candidate to run M&S. But he did not believe M&S was remotely serious about employing him.

> The fact that they hadn't [till then] even made an approach to me and had written me off publicly and had not even inter-viewed me would have made it difficult for them. Because when they did appoint someone the papers were bound to ask whether they had approached me. Had Philip's bid not happened and they had chosen somebody, someone like Kate Rankine (then a formidable City journalist at the *Daily Telegraph*) would have asked: 'Did you interview Stuart?' And they would have looked

stupid because I would have made it quite clear they didn't interview me. So they had to interview me.

The penny must have dropped the week before Philip made the [bid] approach because I had a phone call from the head-hunters Russell Reynolds. It was an American woman, Rae Sedel. She said: 'I just want to talk to you about Marks & Spencer and the ethos and the philosophy of this business.' I remember her saying 'ethos and philosophy'. And she said: 'Would you like to have a conversation with me?' And I said: 'I don't think that will be possible.' And I said – and I was a bit rude to her – I said: 'There is nothing that you can tell me about the ethos and philosophy of Marks & Spencer that I don't already know. However, if one of the board would like to see me, I'll be very happy.' And she said: 'That won't be possible.' So I said: 'This will be a very short conversation.' . . . But the following day the headhunter called me back and said: 'It might be possible for you to have a conversation with one of the non-execs.' [Stuart Rose interview, 4 July 2006]

Rose agreed to meet Kevin Lomax, the M&S non-executive charged with leading the search for a replacement for Vandevelde, on the morning of 27 May. Lomax is a forthright individual who created one of the UK's leading software companies, Misys, which has gone through a sticky patch in the past few years (Lomax quit the company in October 2006 after he failed in an attempt to buy it). Rose met Lomax in Misys's Kensington office at 10.30 a.m. He could not and did not disclose to Lomax his knowledge that Green was thinking of making a bid because he had signed the confidentiality agreement.

I went in there with no notion that a bid was coming, although I had had the conversation with Philip that one might happen at some point, to have a chat with Kevin which I thought was a routine 'tick in the box' so they could say: 'Now we've seen Stuart Rose we can tell him to fuck off and we can announce whoever it is we want to announce.' [ibid.]

By coincidence, Rose had also arranged to have a cup of tea at 3 p.m. on the same day at Claridge's, the West End hotel, with Tony Ball, the television executive who had quit as an M&S non-executive in September 2002 because of his concerns that Vandevelde was being paid too much to do too little.

> I came out and my phone was red-hot. And that is when I found out there was a bid for Marks & Spencer. Twenty-four people left me a message there had been a bid for Marks & Spencer. I rang a couple of mates and said: 'What the fuck's going on?' I rang a few people in the City. Later in the day I had a call from Cazenove – Richard Wintour – who asked me would I be prepared to go and have another conversation with the board of Marks & Spencer. [ibid.]

At the time, Cazenove was the sole survivor of the old City of London. Founded in 1823 by Philip Cazenove, its origins are traceable to the Huguenot financiers who left France in 1685 after the revocation of the Edict of Nantes. Its métier was as a 'corporate stockbroker', which means it advises companies on how to raise money on the stock market. In practice, its remit is much wider. In particular, its Old Etonian chairman, David Mayhew, was the trusted confidant of the directors of many substantial British companies. His judgement was often sought on whether a business could successfully fend off a takeover bid or at what price that business should sell out.

Cazenove was also notable because, unlike most of its serious rivals, it had remained an independent business. The vast majority of the other leading UK investment banking and securities businesses – from SG Warburg to Schroders to Morgan Grenfell – were in the hands of overseas banks. Cazenove, however, believed it could prosper without the access to overseas markets and the vast amounts of capital that were provided to a Warburg or a Schroders by their enormous international parents – which were UBS of Switzerland for Warburg and Citigroup of the US for Schroders. However, 2004 was the watershed year for Cazenove.

As an adviser to Marks & Spencer, it appeared less comfortable than Citigroup or the leading US investment bank, Morgan Stanley – who were also advisers to M&S – when giving counsel on the implications of what hedge funds or US investors were doing in M&S shares. This takeover battle was the definitive confirmation of how financial markets had gone global, that the concept of a London market was a bit quaint and old-fashioned – which in turn made Cazenove's proud independence look anachronistic. At the end of 2004, Cazenove announced that it would merge its investment banking business with that of JP Morgan, the huge US bank. And it is now reinventing itself as big, international and loving it.

In the conversation with Richard Wintour of Cazenove, Rose agreed to have a breakfast meeting the following day with three M&S directors – Paul Myners, Stella Rimington, the former head of MI5, and Brian Baldock – at Myners's house in Chelsea. But that evening he went to the annual summer party held by Brunswick's founder and chairman, Alan Parker, at the modish Hempel Hotel in Bayswater.

> It was then I got taken aside by David Mayhew, who stuck his finger in my chest and said something to the effect of: 'You are seeing the M&S board tomorrow; just remember you are not as smart as you think you are.' Which I thought for a company which was in a bit of fucking bother was a bit fucking rude, actually. [ibid.]

At the breakfast meeting on 28 May with Myners, Baldock and Rimington, Rose made clear that he was not prepared to be a part-time or non-executive chairman. He would want far greater responsibility than Vandevelde held. He would want to run M&S, which meant that he wanted Holmes's job. This was no great shock to Myners, who had already concluded that the company could not fight off Green unless Holmes was replaced: investors would take the certainty of Green's cash rather than the uncertainty that Holmes would be able to turn around a business to whose woes he had contributed. The logic of this analysis gradually persuaded the rest of the board that Holmes had to go. But if Rose was to replace Holmes, who would then become chairman? Vandevelde could not remain, even for a short time, given that he had already announced that he wanted to leave. Investors would have no confidence in his judgement after he had said that he would rather be elsewhere.

There was a credible internal candidate, at least for the period of the fight with Green. That was Myners, who knew the workings of the City better than anyone else on the board. He agreed to fill the breach.

> I said I would take the chair for the duration of the bid. And then I said we would see after that. [Paul Myners interview, 20 July 2006]

But when he left Myners's home, Rose did not yet know the job was his. 'I did not have an offer on the table,' he says. 'I did not know I was going to Baker Street. I did not get an offer till the weekend.'

Rose makes a point of the uncertainty about his future, to explain why he felt able to go round to Philip Green's office for a chat that same Friday morning, 28 May. Their conversation was characteristically combative:

> At the end of the day, I kept saying: 'Philip, I don't want to play [join Green's bidding team].' . . . I'll tell you exactly what he said to me: 'If I come bumper-to-bumper with you on Monday morning, I'll punch your headlights out.' That was the conversation. It became quite clear to me he didn't want me there [at M&S]. He can be quite intimidating when he wants to be.
>
> I'm my own man. I didn't want to work for him but I did not have an offer from Marks & Spencer on the table. I was acting in good faith. I was like any bloke who's selling his wares. And a bloke was trying to hire me to work on the one side and I was

thinking to myself that maybe there's a chance I might get hired on the other side.

I would rather run M&S as a public company, running the business myself, than run it with Philip Green. If I had gone in with Philip, I would not have been running the company. I would have been one of his gofers; I don't want to be a Philip gofer. [Stuart Rose interview, 5 June 2004]

Negotiations between M&S and Rose moved swiftly. Rose has an admirable sense of his own limitations and insisted on bringing two long-standing colleagues into the business with him. They were Charles Wilson, whose expertise is in implementing financial controls and minimizing costs; and Steven Sharp, a marketing expert. On Monday 31 May, the appointment of all three was announced by M&S. Rose was to replace Holmes as chief executive with immediate effect and Myners was to become interim chairman.

Green was livid. M&S now had a credible management team. It would not be impossible to buy the company but the price he would probably have to pay had risen by at least £1bn, possibly more. If he was furious with Rose, Green was also angry with himself for not blocking Rose. The ferocity of his fury became clear at the end of that week, on the morning of Friday 4 June, when he accosted Rose outside M&S's Baker Street headquarters.

I got out of my car. He grabbed me by the lapels and said I was a complete cunt. The upshot was I had gone into Marks & Spencer, was causing him difficulty and if I had been intelligent I could have had a quarter of a billion pounds working for him. And why did I want to work for that company as chief executive? . . . Did I realize that he was risking a billion pounds of his money and could lose it? I said: 'If you're that worried, don't risk it.' [ibid.]

Even now, Rose is bemused by how Green found him that morning. Rose is slightly unnerved by Green's remarkable ability to know what is going on and where to find people. 'He says to me quite openly: "Listen, son, there is nothing goes on in this town that I don't know about",' says Rose.

By a combination of admonition and flattery, Green has an uncanny ability to extract information. Rose was thrown, for example, when Green divulged to him that he knew he had spoken to a particular reporter on the *Financial Times*, since this was an unusual event. 'Philip knew precisely who I had been speaking to,' Rose says.

Marks's battle to remain independent was sliding into a personal confrontation between Stuart Rose and Philip Green – and Rose found himself fighting to preserve his name. On 27 June, the *Sunday Times* disclosed that a friend of Rose, Michael Spencer, had acquired an interest in two million shares in Marks & Spencer on 11 May through contracts for difference. What added frisson to the report was that on the previous day, Spencer had met Rose for lunch at the George Club, a flashy private members' club in Mayfair. At the time, Spencer said to me that he had bought the shares because he is 'a frequent punter in equities', M&S shares had looked cheap, and he hoped that the 'muppets' on the M&S board had the good sense to 'choose Stuart' to run the company. These dealings in M&S shares and those of Rose were probed by the Financial Services Authority. Spencer and Rose were both cleared of any wrongdoing, of having profited illegally from inside information – which was hardly surprising, given that Green did not tell Rose of his plans to bid for M&S until 12 May, after Rose and Spencer had bought their stakes. Nevertheless, uncomfortable questions were raised for Rose about why he and his friend dealt, and that made it harder for Rose to focus the attention of the media and investors on what he saw as the inadequacy of what Green was offering for Marks & Spencer.

This was one of those takeover struggles where the weapons were money and innuendo. The fate of this national institution, Marks, would be determined partly by what shareholders thought of the cash Green was prepared to offer them and partly by whether they regarded Stuart Rose as a credible steward of the business. The tone and content of coverage in the press and on television mattered even more than it usually does in this kind of corporate contest. Although Green continued to nurture relationships with specific journalists he had built up over years, he also hired a public-relations firm, Finsbury, as his adviser. Finsbury, founded by Roland Rudd, vies with Alan Parker's Brunswick for the position of the UK's leading financial PR firm. Rudd and Parker are arch-rivals, though this would not be a Rudd-versus-Parker contest. Rose felt that Parker was too associated with the deposed *ancien régime* at Marks. Also, Rose is immensely loyal to his long-standing friends in business. One of his first acts as M&S chief executive was to dump Brunswick and bring in his old friend, Andrew Grant – which was a little painful for Brunswick, since Grant was a former Brunswick executive. If Brunswick had retained the mandate, it would have raised the stakes even higher, since Green holds Parker personally responsible for the negative publicity about his wife's purchase of M&S shares during his previous tilt at the company.

Green had created a new company, Revival Acquisitions, to buy M&S, and he acquired enhanced credibility for Revival by persuading Lord [Dennis] Stevenson, the chairman of the leading bank, HBOS, to join Revival's board with a mandate to recruit an independent chairman and other independent non-executives. Stevenson was also then chairman of the education and media company Pearson and is chairman of the Lords Appointments Commission – which vets whether nominees for peerages are fit and proper. He is one of the UK's more influential and respected businessmen, so it was shrewd of Green to enlist him. And it showed Green's pragmatism, because in the late 1980s Stevenson had been instrumental in ousting one of Green's closest friends, Tony Berry, from the international recruitment company he then ran, Blue Arrow.

> Kicked Tony in the bollocks. Never discussed it with him [Stevenson]. Look, I've always believed, in 99.5 per cent of the time, there's always three versions. Not my business. I don't

think Dennis is the kind of guy you would enquire of. [Philip Green interview, 31 May 2006]

As the weeks progressed, Green modified and increased his offer to take account of what he thought shareholders wanted. Gradually, he began to win support from investors, although the board of M&S was resolute in arguing that he was not offering enough. What was striking, however, is that the more that Green in fact gained the upper hand, the more he saw obstacles in his way. In particular, he became extremely concerned about whether he could afford to finance the deficit in M&S's pension scheme – although he was convinced that the company and the trustees of its pension fund were exaggerating the pension liability to undermine his ability to finance his offer. The fund's trustees announced on 10 July that if M&S's borrowings rose sharply following a takeover, they would be concerned about the cost to the company of servicing all that debt and its ability over the longer term to support the pension fund. In those circumstances, it would insist that any new owner of the business should pump in vast amounts of cash by way of insurance. In an extreme case, the trustees might demand that M&S under Green's ownership should put £785m into the pension fund every year for three years – compared with £105m per annum over 12 years, which was what M&S as a public company had agreed to inject. Such a sharp rise in payments would have more than have wiped out the company's entire profits.

By contrast, just three days earlier, on 7 July, there had been a significant breakthrough for Green. Having said he was prepared to increase what he would pay for M&S, he won the support of the retailer's most important shareholder, Brandes of the US, which said that it would accept an offer for the 11.7 per cent of M&S's shares it owned. Green had announced that he was now ready to pay 400p in cash per M&S share or 335p in cash plus shares in Revival, his bidding company. If they had taken those Revival shares, M&S's investors would have ended up with 30 per cent of Green's new company. But with the offer now pitched at 400p per share, Green had obtained £12.5bn of finance for the deal, up from £11.9bn. That included £3bn of equity, of which £1.6bn came from Philip Green and his family alone – which was a colossal sum for any single individual to put into a deal. But enough was enough. He decided to cap the bid at that level, saying he would not pay more than 400p per share.

> Many great entrepreneurs have fallen over doing a deal too far . . . As far as I was concerned it was fully valued at £4, there was nothing left to give. But it was a great personal achievement, Herculean, raising £12.5bn on my own. [Philip Green interview, 15 July 2004]

Myners and the M&S board contended that 400p was still too little. On 12 July, Rose announced his own strategy to revive the company, which was to sell its financial services business to the giant bank, HSBC, refocus the group on its core businesses of clothing and food, cut costs, return £2.3bn in cash to M&S shareholders (equivalent to 100p per share) and make George Davies a wealthier man by acquiring his Per Una brand for £125m.

Even so, Brandes continued to back Green. What's more, by 14 July, Green could claim that investors controlling 34 per cent of M&S's shares either unambiguously supported his desire to buy M&S or wanted M&S at least to give him access to the company's books to facilitate his bid. This was not overwhelming support but momentum was moving in Green's direction.

There was an M&S board meeting at 6 p.m. on the evening of 14 July, which took place a few hours after the company's annual meeting. Green had made up his mind this would be the decisive moment. He wanted to hear from Myners and M&S that very night that it would recommend shareholders accept his 400p per share, that it would allow him to negotiate directly with the M&S pension fund trustees and that he would have access to some of the company's confidential financial information. He and his two Goldman colleagues, Sharp and Sherwood, piled the pressure on Mayhew to secure a response from Myners; though this was harder than it might normally be, given that Mayhew was communing with Scottish salmon. 'The day of the AGM and the biggest deal in Europe and he's fishing,' says Green. 'It's arrogance deluxe. I was furious.' [*Financial Times*, 5 October 2004]

The day wore on and Green had still heard nothing from Myners. He was becoming more and more exasperated. From two journalists, Kate Rankine of the *Daily Telegraph* and Lina Saigol of the *Financial Times*, he was hearing that the opposition of the M&S board to his proposed offer had not been dropped. He interpreted this as a hardening of M&S's position, although, in fact, this was not the case. At 8.30 p.m., when he had still heard nothing directly from M&S, he decided to call it a day. He put out an announcement saying he was – once again – abandoning his attempt to buy the UK's leading clothing retailer.

Rose, for one, had not expected him to withdraw. He was by no means certain that M&S could see off Green.

> I'm still surprised that Philip pulled out when he did. I think if he had waited another 24 hours the pressure might have intensified to the point where we might not have been so robust. I dunno, I can only speak for myself. If you remember, that's when he was claiming he had 35 per cent, 33 or 38.
>
> We were sitting in the board meeting, which had adjourned for a 10-minute, 15-minute period because it was a late-evening board meeting, and we came back in and a specific subject was due to be discussed when Robert Swannell [a banking adviser from Citigroup], sitting on the left-hand side of the table, said: 'Seems like it's all over.' [Stuart Rose interview, 4 July 2006]

Why did Green pull out? My view is that the balance between risk and reward had moved against him more than he found tolerable, especially in respect of the cash he might have had to inject into the pension fund. He had made an immense fortune from Bhs and Arcadia, and although Rose and Myners believe

Green was aiming to make an additional £5bn or so of personal profit from M&S, I think Green became less and less sure this was do-able. This is what he said to me hours after throwing in the towel:

> This was personal money, family money, £1.6bn. Twenty-five years ago this September I started with one shop selling discount ladies' fashions. This [£1.6bn] is new money that's been earned going in the trenches. And as you know, I've fought a few wars, haven't I? I said to my wife last Sunday morning – about a quarter to six I woke up – I said to Tina how lucky we have been to somehow get through this jungle to end up with a private business turning over £3bn, virtually no debt, nobody to answer to. [Philip Green interview, 15 July 2004]

After all the turmoil and excitement of the preceding few weeks, Green suddenly realized that the grass was already pretty green on his side of the fence. He had one of the largest private business empires in Europe, he was wholly independent and he was answerable to no one. M&S would be a great prize, but not so great as to be worth jeopardizing everything he had built.

Initially, it looked as though Green's attack of risk-aversion was an impressive manifestation of self-preservation instincts. Rose did not find it simple or quick to restore the fortunes of M&S.

> During the height of the battle the adrenalin was flowing 24 hours a day. But then you suddenly realize you have to run the business and deliver the promises. And that period – July, August, September, October, November, December – was a very grim period because everything was going backwards and in fact went backwards well into 2005. It was a lot of pressure and I don't deny there were a few dark moments. [Stuart Rose interview, 26 July 2006]

To make matters more complicated for Rose and Myners – who worked together exceptionally well – there was uncertainty about how long Myners would remain as chairman. Originally, he had said he would stay only for the length of the contest with Green. The board then asked him to stay on for a relatively short but indeterminate period while it considered whom to appoint as a permanent chairman.

> The criticism of me is that I should have been more confident at that point and should have said I could make a good job of it. But I had never done a job like this. I had been on boards of big companies but I had never chaired or led a company of this scale. Gartmore employed 400 people. [Paul Myners interview, 20 July 2006]

Leading the search for a permanent chairman was Kevin Lomax. In January 2005, Myners told him that he wanted to be a candidate but met fierce resistance from Lomax.

> When in January I said I wanted to go on the list, he said: 'We're not going to put you on the list.' And I said: 'In that case, you must have a very strong list.' He declined to share it with me. And I said: 'I am a member of the board and if you are not going to put me on the list you should share the list with me.' And over a period of time he did share the list with me. [ibid.]

It turned out that there were three names on the list: Chris Gibson-Smith, chairman of the London Stock Exchange, Baroness Hogg, chair of 3i, and Lord Burns, the former Treasury Permanent Secretary and erstwhile chairman of Abbey National, the bank. Myners, with some justification, felt his credentials were as strong as theirs. The dispute between Myners and Lomax then exploded into the media. Both sides were briefing journalists, and damaging stories were written about a split on the M&S board. Myners says: 'At that point, it became very personal . . . because I had triggered the backing of the press that a process had to occur, as it should have done.'

Rose says the dispute made life very difficult: 'It was very, very,

very ill-judged, it was very, very, very unhelpful and it was very, very, very difficult to manage internally. It was a fucking nightmare.' Myners's failure was in not winning over the other non-executive directors.

> Where I went wrong was that Kevin got the support of Jack Keenan and Steve Holliday, the other two non-executives. It was a very small board, remember. They became nervous that the share price was still 335p, 340p, in the spring of 2005. We had had four successive quarters of declining sales, we were still losing market share. But Stuart had told them that was going to happen. I remember Steve Holliday saying in a meeting: 'Where's the top-line growth?' and Stuart said: 'I told you, there will be no top-line growth until Year Three. We have things we need to fix first.' [Paul Myners interview, 20 July 2006]

Rose still winces when he remembers Holliday's implicit criticism. At the time, he was certain he could increase profits in the short-term by making the business more efficient, but he was uncertain whether sales could be grown again in a meaningful way. Meanwhile, as Myners recalls, Green was revelling in M&S's discomfiture, pointing out to the media that its share price was well below the price he had been prepared to pay.

> There were worries about individual reputations. And of course Philip was on the phone all the time to you guys in the press. He used to ring me and say: 'I've been round your store in Croydon. It's bloody awful. They are throwing the frocks on the ground and stealing the coat hangers.' [ibid.]

In the end, what did for Myners was the fear on the board that he had become too close to Rose. The primary duty of a chairman is to review the performance of a chief executive and sack him if he or she is not up to the mark. According to Myners, however, Lomax persuaded the board that he [Myners] would not feel able to dismiss Rose if a recovery at M&S

did not materialize. Myners, however, insists that although he had become friendly with Rose, he had the backbone to dismiss him had that become necessary.

> Kevin was able to say to them: 'If this doesn't work, perish the thought, and we have to part company with Stuart or we have to go back and try to re-initiate talks with Philip Green or something, Paul is going to absolutely refuse to do that. So we need to have somebody who will keep options open.' [ibid.]

In the end, there was a compromise. Myners was to serve a full two years as chairman, giving him the opportunity to prove that he could do the job. He would leave after the annual meeting on 11 July 2006, when he would be replaced by Lord Burns. Lomax retired on 31 August 2006, to be replaced as the senior independent director by Sir David Michels, the former chief executive of Hilton Group.

As it turned out, the timing of Myners's exit was perfect. From the autumn of 2005, the City began to believe that M&S was on the mend and its share price took off. Although consumer confidence in the UK as a whole deteriorated, M&S's sales performance started to improve. There was a much-needed rise in underlying sales over the Christmas period of 2005, and in the succeeding six months growth accelerated. That said, the rise in sales was exaggerated by a lamentable comparative performance in the previous year. By the time Myners left, M&S's shares were nearer to 600p than the 400p that would have been Green's takeover price. His refusal to sell to Green seemed justified.

By 2007, M&S was making serious market-share gains. While old arch-rivals such as Next and Debenhams were losing momentum, Marks's sales were growing strongly. The marketing campaigns for clothing and food, overseen by Rose's old friend, Steve Sharp, were imaginative, populist and seductive. The product range across the board was widely seen as vastly improved. Rose never seemed to be off the TV or radio – and had some success reclaiming M&S's traditional image as a paternalistic, socially responsible business, with a campaign to reduce the business's contribution to global warming. The share price soared through 700p – before drifting down towards 600p again. Towards the middle of the year, the rocket that was driving sales fizzled a bit: clothing sales were dampened by dismal summer weather and shoppers in general were becoming just a little less liberal with their cash. Marks continued to grow its underlying sales, albeit at a much decelerated pace. And in the autumn it became clear although the company was still doing a bit better than many of its peers, the margin of difference would narrow and progress would be slower.

As M&S recovered, so too did the relationship between Rose and Green. They started to gossip again on a regular basis. For Green, business comes first.

> Tony Grabiner [the distinguished lawyer who chairs Arcadia] said to me: 'You are the only person who would have mended a fence with Stuart Rose after what he did to you.' . . . I try not to fall out with people. There are odd people . . . But I am just trying to say, in the main, you know what they say: 'Keep your friends close, your enemies closer.' [Philip Green interview, 31 May 2006]

Green even turned up at Harry's Bar, the stylish private members' club in Mayfair that serves Italian food and is favoured by celebrities of a certain age, for a small party to mark Myners's exit from M&S.

> I had all the people from M&S and the advisory team who were in the room when we got the phone call that said that Philip had withdrawn his bid. I don't know how Philip found out we were having this dinner but Stuart said to me that Philip was keen to come along. And I said I'd be happy and we agreed that Philip would stumble in at about 11 o'clock, which he did.
>
> He stayed till 1.30 a.m. and we had a good time. He and I are all right now. It ended up with him saying: 'You know what,

Paul, you should become chairman of Bhs. That would upset that cunt Burns [who had replaced Myners as chairman of M&S].' [Paul Myners interview, 20 July 2006]

So Myners, Rose and Green are now one happy family. Green did not recruit Myners to chair Bhs, the competitor to M&S which he owns, but Rose played a role in landing for Myners a decent chairmanship that kept the double-act going. Rose is on the board of the UK's largest property company, Land Securities, and is a member of its two-person 'nominations' committee – which in July 2006 appointed Myners to be Land Securities' new chairman. They are an impressive troika: Green has a mind-boggling amount of personal wealth, one of the largest private businesses in Europe and a unique ability to raise finance for deals; Rose has one of the swankiest and most powerful public-company jobs in the UK and has been appointed to the Prime Minister's Business Council for Britain; Myners has a uniquely diverse collection of top-drawer commercial and public-sector jobs, and the ear of the Government. They have all done it for themselves, more or less. With their unconventional backgrounds and sophisticated understanding of how to use the media, they are the New British Corporate Establishment.

And if there is one big lesson of Marks & Spencer's great soap opera of City life, it is that a mature business can benefit from the threat of being taken over by a Philip Green or the institutional version of Philip Green, private equity. Marks & Spencer would today be in a lot worse shape if it hadn't reacted to the shock of Green's attempt to buy it. So if Philip Green did not exist, the health of the economy would probably require him to be invented. However, M&S's renaissance under Rose also demonstrates that there is no new law of history which says that an essential condition of reviving a mature company like Marks & Spencer is that boundless booty simply has to go to private equity or to Green. It proves that the great businesses that underpin the British economy can survive and prosper as public companies. That matters. The aggregate value of shares bought back by Marks and the increase in the market value of the business since the summer of 2004 is more than £6bn. That £6bn would have gone to Green and his supporters. Instead a healthy slug of it has enriched the millions of us who still have a stake in it through our pension schemes.

CHAPTER 5
POISON MANUFACTURERS

Investment banks, hedge funds and the other titans of global financial capitalism will save the world. That seemed to be the thesis of the distinguished US economist Robert Shiller, who wrote a persuasive book about the golden age of creativity in financial markets that we have been living through. Called *The New Financial Order*, it implies that those who long for the days of interventionist, socially progressive government may be able to find new heroes in the great investment banks. These, he says, are creating products and services that should enhance social welfare. Among the examples he gives of a possible innovation is a form of insurance that would provide protection against falls in the price of our homes, thus preserving the value of what for many of us is our most important asset. He also writes of young students being able to embark on highly specialist careers in, say, medicine or science with less fear that they may have opted for a vocational dead-end, by – again – insuring against the danger that a particular branch of medicine may become supplanted by another. Shiller also has clever ideas to promote equality within individual countries and to reduce the gap between the income per head of wealthy nations and developing ones, all through sophisticated financial engineering.

It is a seductive vision of how financial markets could promote equality. And it is a vision which delighted investment bankers: how wonderful that their own enrichment should be the underpinning of true social justice. Perhaps one day good government will simply be a matter of nudging the markets to shower their gold on this or that deprived social group or on poverty-stricken countries. As Shiller says, the innovation of markets in recent years has been magnificent. There has been an explosion of new financial products and services of astonishing complexity. But since the summer of 2007, the most conspicuous effect of all this imaginative financial toil has been a crisis in money markets of a depth and breadth without modern precedent. For the best part of two months, banks and other financial institutions more or less stopped lending to each other – and, at the time of writing, conditions had improved but were still not back to normal. There was a soaring in the cost of what little credit was available. And where before banks and institutions were prepared to provide loans to each other for months, now they would lend for only days at a stretch. The world's biggest banks suffered write-downs and losses running to tens of billions of dollars. Severe financial difficulties afflicted a couple of banks in Germany. There were humiliating losses at the world's biggest bank, Citigroup, and at the Wall Street 'bulge-bracket' investment bank, Merrill Lynch – both of whose chief executives quit, as blame from the media and the ire of shareholders rained down on them. And there was a run on a big British bank, Northern Rock, the first run on a major bank in the UK since the collapse of Overend, Gurney in 1866 (the failure of the City of Glasgow Bank in 1878 wreaked less havoc on the financial system than the Overend, Gurney debacle). The Rock was forced to borrow more than £20bn from taxpayers in the form of emergency funds provided by the Bank of England and underwritten by the Treasury. The Bank anticipated it would eventually lend the Rock at least £30bn, or £1,000 for every British taxpayer. An unprecedented pledge by the Chancellor that no Rock depositor would lose a penny meant the total financial exposure of the

Government was more than £40bn, equivalent to 3 per cent of the annual output of the entire British economy.

The effects of this crisis are still rippling through the global economy. But what is already clear is that the impact will be negative for most of us, in that the price of borrowing money is rising and the availability of loans is diminishing – which in turn will lead to a reduction in economic growth. How severe will the downturn turn out to be? That is uncertain, but it will not be negligible. The evidence suggests that the relentless, unfettered determination of players in the markets to invent new investment products offering better returns for less risk has been anything but benign. They pocketed the fees when the products were sold. But all of us will be poorer than we would otherwise have been, due to a reduction in growth caused by the fear engendered throughout the world by the toxicity of many of these products.

Until August 2007, the conventional view was that the globalization and growth of finance had helped the world to grow faster. And that turned out to be true, while the good times rolled. It is also plausible that economic growth may in recent years have been smoother, less vulnerable to shocks, less prone to blips, as a result of the way that bankers had seemingly become more expert in assessing, dividing and distributing the many risks that confront businesses, countries and individuals. Such was the view of no less an authority than Alan Greenspan, former chairman of the US Federal Reserve, widely revered as the greatest central banker of his age. But, in retrospect, we were living through an era of collective delusion about the risks being run. And the longer those risks failed to be exposed, the bigger they became – and the greater the price we are all now paying.

LOANS FOR LIARS

One of the underlying causes of the mess we find ourselves in was the decision of central banks – and notably that of Greenspan's central bank, the Fed – to keep interest rates too low for too long. The US central bank cut its main policy rate to 1 per cent in 2003 and held it at that negligible level for a year. Borrowed money was more or less free – especially in Japan but also in the US. That engendered confidence bordering on arrogance among bankers that the boom would go on for ever. Much of the money that was sloshing around the place had its source in the enormous financial surpluses of the world's great exporting countries: manufacturing giants in Asia, led by China and Japan; the oil and gas exporters, notably those in the Middle East and Russia. Trillions of dollars were pumped to the West, where the clever financial engineers of the investment banks and hedge funds promised they would put it all to work in places that would offer a decent rate of return.

A good chunk of that money was lent, in what appeared to be a socially progressive way, in the form of sub-prime loans to those in the US with poor credit records who wanted to buy a home. That may seem odd. But the basic explanation is simple. Bad credit risks have to pay more to borrow. So if you as a lender want to earn a bit more for your money, give credit to those who will find it hardest to repay. But, of course, you still want them to repay. And the problem with these sub-prime loans in the US is that – as a result of a whole series of cock-ups – the system of providing this money guaranteed that a disproportionate amount would never be repaid. Though the lenders did not find that out till it was far too late.

First, the processes and institutional structures for making those loans were deeply flawed. In the US, some half a million mortgage brokers were incentivized to 'sell' mortgages to potential homebuyers. They were not employed by the providers of the loans. The credit did not sit on the balance sheets of the institutions for which they worked: if the loan went horribly wrong, that would be someone else's problem. They were paid commissions for the volume of mortgages they arranged. So, of course, they tried to arrange as many mortgages as they could, not minding the consequences. In 2006 alone, more than

$600bn of sub-prime loans were provided to American home-owners. And if the customer wanted to borrow more than he or she could afford, then that could be glossed over, due to an innovation called 'stated income, stated assets' loans. These allow US homebuyers to give a personal undertaking that their income is a certain level, even if they don't provide any proof. Such loans were taken out by hundreds of thousands of US citizens who were pay-as-you-earn taxpayers and could there-fore have easily provided proof of earnings, had they wanted to do so. It is little surprise, then, that studies have shown 'dis-crepancies' between what such borrowers said they earned and what they actually earn, in 95 per cent of these loans.

Such mortgages became known as 'liars' loans' – and it is easy to see why. But it wasn't just some of the borrowers who lied. Deception was built into a global system for raising money on a colossal scale and then providing it to all manner of unsuitable borrowers, of which these US homebuyers were just one important group.

At the lending end of this global system, liars' loans were the extreme manifestation of a US process for manufacturing sub-prime mortgages that was predicated on turning a blind eye to economic reality. When a borrower had difficulty making repay-ments on a loan, a mortgage broker would typically encourage them to pay off that loan by taking out a new one for an even greater amount. These became infamous as 'rolling loans' which 'gather no losses'. When a loan was rolled over, no one needed to know that default was looming. Although painful economic reality could not be avoided for ever.

Now, here is where we link the Wal-Mart employee in Arizona, who has bought a house he can't really afford, to the seizing up of global financial markets, the meltdown (and subsequent rescue) of a couple of German banks and – ultimately – that dramatic flight of capital from Northern Rock. The point is that somewhere close to a trillion dollars of these loans to financially stretched American homebuyers were sold to investors all over the world in a process known as securitization. The debts went into a giant mincing and mixing machine on Wall Street and in the City. It was operated by the biggest US investment banks, which included Morgan Stanley, Merrill Lynch and Goldman Sachs, as well as giant global commercial banks, such as Citigroup, UBS and Barclays. They took thousands of these mortgages, pooled them, and then created tradeable bonds out of them, called asset-backed securities, which appeared to offer a decent rate of interest (the interest paid by the home purchasers with poor credit records) for a specified level of risk.

You might wonder why banks prefer to sell these loans in the form of asset-backed bonds rather than keep them on their own balance sheets. Well, here's one reason. When they sell a loan, they are selling a stream of future payments from the borrower. So in selling the loan, they book a big one-off profit, as opposed to a stream of future profits. And a big profit today means bigger bonuses and fatter remuneration for the bankers that create and sell the relevant bonds. Nothing wrong with that, in principle. Except that some of these securities – especially those which went through a further reprocessing into collateralized debt and loan obligations (see below) – were sold at the wrong price. They were priced as solid gold investments, when many of them were altogether smellier than that. And some of these banks subsequently suffered substantial losses on bonds they either could not sell or chose not to sell. But there is an asymmetry to the bonus system at banks: bankers, who had already received fat rewards for creating this stuff, could not be asked to return this money when the banks' shareholders were batterd as the poo hit the whirring blades (though some bankers have paid with the loss of their jobs).

Note that Merrill, Morgan et al had no direct connection with any individual borrower and no idea whether any such borrower was a good risk or a bad risk. But they believed that data on the past behaviour of other borrowers meant they could predict with near certainty how these new borrowers would behave. This data allowed them – or so they claimed – to assess the riskiness of a bond and therefore to price it for consumption by international investors. What's more, verification of the riskiness of a bond was provided, for a fee, by the specialist credit-rating agencies, led by Moody's and Standard & Poor's – although there was a potential conflict of interest for the rating agencies, since their fees are paid by those who are trying to sell the bonds. However, the biggest defect in this measurement of risk was that the sub-prime market was growing like Topsy. In the mid-1990s, only 5 per cent of new US mortgages were in the sub-prime category. That rose to between 15 and 20 per cent over the following ten years. By the spring of 2007, there were $1,300bn ($1.3 trillion) of sub-prime loans in existence, of which just under half had been created in the frothy market conditions of 2006 alone. The point is that data on how many borrowers defaulted when the market was younger and much smaller would not necessarily be a guide to default rates in a market that had more than doubled in size over a few short years. So it proved, and painfully for us all. Nevertheless, the big investment banks cited this question-able data to convert sub-prime loans into bonds that they claimed were risk-free and which had a so-called triple-A credit rating.

Here's how they do the clever engineering, which turned out to be lethally flawed. For argument's sake, let's say that they estimate that as many as one in two home loans will default and that on average there will be a 40 per cent loss on those defaulting loans. That, in turn, gives a maximum risk of 20 per cent losses on a portfolio of these loans. Bad news? Not for creative investment bankers. Out of this portfolio of low-quality loans, they can create supposedly high-quality bonds by putting in place covenants which stipulate that the first 20 per cent of losses would be attributed to one bunch of really poisonous bonds, usually called toxic waste, leaving most of the rest of the bonds almost as safe as US Treasury bonds (in theory). So out of lending to US home-buyers widely considered to be a bad risk, to whom many con-servative banks would not extend credit under any circumstances, the investment banks created hundreds of billions of dollars of bonds viewed in the market as almost as safe as the debt of the most powerful state in the world. It seemed to be genuine alchemy, turning ordure into gold.

Before we move on, it's probably worth recapping the phoney assumptions made by the investment banks as they created these bonds: that historic data on default rates was useful even though the market had exploded in size; that data of any sort was useful even though the system for originating the loans, with mortgage brokers paid by the volume of loans they sell, actually encouraged fraud.

So far, so disturbing. But it gets worse.

Because the demand for toxic waste isn't as huge as all that (some purchasers of this poison have suffered horrendous losses), investment banks looked for ways to slice and dice the toxic waste, to create something almost edible. They've mixed it up with other securities in collateralized debt obligations, which are structures for creating bonds out of other bonds – or sometimes bonds created out of bonds that are in turn created out of other bonds (collateralized debt obligations squared, as if you wanted to know). Here we are looking at one of the great phenomena of our age, the creation of 'structured credit vehicles', into which hundreds of billions of dollars poured – including cash that we gave in trust to our pension funds – but which were barely known outside a circle of financial experts at investment banks, commercial banks and hedge funds. And, again, the main cause of the explosive growth in structured credit was the very basic desire for those controlling vast pools of cash to earn a better-than-average return for minimal risk – though it turned out that all this financial creativity disguised the risk, rather than reducing it.

Although these structured credit vehicles have different names – collateralized debt obligations, collateralized loan obligations, structured investment vehicles, conduits – and they finance themselves in different ways, they have one big thing in common: they turn one lot of debt into different kinds of debt. So, in a collateralized debt obligation, a collection of asset-backed bonds – such as bonds based on sub-prime loans – may be turned into bonds of varying specified risks and varying specified interest rates. Within a collateralized debt obligation, some of the new securities were priced as though they were the best quality assets in the world – thanks to the willingness of specialized insurance companies to insure them against default. Which created the illusion that the risk of losses had vanished on what had started life as high-risk loans to US homeowners, many of whom were in low-paying, insecure jobs. In fact, the risk still existed: it had simply been transferred, much of it to these specialized or monocline insurers, whose share prices slumped in the autumn of 2007.

That probably sounds confusing and difficult to comprehend. Which may – against all my instincts as a writer – be a good thing. Because it demonstrates that what were being manufactured on a colossal scale were investments whose intrinsic risks even sophisticated investors did not understand properly. Once the original sub-prime loan was in a collateralized debt obligation or some other structured credit vehicle, that loan could be one of perhaps a million different loans all mashed together to form this new bond. And, of course, even these bonds-made-of-bonds rely to a worrying extent on all that dodgy historic data to determine their risk of default. So the eventual purchaser of the collateralized debt obligation had no more idea what was in that new bond than a child at primary school eating a Turkey Twizzler knows what he or she is eating. Little wonder that when there was a global scare about what may actually be in these bonds, no one wanted to touch them – just in case they all turned out to be poisonous. That said, the investment banker would argue, on the basis of portfolio theory, that if you put one load of debt with a risk of going bad together with another seemingly independent load of debt, the risks attached to the resulting melange should be lower than for the individual loads. But for that to be true, each original parcel of debt would have had to be uncorrelated to the other parcels – and the absence of such a correlation turned out to be yet another illusion in a market built on systemic self-delusion.

So, for the past few years, Wall Street operated a giant machine for turning mind-boggling amounts of US home loans – which were hugely vulnerable to losses from fraud and the inescapable cycles in interest rates and house prices – into supposedly risk-free investments for risk-averse investors in Asia, the Middle East and (as it turns out) for Europe's big banks. But Europe's banks were hardly blameless either. If the underlying cause of the global financial crisis was fraud and greed in the US home-loans system, there was also chronic folly by big international lending banks, especially European ones. Banks thousands of miles from America – as well as US banks – tried to make incremental profits and get round rules limiting their lending activities by buying bonds linked to sub-prime loans and putting them into enormous special funding vehicles, the conduits and structured investment vehicles (SIVs).

These were off-balance-sheet entities for borrowing cheap short-term funds from the money markets in the form of securities known as asset-backed commercial paper. Now, as their name implied, the commercial paper was secured against asset-backed securities, such as mortgage-backed securities and collateralized debt obligations (CDOs). Banks that set up these conduits and SIVs thought they were making easy money: they paid out less in interest on the commercial paper than they received from their holdings of asset-backed bonds and CDOs. According to Citigroup, European conduits alone held more than $500bn of assets as collateral for commercial paper at the end of March 2007. But there was an intrinsic weakness to this funding: commercial paper of short duration had been sold by banks to finance their purchases of long-dated bonds whose underlying assets included those dodgy sub-prime loans to US homeowners. It represented a classic liquidity mismatch, or borrowing short to lend long – although that mismatch was disguised when there was a reliable, active market for such bonds, when they could be bought and sold fairly easily. But when and if they could not be sold, European banks would find that they had been borrowing money that typically had to be repaid or rolled-over every 90 days or less to fund their ownership – direct or indirect – of 30-year US home loans.

Such funding schemes only worked when the market had

confidence in the value of the collateral backing the commercial paper. When investors started to become aware of the scale of defaults in the US sub-prime mortgage market, they began to fear that all those asset-backed bonds and collateralized debt obligations might be worth less than they had thought. And that meant that they were much less interested in purchasing asset-backed commercial paper issued by SIVs and conduits, which was backed by bonds and CDOs linked to sub-prime mortgages. When the demand for such commercial paper disappeared, the managers of SIVs and CDOs found they had to repay billions of dollars to holders of commercial paper they had sold earlier, which was falling due for repayment in the normal way. But they did not have the money to do so, because no one wanted to buy the asset-backed bonds and CDOs that were supposed to be the security.

It was a fully fledged financial crisis, which forced many banks to put vast amounts of their own resources into SIVs and conduits to prevent them going bust and precipitating an even bigger crisis. What triggered it was an extraordinary statement made on 9 August 2007 by the giant French bank BNP Paribas, that it could no longer value with any great confidence the US asset-backed bonds in three of its funds. It was like the little boy shouting out that the emperor has no clothes. All of a sudden, huge banks, hedge funds and professional investors woke up and recognized that they too did not know the proper value of hundreds of billions of dollars of assets they owned. There was an epidemic of fear. And, almost in an instant, something happened which had no modern precedent. These institutions stopped lending to each other.

There was a lending freeze for two main reasons. First, no one knew whether any particular bank had so many bad assets on its books that it might go bust. So, if there was a chance that any bank could collapse, why lend to one? And secondly, those banks which thought they were being clever by making seemingly easy profits through their SIVs and conduits discovered that they would have to put their own precious cash into these vehicles to keep them afloat. So banks hoarded cash, in case they needed it to replace the asset-backed commercial paper that had hitherto funded SIVs and conduits but could no longer be sold. Everyone had woken up to the idea that the allegedly safe collateral of mortgage-backed securities and collateralized debt obligations was the equivalent of a palace built on paper foundations. And as the foundations crumpled, all financial institutions panicked.

The casualties have included a couple of German banks, Sachsen and IKB, which had bought excessive amounts of bonds linked to US sub-prime borrowers. Both had to be rescued in operations initiated by the German authorities. Also, predictably, a string of US banks specializing in sub-prime lending have suffered huge losses and some have closed down. In the UK the crisis brought a substantial bank, Northern Rock, to the brink of collapse, even though it had no direct exposure to US sub-prime debt.

Northern Rock was vulnerable because it was unusually dependent on the money market for financing the ordinary mortgages it made to British homebuyers. The mistake made by its directors was that they believed these markets would always be open for business. They never believed that one day these markets would put up a 'gone for an extended holiday' sign. The point is that Northern Rock took in proportionately less money than other British banks from retail depositors, savers like you and me. In the first half of 2007, only 14 per cent of all the money it raised came from retail depositors. Some £12bn came from what are known as the wholesale markets, including £5.6bn from the sale of its very own mortgage-backed bonds.

So on 9 August, when those money markets seized up, Northern Rock had a problem. It could no longer sell any mortgage-backed bonds. There was a global buyers' strike for all mortgage-backed bonds, whether or not they were linked to US sub-prime lending. Nobody wanted them. And that was a disaster for Northern Rock. It was as though someone had turned off the tap that kept it alive. It had been the fastest-growing mortgage bank in the UK, granting one in five of all new mortgages during the first six months of the year. But you can't stay in business as a bank if you haven't got the cash to lend or to repay depositors. And Northern Rock was running out of money fast. Not only was it impossible to sell the mortgage-backed bonds, but other initiatives for raising long-term funds also flopped. As its own debts came up for renewal, they were replaced by loans of very short-term maturity, lasting just a day at a time. There was a growing mismatch between the long-term mortgage loans it had made and the shorter term money it was able to borrow to finance these loans. That mismatch was potentially very dangerous. It increased the risk – which all banks face – that one day a depositor would ask for its money back and there would be no cash available. So on 10 September, when Northern Rock's final attempt to sell asset-backed bonds had collapsed, the bank was forced to go cap-in-hand to the Bank of England for emergency support under the Bank of England's role as lender of last resort.

When, on the night of 13 September, I reported on the BBC that Northern Rock was no longer able to finance itself in a conventional way and had asked for help from the Bank of England, depositors became anxious. Thousands of them queued at branches and logged on to Northern Rock's website to withdraw their precious savings. In the absence of a formal guarantee that all their money would be safe, this was a rational reaction – as the Governor of the Bank of England, Mervyn King, told me in an interview for BBC Radio 4's File on 4 programme. Because of the shortcomings of the official system for insuring deposits, King felt unable during the run to stand up in public and tell the Rock's depositors they had nothing to fear. To have done so would have been 'dishonest', he said. After four days, during which television pictures of the shocking run at Northern Rock were beamed around the world, the Chancellor of the Exchequer, Alistair Darling, belatedly gave a Government guarantee that no depositor would lose a penny. And he initiated a process of reforming the entire system of insuring depositors' money to provide greater protection to ordinary savers.

But damage had been done. The reputation of the British banking industry and the City had taken a serious knock. During the autumn, financial institutions refused to roll over or extend their loans to the Rock as they fell due for repayment. So the Bank of England had to fill the breach and expected to lend at least £30bn to it. Because the Bank's credit facility for the Rock is guaranteed by the Treasury, each British taxpayer would in effect lend this mortgage-provider £1,000. But the repercussions went much wider. The chairman of one of the UK's biggest banks told me that those brainy young business-school graduates who control billions of cash from their offices on Wall Street and Dubai and Singapore were spooked by the TV images of anxious Rock savers desperately trying to get their money out of branches. So, for no other reason than that the world is their oyster when it comes to deploying their cash, in the febrile conditions of mid-September they boycotted the UK. In other words, the tap was turned off for almost all British banks regardless of size. There was acute anxiety at the very highest level within the British banking system about a possible domino effect of bank collapses. After a few days, the tap was switched back on – but the flow of money through the pipes is less than it was. And because money has become tighter for the banks, they are more reluctant to lend to all of us.

At the time of writing, what started as a liquidity problem – or a shortage of cash for banks – is transforming into a credit problem. The fuel that kept house prices rising is running low, because banks are lending less and charging more for what they lend. And if house prices fall over a sustained period, consumers would feel less confident. They would spend less and economic growth would slow down such that jobs could be lost. Unemployed homeowners would have difficulty repaying mortgages. And even those in work could face difficulties in meeting mortgage payments, as their cheap mortgage deals expire, to be replaced by pricier loans. The providers of mortgages could incur losses on their loans – which would eat into their capital resources, further constraining how much they can lend. Few of us would emerge unscathed from such a vicious cycle.

We are all the victims of a sort of global warming in the global financial markets – bubbles in the value of assets, concentrations of toxic financial products whose dangers were poorly understood. Invisible financial risks accumulated, ultimately precipitating crisis. The losers are us, while many of the plutocrats who made fortunes during the good times – rocket scientists at investment banks that manufactured the lethal products, founders of hedge funds who helped to create the market for them – have cashed in and protected much of their gains. In fact, many investment banks and hedge funds spotted the risks of sub-prime early and made out like bandits by selling all and any asset linked to sub-prime before it became fashionable to do so. Those which used derivative instruments in 2006 to bet against low-quality loans to US homeowners made profits estimated at $20bn in 2007. They did this by short-selling securities linked to sub-prime – or borrowing those securities, selling them and then buying them back much cheaper after the market had collapsed. The biggest winners were Paulson & Co of New York, whose funds are reported to have made profits of at least $12bn from short-selling sub-prime, and California-based Lahde Capital, which is said to have increased the value of its investors' money by more than 11 times in 2007 by speculating on a sub-prime meltdown.

The enrichment of the few takes many forms in today's complex world. But it's from hedge funds and investment banks that many of the new members of the super-wealthy class emerged. This chapter and the next one are about who they are and what they do.

A QUESTION OF TRUST

There is a confidence, swagger and arrogance about many stars of the hedge-fund world. And in 2005 there was a very rare opportunity to gaze on this world during a surreal court case over the stewardship of a chain of shops selling electronic gizmos, called the Gadget Shop. The minority owners of the Gadget Shop were suing the major shareholders because they felt aggrieved that the Gadget Shop hadn't bought another chain of stores, Birthdays, which sells greetings products. It was all a bit odd in that the Gadget Shop subsequently collapsed and Birthdays performed pretty badly. But these minority owners felt that their rights had been trampled and wanted compensation.

One of the plaintiffs was Jon Wood, who at the time was a superstar banker at UBS and has since created a substantial hedge fund. And one of the defendants was Sir Tom Hunter, an immensely wealthy purchaser of businesses who operates much as private-equity firms do. Wood's great achievement was that during the previous six years at UBS he helped the Zurich-based bank earn $2.4bn and he apparently never lost money for his clients during his 16 years at the firm. Since the court case, he has raised $3bn for his own Monaco-based hedge fund, SRM Global Fund. As for Hunter, this son of an Ayrshire grocer shot to prominence in 1998 when he pocketed £250m from the sale of Sports Division, a business he had bought for a relative trifle with Sir Philip Green. He has since become more famous as a leading philanthropist.

It's a little misleading to describe the court case as a contest between a hedge-fund heavyweight and a private-equity-style entrepreneur. But it exposed the calculation and ruthlessness of a modern breed of investor. In the end, the hedge-fund man got the worst of it. In his summing-up on 21 December 2005, the judge, Mr Justice Warren, said:

> I found Mr Wood an unreliable witness. As will be seen from the detailed consideration of many aspects of his evidence, I do not consider that he is being honest in everything he says. I found him evasive in the witness box. I found his ability to remember matters favourable to him but not those unfavourable surprising. He came across as a very hard and calculating man albeit attempting to present himself in a much softer way. Where his evidence differs from those of other witnesses, I prefer theirs.

Wood lost, but fights on in global markets – backed by $500m from his former employer, UBS. He may not have impressed Mr Justice Warren but his reputation for making money matters more to investors. In late 2007, he became influential in deciding the fate of Northern Rock after his hedge fund, SRM, acquired a stake of more than 6 per cent in the battered bank – and he campaigned against attempts to sell the bank in a hurry.

In hedge funds and in the investment banks which provide them with the infrastructure and services that support them, thousands of individuals are accumulating personal wealth running to tens of millions of dollars each. And to what purpose? Enormous markets have developed in products that in theory allow investors and lenders to analyse the risks that they are taking in making an investment or loan, and then sell the risks that they do not want and repurchase other risks they do like. That may sound like a boon, an aid to rational investment. But, in practice, complex new products have been created that are understood only by a relatively small number of specialists. It is the opposite of the democratization of finance, which is what appeared to be happening in the great years of mass-market privatizations in the 1980s.

Those with the requisite specialist expertise in these new markets worth trillions of dollars can earn massive, disproportionate returns. The personal earnings made by the partners who run hedge funds can be mind-boggling, more than a billion dollars per annum in a few cases. They may be worth it, if their activities have allocated capital to those who can use it best and in the process have made the world a safer and more prosperous place – which for years is what their supporters argued. Certainly, the theory is persuasive: if they can deconstruct the risks of lending in a more scientific way, that should be good for all of us. There was a time, for example – which really ended only about 15 years ago – when big banks regularly came perilously close to collapse because they simply lent too much money to certain kinds of company or to borrowers in certain fragile countries. Within the past 25 years, Barclays has incurred huge losses because of its exposure to property companies; Lloyds took a big hit as a result of being over-extended in South America; and Midland was actually taken over, in part because it miscalculated the risks of buying an American bank. If any of these banks had actually gone bust – and NatWest skirted calamity in the 1970s – the impact on millions of depositors would have been horrific. But, for more than a decade, banks have been able to break up their big loans to companies into small parcels and then sell them on to other investors, such as pension funds and insurance companies. Today, if a big company were to run into difficulties, the impact on the bank that arranged the original loan would be limited.

In an analogous way, banks can also limit their exposure to particular categories of loan, such as the mortgages they provide or loans to buy cars. In this case, rather than breaking up the smallish individual loans that they make to people like us, the banks package them together, convert them into special bonds – such as mortgage-backed securities – and again sell them on to other investors. Now, this kind of 'securitization' has been going on for a couple of decades. And it has worked pretty well, in providing pension funds and insurers with new investments and in helping lending banks to control and limit the risks they take on when they lend.

But recent innovations in the identification and distribution of lending risk are much more complex. For example, there is now a booming market in products that insure against the risk that a company will default or be unable to repay a loan. These products are called credit derivatives, of which the most popular versions are credit default swaps. It is a big and booming market, which is growing at about 45 per cent a year. According to the Bank for International Settlements, the institution that monitors banking activity, the 'notional amount outstanding' of credit default swaps at the end of 2006 was $29 trillion – or about a third less than the value of the total global economy.

Now there are three reasons why these products, which are supposed to provide insurance against dangers, actually increased the risk of a crisis in financial markets. First, the market for credit default swaps is huge and opaque, which makes it very hard for regulators – whose job is to try to prevent meltdowns – to work out which hedge funds, or pension funds, or insurers, or banks are actually holding these instruments and are therefore exposed to the risk of companies going bust. Secondly, the intrinsic creativity of markets is operating to further obscure the precise location of this risk. These credit default swaps are not being sold in a plain vanilla way. They are also being chopped up and reprocessed, often ending up as part of collateralized debt obligations or collateralized loan obligations. But the final and perhaps more important reason why the development of credit derivatives is bad for the health of the financial system is that they provide false comfort to banks and investors about the credit-worthiness of companies and other institutions that borrow the money which is then reprocessed into bonds, credit derivatives and collateralized debt obligations.

Here is why. For centuries, a lender controlled the risk of lending by getting to know the borrower, looking at his or her business plan, assessing his or her business history, and looking him or her in the eye. However, in a world where innovation and technology has allowed a lender to insure against the risk of a loan going bad, it is no longer so important for the arranger of the loan to make such a meticulous assessment of the credit-worthiness of the borrower. The personal link between lender and borrower has been broken. The result is that billions of pounds in loans have probably been provided to borrowers who may in the end have enormous difficulty keeping up the payments, on the false premise that the risk of default has been insured away. There is, for example, lots of evidence that huge loans were being provided to finance private-equity takeovers at interest rates well below what may be justified by a proper assessment of the risks – and also relatively few conditions were being imposed that would allow the lenders to seize control of assets if it all went horribly wrong. Also in this complex world where risk is being sliced, diced, packaged, sold and re-sold, the bank that arranged the original loan to a private-equity borrower may find it has exposure to that borrower even when it believes it has insured away the risk of default.

It was a combination of all these fears which, in the early summer of 2007, precipitated a shutdown in the market for so-called leverage, or loans to finance private-equity takeovers. Big banks had already provided more than $300bn of loans for such buyouts, including the UK's biggest one ever, that of Alliance

Boots, owner of the famous high-street chemist, Boots. But when they tried to do what they normally do, which was to sell these loans on to other investors, they could find no takers. All of a sudden, they found that they had lent money too cheaply and on terms which gave them far too little influence over the borrowers. This discovery – that loans the banks thought of as bridging loans were stuck on their balance sheets – contributed to the wider freezing-up of money markets. Subsequently, the lending banks have had to acknowledge that they will incur losses that may turn out to be $13bn in aggregate or more. And there has been a gradual process of selling this debt to other financial institutions, but only on terms that have been very costly to the banks that extended the credit in the first place.

So when investment bankers and hedge-fund managers say to me that all this innovation has actually made markets a safer place for all of us, they seem to me to be no more reliable as witnesses than Mr Justice Warren found Jon Wood.

WE HAVE BEEN EXPECTING THE WRONG KIND OF CRISIS

In the autumn of 2006, a US-based hedge fund, Amaranth, lost more than $6bn, largely because it made bets that went badly wrong on the price of natural gas. That's a considerable sum to be wiped out, and Amaranth's investors suffered pain. It was the largest hedge-fund failure in history. But there was no serious contagion. Hedge funds in general were not hurt. Investment banks that dealt with Amaranth continued on their path to record-beating profits. And in the spring of 2007, Brian Hunter – the energy trader whose gas bets triggered the disaster – formed a new fund, Solengo Capital, and solicited cash running to hundreds of millions of dollars from overseas investors.

But what if there are lots of Amaranths out there? What if hedge funds are less brilliant at understanding risk than we hope? And what if they turned out to be betting on the same outcomes – such as a fall in the natural-gas price, or a rise in the dollar – and they all lost at the same time? What if a whole load of them ran into trouble? That would be the financial equivalent of a tsunami.

To be clear, what's going on in financial markets isn't the same as the current debate on the environment, to the extent that there's not the kind of consensus we've seen in the scientific community on the causes and consequences of global warming. But there is a growing consensus about the paradox of the hedge-fund boom: that the financial 'science' of creating investment products with very specific risk characteristics – a bit like genetically engineering a 'designer' baby – has engineered a world where the net overall risk is almost impossible to calibrate. Any particular hedge fund typically claims that it has a more precise understanding of the risks in its investment portfolio than any conventional investment manager or banker. The owner of a successful hedge fund puts it like this:

> The big differentiator between hedge funds and other asset managers is all we ever think about is risk. You hear conventional fund managers talking about their asset weighting, do they own too many UK stocks, too few pharmaceutical stocks – those sorts of issues. But if you listen to a similar discussion here it is all about how much we can lose, what scenario would we lose it under, how we can protect against that. We're most interested in understanding how we can lose money. That happens to be our psychology.

Which sounds reassuring. Except that in practice they have brought darkness where before there was light, and complexity where there was relative simplicity. Also, the torrent of cash cascading into the industry and the magnificent rewards are attracting cowboys. According to the research firm Hedge Fund Intelligence, the value of assets in global hedge funds rose from $1.5 trillion in January 2006 to $2.1 trillion in January 2007. And with funds under management rising so fast, our putative protectors, the regulators, find it almost impossible to know all the interconnections between the funds and the rest of the system, whether serious vulnerabilities are being created. In early 2007, a fall in the Shanghai stock market seemed to generate huge falls in share prices all over the world – except that it fast became apparent that the Shanghai fall was the trigger of the volatility rather than the fundamental cause, which owed more to the appreciation of the yen and the woes of banks that had been lending to the riskier end of the US housing market. There were moments when US share prices were in freefall – and it was scarier precisely because there was no single, easily identifiable cause. In the event, no fundamental damage was done. But it added resonance to remarks made only a few weeks earlier, at the World Economic Forum in Davos, by the president of the European Central Bank, Jean-Claude Trichet:

> We are currently seeing elements in global financial markets which are not necessarily stable . . . There is now such creativity of new and very sophisticated financial instruments . . . that we don't know fully where the risks are created. We are trying to understand what is going on, but it is a big, big challenge. [Jean-Claude Trichet, 27 January 2007]

Trichet, and a handful of other central bankers and financial regulators, are the safety engineers of the global financial system. They are supposed to find a solution when things go wrong. So it mattered that he could not be confident of having identified the weak links in that system.

Here is the paradox: Trichet's unease, and that of banks and other market participants, *was* the weakness in the financial system. Regulators, bankers, traders had all been trying to protect themselves – and us – from losses on investments or from lending, of the conventional sort suffered by Amaranth. But when the storm broke in August 2007, it turned out – to use the cliché – that participants in the money market had nothing to fear but fear itself. It was the possibility of losses that exposed quite how quickly highly liquid markets could become illiquid. There was inadequate insurance in place against a contagious collapse in confidence. The mains system of the global economy – the process of borrowing and lending between banks themselves – ran dry. Anyone turning on the tap found there was only a trickle. What it showed was not that any individual institution had taken on excessive risks, but that the architecture of the system was seriously flawed.

CHAPTER 6

SUPER-RICH, SUPER-CAPITALISTS

One bank which understands risk better than most is Goldman Sachs, which has exploited this understanding for massive profit. In the autumn of 2007, when almost every other bank was disclosing that its profits had taken a knock, Goldman's surged forward again. It is the world's most successful investment bank by a margin, a financial institution of influence and reach unrivalled probably since the highpoint of Rothschild power in the nineteenth century. But Goldman is not just a bank: it is a way of life, almost a cult as much as it is a money-making machine.

'They look after you, in ways that you can't imagine; it's all a bit spooky,' says a former director.

If you go on holiday, you have to tell them precisely where you are going – because they insist on being able to airlift you out if there is a natural disaster, or a terrorist outrage or a world war. And you are expected to buy all your food inside the building, on electronic cards they issue you. These cards give them the information that allows them to monitor what you eat. If they think you are not eating healthily – perhaps you are eating too many snacks or too much starch – you are contacted by one of their dieticians. I used to hate the idea of having my habits monitored, so I used to buy a sandwich from a shop down the road. Inevitably, they thought I had an eating disorder and they got in touch to see if they could help. It's all a bit nuts. [Interview with former director, September 2006]

Nuts? Possibly. But it works. Goldman makes its partners, directors and staff wealthy beyond most people's wildest dreams. As a rule, Goldman tries to give its employees up to 50 per cent of all the revenues generated by the firm (net of paying interest on borrowings and the cost of keeping the lights on). It says this is a lower proportion of revenues than is typical of its competitors. In other words, it claims its executives are not being greedy. However, by making this point all it really does is highlight quite how spectacularly profitable it is. In 2006, it paid out $16.5bn in remuneration to the 25,000 people it employed that year (this is the average number it employed; employee numbers have been rising fast and in November 2006 the total employed was 26,467). That equates to average pay per employee of $660,000. Think about that number for a second, because it is truly remarkable. The average pay at Goldman for all of its 25,000 members of staff, from secretaries up to senior partners, was nudging $700,000.

Goldman's senior directors say that this way of analysing its compensation statistics is annoying and misleading, because it implies that secretaries and administrative staff are earning hundreds of thousands of pounds each, which they are not. Cleaners at Goldman's London office, who are employed by an office-cleaning sub-contractor, are in fact paid £7.05 per hour, or the equivalent of £14,500 per annum, well below the median wage for British workers (the median wage is the point in the income scale at which half of all workers earn more and half of all workers earn less). By contrast, the 300-odd Goldman partners typically take home between $3m and $20m in a decent year. And the top earners make multiples of that: in 2006, more than ten partners pocketed more than $50m each (the remuneration of Lloyd Blankfein, the chairman and chief executive, was $54m in

2006, and he was by no means the highest-paid employee at Goldman Sachs). A successful banker at Goldman would expect to retire at around 50 – perhaps earlier – having accumulated hundreds of millions of dollars of personal wealth. When its former chairman, Hank Paulson, left Goldman in the summer of 2006 to become President Bush's Treasury Secretary, his net worth was comfortably over $700m and his compensation in the previous year had been $38.8m.

It is little wonder that Goldman people behave like the Moonies. Their allegiance to Goldman is total and they are ruthlessly focused on how to make money. There is an *esprit de corps* which is second to none. If they have a competitive advantage it is that no one is permitted to hide information. There is a team culture of sharing wisdom, insights and information that is – in my experience – unlike that of any rival firm. And what they have collectively undertaken in recent years is to direct their efforts at the booming financial industries of hedge funds and private equity, where, in true Goldman style, the firm has had its cake and eaten it. Not only has it advised and provided services to hedge funds and private-equity firms, but it has sold services and advice to companies defending themselves from the unwanted attention of private equity and hedge funds. Also, it has created its own private-equity and infrastructure funds to buy and sell companies in just the way that a private-equity firm would. It recently raised around $20bn to create one of the world's largest-ever private-equity funds. And at the time of writing, it was raising billions more to buy unwanted financial assets that firms like itself had created and whose creation had contributed to the money-markets freeze of 2007.

Whatever the weather, and even if its own behaviour has contributed to inclement weather, Goldman always seems to make money. It is the definitive modern financial institution. And although its origins are very much New York Wall Street, it is also the dominant firm in the City of London – and powerful in almost every financial centre all over the world.

Goldman's critics – which in this case is often a synonym for 'less successful competitors' – complain that it puts its interests ahead of clients'. They say, for example, that Goldman's own private-equity funds are in direct competition with the private-equity funds it advises. Or they point out that the public companies advised by Goldman cannot generate as much revenue for the firm as private-equity transactions or hedge-fund business and so claim that they must receive an inferior service. But the problem for those who point to these theoretical conflicts of interest is twofold: the first is that firms of all kinds, including public companies, continue to employ Goldman, although every now and then one will stomp off in a huff; and the second is that its breathtaking financial results do not suggest that potential conflicts of interest are having a materially deleterious impact. What is striking is that its keenest competitor for decades, Morgan Stanley, carped *sotto voce* for many years as Goldman generated larger returns than it did – and has latterly attempted some kind of emulation, by buying assorted stakes in hedge funds.

As joint head of Goldman Sachs in Europe, Mike 'Woody' Sherwood is one of the City's most powerful individuals. Sherwood is loud and direct, a trader by background. An enthusiastic Tottenham Hotspur supporter, the richness of his language in support of Spurs led the head of a leading international bank to blanch when sitting behind him in the Directors' box at White Hart Lane. Sherwood is not even from the same planet as the kind of bankers who ran the City twenty years ago. They were equally ruthless, but in a public-schoolboy, self-deprecating sort of way. The senior directors of Goldman Sachs are ferociously bright, supremely confident and frequently swagger around as if they own the world – which they do not quite do, yet.

Sherwood grew up in Highgate in north London and went to Manchester University before joining Goldman in 1986 to work in capital markets (the business of buying and selling debt issued by companies and governments). For much of the 1980s and 1990s, the so-called fixed-income business at which he excelled was unglamorous compared with advising companies on mergers and acquisitions or underwriting issues of shares. But he had a genius for it and rose rapidly through the Goldman ranks. His ascent was little noticed until 2003, when he worked closely with the billionaire Philip Green on a controversial and failed attempt to acquire Marks & Spencer (see Chapter 3). That deal epitomized the transformation of Goldman into an institution as keen to invest its own money for gain as to hire out its brains to clients. And it is in that sense that Sherwood and Goldman are the quintessential 'new' City.

One of the few rivals to Sherwood in the City is Anshuman 'Anshu' Jain, a 44-year-old banker who graduated in economics from Delhi University in 1983. As head of global markets at Deutsche Bank – the leading German bank – the London-based Jain is a towering figure in global capital markets. What propelled him there was that right at the end of the 1980s he created and ran a business aimed at providing a service to hedge funds for Merrill Lynch, the US investment bank. He has helped to transform Deutsche from a stodgy 'universal bank' – offering inefficient and expensive services to German companies and individuals – into what looks increasingly like an investment bank (its corporate and investment banking operations generated two-thirds of the group's pre-tax profits in 2005). As both an Asian and an enthusiastic creative thinker, he is a million miles from the stuffy British bankers of yore:

> I bounce out of bed every morning still as excited about going to work as I did in July 1985 when I started working on Wall Street from my tiny apartment in New York. Investment banking is truly an exhilarating profession. You work with some of the brightest people in the world who can be rapier sharp. The stimulation you get from that is enormous. The feedback cycle is very rapid. The time lapse between taking a decision and experiencing the pleasure of getting it right or the pain of getting it wrong is very rapid. I have also been fortunate that every two or three years, I have been given new assignments, new challenges, new tasks. That keeps the juices flowing and the energy levels high. [Interview with the *Economic Times*, 4 January 2006]

Jain is a symbol of the cross-border mobility of human capital that is a feature of globalization. He came to the UK for the first time in 1995, when he joined Deutsche, having previously been educated in India and the US and having worked on Wall Street.

INVASION AND ASSIMILATION

Jain's and Sherwood's equivalent 20 years ago was Sir David Scholey. He was the chairman of the last British investment bank that had any claim to be a world leader, SG Warburg. In those days, such institutions were called merchant banks. This one was a latter-day interloper, created after the Second World War by the legendary Sigmund Warburg, a Jewish German émigré. At its inception it was widely regarded as a rebel, a manifestation of the City's ability over hundreds of years to reinvent itself. Warburg created the Eurobond market and played an important role in the development of what is now called mergers and acquisitions, the business of advising companies how to buy other companies or be bought. But, by the end of the 1980s, Warburg had transformed itself from a creative outsider into an establishment firm. And in this transformation it bought a very public-school stockbroking firm, Rowe & Pitman; the Government's broker in gilt-edged stock, Mullens; and a leading stockjobber, or wholesaler of shares, Ackroyd & Smithers. Scholey was the antithesis of Sherwood and Jain. Educated at Wellington – a public school with a slightly military flavour – he is a bon-vivant with a cut-glass accent, who was rarely to be seen without a fairly substantial Havana in his gob. Under his stewardship, Warburg was the adviser of choice for Britain's best-known and most conservative companies. The bank was widely viewed as the only British merchant bank which might challenge the might of its great US rivals, Goldman Sachs and Morgan Stanley, and the Japanese colossus, Nomura (whose international power and reputation was soon to deflate, just like the Japanese economy). Scholey was talked of as a future governor of the Bank of England, although the job, when it came up in 1993, went to Eddie George (who in fact, according to a Downing Street chum, was always a shoo-in).

Warburg announced record pre-tax profits in 1990 of £187.5m, but it was the beginning of the end for the firm. In the process of entering the mainstream, it had lost much of the creativity that had made it great. And it lacked the sheer scale of its international rivals that would allow it to invest sufficient capital in the fast-growing new 'derivative' financial markets (the ones that would be so brilliantly exploited by hedge funds, as they bet on almost any imaginable eventuality, from changes in the price of a share to changes in the weather). In December 1994, Warburg was made to look vulnerable and strategically challenged when it engaged in abortive merger talks with Morgan Stanley, the US investment bank. Just six months later, Warburg agreed to be taken over by the Swiss Banking Corporation, which in turn announced a merger with Union Bank of Switzerland at the end of 1997. Warburg had become just another subsidiary of a great multinational with headquarters in Zurich – and its name would soon vanish altogether. As for Scholey, his latter years were spent as chairman of Close Brothers, an unpretentious, medium-size British bank which had none of Warburg's global ambitions.

Quite as striking as Warburg's decline and fall has been the humbling of Cazenove. In the mid-1980s, no institution knew more valuable secrets about Britain's great businesses than this stockbroker, which had been founded in 1823 by Huguenot immigrants. Owned by its partners, who were typically Old Etonians, it was the trusted adviser to the chairmen and chief executives of Britain's most substantial companies, and benefited from deep and strong relationships with the City's largest investment institutions. If a large bank or manufacturer wanted to buy another business or raise cash by issuing shares, Cazenove would inform the chairman whether the City would tolerate the deal and at what price.

In those days, the pokey vestibule of its rambling headquarters in Tokenhouse Yard was bustling with footmen (it has since moved to hi-tech premises a couple of hundred yards to the east). The servants would usher the chosen few down gloomy corridors into a room the size of a pantry, with deafening, dysfunctional air-conditioning, for an audience with its senior partners, who in the 1980s and early 1990s were Anthony Forbes and John Kemp-Welch. It was a privilege to be talked at by them – or so they implied, at any rate. They had perfected the trick of saying nothing out of the ordinary, but somehow implying that they were divulging great truths. This was entertaining theatre.

Such was their sangfroid, they remained an independent partnership while almost every other London stockbroker or merchant bank was selling itself to foreign banks or bulking up by merging with another. By the mid-1990s, there was barely a famous City name from 1980 extant, apart from Cazenove, Rothschild and Lazard. But, in November 2000, Cazenove took the revolutionary decision to incorporate. The first chairman of Cazenove Group Plc would be David Mayhew – the most influential broker of his generation and an Old Etonian.

Mayhew remains a substantial City figure, though much less powerful than a decade ago, when he was peerless. His advice is still sought by the boards of leading companies. But, under his stewardship, the veils that sustained the illusion of Cazenove's greatness were removed. Thus, in its first full year as an incorporated business – the 12 months to 30 April 2002 – it generated a pre-tax profit of just £60m, which was a fraction of what its US rivals, Goldman Sachs, Morgan Stanley and Merrill Lynch, were making. In fact, their trading operations would routinely make (and occasionally lose) that kind of money over a day or two. For all its mystique, Cazenove turned out to be a small business. And the shares in the firm held by Mayhew and his senior colleagues were worth a few million pounds each, too little to buy them membership (whether they wanted it, or not) of the UK's proliferating rich lists.

Seemingly overnight, Cazenove started to look frail. One problem for Caz is that its historically strong relationships with traditional fund managers, like those at the insurers the Prudential and Aviva, had become less useful in markets bossed by hedge funds – with whom it had no special ties. What compounded its woes was that it was so small that it could not make up for its competitive disadvantage by providing capital from its own balance sheet to clients.

In other words, independence was no longer a viable option, so Mayhew set about finding a partner from among the world's great investment banks. He had formal and less formal conversations with most of the top names in the industry before forming a joint venture with JP Morgan, a giant US bank, in November 2004. JP Morgan Cazenove, as the new firm is called, has established a new identity in the highly competitive corporate advisory market. And although it retains a substantial market share in the corporate broking market, important clients – from Marks & Spencer to Centrica, the owner of British Gas, to HBOS, the bank – have defected. One of the most famous of its City clients, the Prudential, took it off its list of official corporate brokers at the start of 2006. And Caz did not look altogether comfortable when another of its oldest insurance clients, Aviva, subsequently tried – with Caz's help – to put the squeeze on Prudential to agree to a merger. When the Pru said no, Aviva and Caz scuttled away faster than seemed altogether dignified or necessary. It was as if they did not quite understand that big, bold and brash is *de rigueur* in the new City.

Latterly, Cazenove, or rather JP Morgan Cazenove, has adapted to the imperatives of the new markets. It has helped interloping overseas companies list on the London Stock Exchange. It has advised aggressive private-equity firms trying to buy old, established British companies. Previous generations of Caz senior partners are probably rotating in their tombs, although the business is now seriously profitable – and for all their snootiness, Caz partners have always understood the imperative of making profits.

So Caz's reinvention illustrates the City's competitive advantage, its ability to adjust to financial change. The City has always welcomed émigrés. There is nothing revolutionary in the proliferation of foreign-owned firms operating in the UK's financial services industry. What is new, however, is the prominence of US-owned investment banks, such as Goldman and Morgan Stanley. In previous generations, a Lazard, or a Rothschild or a Warburg, would arrive from continental Europe and be assimilated into the City of London. Today, it is the City that to a certain extent has been assimilated into a US investment banking super-state. However, the argument that the City has been captured by the US should not be overstated – Britons and other Europeans are filling many of the top jobs at Goldman, Lehman, Morgan Stanley and so on. Wall Street's firms have been Europeanized almost to the same extent as the City has been Americanized.

A STATE WITHIN A STATE

Perhaps the important point to make about the City is that it has become a sort of city state in its own right: it is a very substantial micro-economy, peopled by individuals of every conceivable nationality united by a ferocious determination to make money and 'win'. Indeed, the concept of nationality in the conventional sense has become very nebulous in what has traditionally been called the Square Mile but now encompasses businesses based as far to the east of London as Canary Wharf and as far west as Knightsbridge. What, for example, is the nationality of a typical British-based hedge fund, run by a mixture of English, French and American managers, which operates in Mayfair, but is domiciled for tax and legal purposes in the Cayman Islands? There is something both modern and very ancient about this nexus of global capitalism, perhaps the world's leading entrepot of the financial economy – which in many lines of business is now more successful and more important than an increasingly jealous and anxious New York.

But the City's rise and rise has wrought changes in the UK which many would not see as positive. One is a pronounced increase in inequality, a widening in the gap between the very richest and the poorest – manifested in the transformation of parts of central London into a ghetto for the wealthy, crammed with overpriced hotels and restaurants, and where residential property is among the most expensive in the world. Another is a growing dependence of the UK on financial services, which makes for a degree of potential instability in the British economy. If boom in financial services were to be followed by bust, the damage would go wider than the industry itself: there would be contagion to businesses that support the City, property prices, Government revenues and so on. And the City's supremacy distorts decision-making by Government, because tax and other policies are habitually calibrated so as not to drive internationally mobile financial firms away from the UK.

The economist Doug McWilliams, of the Centre for Economics and Business Research, has compared the role played by the City today and that of manufacturing in the past. Only 20 years ago, manufacturing employed five million people and exported almost enough to pay for our imports. Today, manufacturing has shrunk and exports nowhere near pay for the goods and services we purchase from abroad. As a nation, we now count on the overseas earnings generated by the City.

This economic dependence on the City can be seen in other ways too. In a curious way, Gordon Brown's explicit encouragement of its red-in-tooth-and-claw capitalism has paid for a social-democrat paradise elsewhere in the UK. The massive expansion of public spending in the UK is financed to an astonishing extent by the success of the City of London. Brown needs financial services to flourish, to engender economic activity that provides tax revenues (there are incremental revenues in spite of the tax breaks he makes available to the international plutocratic class). What that means is that Brown's Britain is a bifurcated country, whose equilibrium feels increasingly unstable. In Scotland, Wales, Northern Ireland and much of northern England, the public sector is bigger than the private sector. Their schools and hospitals would not be affordable without the financial support of the one part of the country where the private sector is rampant: a south of England dominated by financial services.

But the City serves as the motor of the economy with only 330,000 direct employees. Or, to put it another way, these 330,000 are astonishingly productive and are therefore hugely well rewarded. So, according to McWilliams, 'The move from being dependent on mass production to being dependent on the City does mean that the prosperity is generated by many fewer people and contributes to the UK being a society with huge variations in disposable income.' However, he insists that 'without the City, everyone in the UK would be worse off'.

He is right, in the unenlightening sense that if the City shut up shop tomorrow there would be a devastating shock to the UK economy. But it does not mean the City's success is an unmitigated good thing. In fact, the rise of financial services may have speeded the decline in manufacturing. How so? Well, management talent has tended to gravitate towards the big money of the City and away from companies that make things. Also, the pound may have been strengthened by the City's overseas earnings to a level that has been lethal for some manufacturers. And the City may have been more interested in financing large multinationals than in providing investment capital for small and medium-size firms.

Then there is the impact on the way that the Government sets taxes. The City's firms and executives are global citizens, not national ones: they are happy to set up shop where the tax breaks are greatest and the pickings are richest. Which means that no British government, nor the rest of us, can take the City's economic contribution for granted. So the interests of the City cannot be ignored when the Chancellor decides what to do with taxes. In the Budget of April 2007, Gordon Brown announced a 2 percentage point cut in the rate of corporation tax from 30 per cent to 28 per cent, in part so that financial firms had less of an incentive to relocate to lower tax economies. However, the rate of tax for small companies was pushed up from 19 per cent to 22 per cent (in stages) – which caused squeals of real pain from young and small businesses. The Chancellor didn't have to fear a mass exodus of corner shops and small software businesses to Dublin or Amsterdam – it's not practical for them to emigrate in the way that it is both possible and realistic for an investment bank or hedge fund. What's more, Brown has done a great deal to help those on the very highest earnings in the City to pay as little tax as possible. And he has shown that he is happy for them to work in London while basing themselves for tax purposes in overseas tax havens.

Gordon Brown – and almost every British Chancellor – has regularly vowed to defend the interests of the City against all possible threats and enemies, especially stifling regulation from Brussels. Which he and they are right to do: it would be a foolish anti-capitalist act of economic vandalism to do otherwise. But as someone who values the City's creativity, Brown could have done a great deal more to spread the wealth around. The success of hedge funds is frequently a giant profit forgone by the rest of us, or – more properly – lost by the pension funds responsible for the retirement income of millions of people. British pension funds tend to be only modest backers of hedge funds: most of the money behind UK-managed hedge funds comes from abroad and from wealthy individuals. Pension funds' historic wariness of hedge funds is just one more reason why, if you are in an occupational pension scheme, the annual contributions made by you and your employer have been rising but are earning diminishing returns. Higher returns have been available, but they have not been seized by your pension fund on your behalf.

BRAIN DRAIN

One noisome consequence of the hedge fund (and private equity) boom is that the riches they offer act as an irresistible magnet to the brightest and the best. This is not to argue that what they do is intrinsically heinous: every time they make a profit on a deal, they should be correcting a market failure; or, to put it another way, they are in theory (although not always in practice) improving the efficiency of the market and helping to ensure that capital is allocated to the right projects and places at the right price. But if someone has a facility for complex analysis, is it better that they should work in a hedge fund or would the world be a better place if they deployed their talents on solving climate change or using the new science of genomics to find cures for fatal illnesses? One leading hedge-fund manager acknowledges that this is not just a rhetorical question:

> I am an engineer by training. I moved out of engineering into the City in the mid-80s. I couldn't believe that people would want to pay you that much money for creating nothing.
>
> At best, when I challenge myself about it, I can argue that it is doing a good thing for the global economy by making financial markets efficient. If we make financial markets efficient then money will be channelled to the most efficient users which in turn will be good for the world. Hedge funds are very good at making financial markets operate efficiently in a liquid fashion, because if they don't someone at a hedge fund will arbitrage that out. So I am not in the category of saying we are leeches on society.
>
> But, equally, what you ought to have is efficient financial markets and then most people creating things. The idea of having all the creative people in the financial markets is rather the tail wagging the dog. Having said that, it's very good fun. [Interview with hedge-fund manager, November 2005]

You have to go to the US, to the headquarters of Renaissance Technologies, to see the extreme version of the brain drain into hedge funds. Renaissance, with offices in Manhattan and East Setauket, New York, is like something out of science fiction. It employs around 80 PhDs – with skills from astrophysics to linguistics – all of whom help Renaissance's founder, James Simons, construct computer programs or algorithms that can identify profitable opportunities in financial markets. Simons is a 70-year-old prize-winning mathematician and former code-breaking cryptologist. His success has been prodigious. Renaissance has about $25bn under management in two funds – and is aiming for $105bn. His original fund, Medallion, has made an average, annualized net return of 36 per cent since launch in 1988, by using computers to spot price anomalies in everything from equities to commodities, futures and options. That kind of return, after fees, is literally astonishing: it would turn $1,000 into more than $250,000 over the life to date of the fund. His new fund, Renaissance Institutional Equity Fund, is not doing quite so well, yet. But Simons's personal rewards almost defy comprehension. According to an annual survey by *Alpha* magazine, Simons pocketed $1.7bn in 2006, making him the best-paid hedge-fund manager in the world.

Simons is not a flashy individual and devotes some of his time and money to initiatives aimed at raising standards of maths education in US state schools. But would the US be better or worse off if the formidable brainpower at Renaissance was applied other than to the remorseless pursuit of trading profits?

What hedge funds tend to have in common is a dedication to an extreme form of capitalism – but not a lot else. Hedge funds engage in a bewildering range of activities. Some buy and sell whole companies, just like private equity. Or they deal in commodities, or individual shares, or bonds, or currencies, or the debt of troubled companies, or complex financial products like credit default swaps and collateralized debt obligations. They are responsible for transactions worth trillions of dollars every year. And what they endeavour to do is measure the intrinsic riskiness of holding a particular asset (which could be some shares, or property, or anything tradeable at all) and then see if that risk has been captured in the market price of that asset. If the price is too low relative to the risk, they would buy the asset. If it is too high, then they would sell the asset.

One of the activities hedge funds have become identified with – slightly misleadingly, because they do so many other things too – is selling assets they do not own, a process called 'short' selling. A 'short' seller borrows shares or other assets and then sells them, in the hope and expectation that the price will fall after the sale, so that the shares or assets can be bought back at a cheaper price to pay off the loan and in the process make a substantial profit. Here is a simplified example. If I borrow 1,000 Marks & Spencer shares when the share price is £6 and then sell them, I will generate £6,000. If the M&S share price falls to £5, it will cost me £5,000 to buy the 1,000 shares in the market to repay my debt to the lender of the shares. So when I repay the 1,000 shares, I will have made a profit of £1,000. Hedge funds engage in short selling on a massive scale, but short selling is not what defines hedge funds. In fact, there is a group of hedge funds, called long-only funds, which never do any short selling – they are always 'long' of assets.

It is, however, possible to put most hedge funds into one of three broad groups. First are the 'macro' funds. These bet on more or less any economically important event in the world at any one time and they do that through currencies, equity market indices, bond market indices and commodities. There are also narrower versions, like pure commodity funds. But what they have in common is that they are a 'directional' bet. They are, in effect, a wager on big things happening the way the hedge-fund manager thinks they will happen, such as when George Soros made his famous and stupendously profitable bet in 1992 that sterling was massively overvalued within the European Exchange Rate Mechanism of managed currencies and would have to drop out.

The next category is 'relative value'. These hedge funds look at the relationship between different asset prices and try to profit from the 'relative' mis-pricing of those assets. So if there is normally a price gap of 'x' between two different kinds of bonds, because the risks inherent in those bonds are so different, then the relative-value fund will see an opportunity to make money when the price gap becomes 'y'. The fund won't necessarily know or care how that pricing anomaly is corrected. It will try to put on a bet that wins whatever way the correction takes place, and irrespective of what happens simultaneously in currency markets, or stock markets or bond markets. This is how the manager of a relative fund describes what he does:

> I don't know how things are going to move, but if this thing is priced here, and that thing is priced there, then one of them is

the wrong price, because they ought to be here. And I don't know whether this is going to go up to there, or this is going to go down to there, but relatively speaking they are the wrong price. If I can put a trade on that is independent of the way that markets in general move, just betting on the relative movements of these two issues, then that is a relative-value trade. [ibid.]

And within the relative-value grouping, there are lots of different micro-strategies. There is what is known as statistical arbitrage, which is based on analyzing historic price data and betting on things reverting to the mean in some way or other. Or there is merger arbitrage, which deals in the shares or securities of companies subject to a takeover offer and tries to profit when the market mis-prices the risk of the deal going through or not going through. So there are many different ways of looking at relative value. Hedge funds and investment banks think of it as a relatively safe way to make money. But, every now and then, historical relationships between assets prices break down in a dramatic way, generating huge losses for those making the relevant relative-value bets.

The third and most famous category, which in a way is an overlap between the two, is the 'long short equity business'. And those are funds, as the name implies, which are both long and short of shares at the same time.

OFFSHORE PARADISE

The best way of distinguishing a hedge fund from a unit trust or a conventional investment fund is in respect of how much it charges its customers (an arm, a leg and any other useful part of the body), how it charges them (a flat fee and a 'performance fee') and where its funds are held (as far as possible from irksome regulators and pesky taxmen). One influential hedge-fund manager puts it like this:

Hedge funds are not a discrete asset class. They have lots of different investment strategies and invest in lots of different things. What they do have in common – and there are very few things they have in common – is that the assets themselves are held offshore. Which means we can do pretty much anything we like with our assets.

That is the real differentiation from a mutual fund [a traditional investment fund]. What it means is that our investors have very little regulatory protection. Obviously, we have a legal agreement with them, an investment memorandum, we have a subscription document, but they are very loosely worded on purpose. So, our investors rely for their due diligence on meeting with us, talking to us, going through our back office, ensuring that we are robust, sensible, trustworthy, etc., etc. They can't rely on anyone else to have done that for them. There is no Government backstop for them. That is the thing that hangs hedge funds together. [ibid.]

Although the hedge-fund managers themselves are in London (or in New York, or in Connecticut), the funds they manage tend to be held in tax havens like the Cayman Islands. That has two advantages. It keeps the tax liability to the bare minimum. But it also gives the hedge-fund manager the ability to take as much or as little risk as he or she likes with the clients' money, free from interference by a watchdog like the Financial Services Authority (FSA). To be clear: these fund managers are authorized and regulated by the FSA (or the Securities and Exchange Commission in the US). And the FSA keeps an eye on them as part of its monitoring of the health of the financial system and to deter them from committing fraud or breaking the law through insider trading or market manipulation, or related improprieties. In fact, the FSA's largest-ever fine of an individual was of a hedge-fund trader, Philippe Jabre. In 2006, the FSA fined him and his then firm, GLG, £750,000 each for market abuse and breaching FSA principles. The punishment followed a probe into Jabre's 'short' sales of shares in Sumitomo Mitsui Financial Group, in February 2003, after he had been told by

Goldman Sachs that there would be a new issue of convertible preference shares by Sumitomo. A furious Jabre has left GLG but didn't have much trouble raising $3.5bn for his first fund at his new Geneva-based firm, Jabre Capital Partners.

There is a perception that hedge funds are much riskier than unit trusts or crude investments in shares. Because of that, hedge funds can only market their services to institutions and to experienced and well-heeled professional investors. They are banned from direct marketing to ordinary retail investors in the UK (though in April 2007 the FSA lifted the ban on retail marketing by funds that invest in hedge funds, known as 'funds of funds'). But the perception that hedge funds are significantly riskier than conventional investments is not quite right. Anyone holding a portfolio of equities in the slumps of 2000 or 2002 learned that only too painfully. It would be fairer to say that hedge funds are more opaque and are little understood. But regulators don't deter consumers from buying laptops just because most of us could not build one or explain how they work. So if hedge funds do what they say on the tin – which is to deliver decent returns whatever the weather – then arguably the watchdogs are being overprotective by keeping them away from the mass market. That said, hedge-fund managers tell me they don't want the mob's money. It would be too much bother administering lots of little investments. They much prefer raising their cash in lavish dollops from the super-rich.

The other spectacular contrast with unit trusts is the fee structure, which will be discussed in greater detail later. Although there are variations, hedge funds tend to charge those who invest in their funds an annual fee of 1.5 or 2 per cent plus 20 per cent of all profits made – which can be twenty times the fees on conventional funds.

THE NEW OLD CITY

According to the research firm Hedge Fund Intelligence, in January 2007, $261bn of hedge-fund money was managed from London by 72 firms that each control more than $1bn (in other words, the smallest hedge funds are ignored). That makes London the second-largest hedge-fund location after New York (which has 123 of these billion-dollar firms). But although they are usually described as City businesses, that is not true in any geographical sense. Most of them are not based in the Square Mile, London's financial district, nor in the towers of Canary Wharf. They live and work in Mayfair, Knightsbridge, Belgravia, Covent Garden and Chelsea. Which means that the journey from overpriced home to overpriced office to overpriced restaurant is often just a short walk. Habitually tieless and dressed-down casual, they sit at computer screens and construct complicated trading strategies. Many of them stay at their desks without pause or interruption from 7 a.m. till 9 p.m. on weekdays and maintain electronic contact with markets at all other times. Not that they are to be pitied, as the co-owner of a young hedge fund that manages a few billion dollars makes clear:

> To my mind being the single mother of four kids on an estate is stressful. Sitting here, walking to work, running a business that I love doing is not stressful. Do I work long hours? Depends how you define it. I am in the office 12 hours a day and I do e-mails from home and worry about it. But then it is my business, so why wouldn't I? We trade global markets so people here work long hours. We are 33 people here, 22 in our office in New York, we will have a Hong Kong office by next year. So we have people up in the middle of the night trading Asian markets.
>
> We have a guy who says this is bliss. He works 12 or 13 hours a day, but used to work in investment banking and never had a weekend to himself. The other thing that is clear here is how everyone gets paid. People see that the more they put in, they more they get. [ibid.]

Now, it is curious that there are so few women running hedge funds or private-equity firms. Elena Ambrosiadou, of Ikos, is a rare exception. The explanation may well be similar to the explanation for why boys tend to be more hooked on computer games than girls: there is a certain kind of obsessive-compulsive behaviour to which the Y-chromosome may be more prone.

The electronic element of the business is new, but the pursuit of dealing profits is as old as civilization. Much of what hedge funds do has been the stuff of swashbuckling banking for centuries, as one hedge-fund executive explains:

> With funds like ourselves, we can provide all sorts of finance, provide a bridge loan, put in riskier debt, provide equity in public or private markets. I haven't thought the analogy through so there are probably a lot of flaws in it. But when Rothschild or Warburgs or Kleinworts were putting together the merchant banks in the old days, they were very flexible financiers of business – and that is what we do. [ibid.]

Perhaps by way of tangible corroboration of this thesis, one of the most successful of the younger generation of hedge-fund tycoons is Nathaniel 'Nat' Rothschild, the son of Lord [Jacob] Rothschild. He is a founder and co-chairman of Atticus Capital, which has $8bn under management. His father, who has an impressive track record as an investor and creator of financial businesses (but may be best known for his arts philanthropy), speaks of the acumen of his 36-year-old son with some envy. Nat Rothschild spotted the potential of the new generation of Russian business leaders and is close to Oleg Deripaska, the young aluminium billionaire. As for Atticus, it made a fortune from identifying early that Europe's stock exchanges were ripe to be taken over and merged with each other. And according to *Alpha*, he earned $240m from Atticus in 2006.

Two other members of the City's new elite are Ian Wace and Paul Marshall, who in 1997 set up a hedge fund, Marshall Wace. These days, it is one of the ten largest funds in Europe, with around $8bn under management at the end of 2006, and a substantial fund listed on Amsterdam's Euronext stock market. It has magnificent open-plan offices, on the top floor of the Adelphi building off the Strand in London, with a glorious view of the Thames. Its great coup came in 2001, when it launched its Trade Optimized Portfolio System (or TOPS), which electronically screens and assesses share recommendations made by analysts at investment banks. The co-designer of TOPS was Anthony Clake, who was in his early 20s and had only just graduated from Oxford when he worked on the project that transformed Marshall Wace. It sifts 800 trading tips a day, or well over 200,000 a year, from more than 1,400 brokers. And on the basis of that evaluation, it trades shares in enormous quantities: Marshall Wace is responsible for more than 2 per cent of all trading in European shares and reputedly pays commissions to brokers worth $250m a year. The formula is attractive to investors: when it opened a new fund focused on North American equities in 2005, it raised $1 billion in a single day.

On the back of all this frantic activity, Marshall and Wace have become immensely wealthy. On the assumption that the business they've created is more than a flash in the pan, they're worth hundreds of millions of pounds each. In the two years to August 2004, their combined pay and dividends was almost £50m according to their published accounts. Marshall has become a significant donor to the Liberal Democrats. He says that he always wanted to go into politics and thinks of his financial activity as very much a second choice. In the mid-1980s, he was a Social Democrat and a researcher for Charles Kennedy, who was then one of the youngest MPs. Marshall has given £30,000 to the LibDems and a further £1m to set up a LibDem-leaning think tank, CentreForum (its first chief executive is Jennifer Moses, a retired Goldman Sachs banker – who was one of the victims of Joyti De-Laurey, the former Goldman secretary jailed for stealing from the bank's executives). Marshall is a conspicuous example of someone who is translating financial success into political influence. He was co-editor of the 2004 *Orange Book*, a collection of essays by Liberal Democrats keen to reclaim the party's Liberal origins (as opposed to its Social Democrat inheritance).

Wace has overcome quite horrific tragedy: in 1994 he watched from his Mercedes as his wife and two children were killed in a car accident. He's also a symbol of what's happened to the City, in that at the start of his career he was a rising star of SG Warburg. In 1988, when he was 25, he was that bank's youngest-ever director. Back then, any opinion poll in the City would have identified Warburg as the pre-eminent British – and European – financial firm, filled with the brightest and the best. But the rise of Wace and the hedge-fund superstars was strongly correlated with the precipitate decline of Warburg and its peer group.

HOW TO EARN A BILLION A YEAR

The decline of Warburg and Cazenove is one manifestation of a dramatic power shift in the City. It can be seen as the corollary of the rise and rise of the US investment banks. These US houses may have become bigger and more profitable over the past few years. But it is arguable that – with the exception of Goldman Sachs – they are less powerful than they were in the early 1990s. Probably the most important trend since the mid-1990s has been the transfer of power away from financial institutions with famous brand names towards individuals. There has been a mass spawning of new businesses, such as hedge-fund managers or private-equity firms. An astonishing number are both highly profitable and capable of influencing markets.

Hundreds of clever individuals have set up hedge funds and private-equity firms. They have secured access to vast pools of capital, running to many billions of dollars, thanks to their putative ability to generate investment returns well above the low yields available on many conventional investments. But for all their cleverness and macho confidence, they shun publicity as if it were pure Kryptonite. Here is the explanation of one of their ilk for withholding financial information about his firm:

> If you publish things like that my children's lives get endangered, and stuff like that. Go and do a Google on Eddie Lampert [a US hedge-fund superstar]. They put a gun to his head and he was

lucky to get away with his life. Do you know how they did it? They [the kidnappers] read articles about things like that, people throwing out numbers [about his wealth]. That's what they do. So it happens. I'm not speculating; it does happen. [Interview with hedge-fund manager, November 2005]

As he says, Lampert, probably the world's most successful hedge-fund manager, was held for ransom for two days in 2003. Famously, he talked his way out. But many in the hedge-fund industry manifest a hostility to the outside world that is not wholly rational, a hostility that is redolent of having a guilty secret to hide. As for Lampert, he has earned $1bn in a single year and now chairs Sears Holdings, the third-largest retailer in the US, which he created through the merger of Sears and Kmart.

According to *Alpha*, there were ten hedge-fund managers who in 2006 earned more than $500m each. This is not $500m per firm but per individual. And five earned more than $900m. They were – in reverse order – Steven Cohen (who pocketed an estimated $900m), George Soros ($950m), Edward Lampert ($1.3bn), Kenneth Griffin ($1.4bn) and the extraordinary James Simons ($1.7bn). Spoils in a single year on that scale are difficult to put into context. But here is one attempt: Simons's pay would have paid the wages for a full year of more than 40,000 US males on typical or median earnings.

Alpha believes the highest-paid UK-based hedge-fund tycoons in 2006 were Noam Gottesman and Pierre Lagrange of GLG, each of whom reputedly earned $240m. But what would be typical annual earnings of a reasonably successful London-based hedge-fund partner? Well, on the basis of industry data, there are probably at least 150 earning at least $40m per annum. A half-decent trader at a hedge fund can expect to earn seven figures in any given year and those who own their firms expect to take home well over $10m in a reasonable year.

The remuneration maths works like this. A typical hedge fund would be owned by between one and four senior partners and would employ perhaps 50. With staff numbers as small as that they would manage around $4bn of other people's money, though $10bn is not unusual – and these investors would generally be charged an annual management fee of 1.5 per cent of funds under management, but the fee can be as high as 2.5 per cent or even, in the case of the legendary Simons, 5 per cent. The point of that fee is to cover all running costs, including basic salaries, information technology and rents on the swanky offices they occupy in Mayfair, Knightsbridge and Belgravia. One Chelsea-based firm, Polygon, simply bills clients for the costs it actually incurs, including the salaries and bonuses of its employees. Anyway, a firm with between $6bn and $8bn under management would generate anywhere between $90m and $160m simply through the annual management charge. The latest accounts from Marshall Wace, for example, show that it generated management fees of £47.5m in the year to 31 August 2005.

However, the big money comes from performance fees. For hedge funds, it tends to be 20 per cent, although the famous Mr Simons reportedly charges a breathtaking 44 per cent. So in the realistic case, where a firm makes a 20 per cent return or $1.2bn on the $6bn it manages for investors, the owners of the firm would scoop 20 per cent of that 20 per cent. So if there were three owners of the firm, they would share $240m between them – which is $80m each. Nice work.

WHY BANKS LOVE HEDGE FUNDS

Hedge funds have disproportionate power within the financial services industry. There are a number of ways of looking at this. One is simply the amount of commission that they place with the likes of Morgan Stanley and Goldman Sachs, which turns those fearsome banks into humble servants.

Here is how it works. Unlike conventional fund-management businesses, which do little else but buy 'long' positions in stocks or bonds, a hedge fund will go long, go short, buy options, purchase futures, play in credit derivatives and do all sorts of other clever deals. Now, a conventional investment fund may trade most of the shares in its portfolio two times in a year, providing two commission opportunities for the bank it deals through. But a hedge fund of the same size tends to be quicker to make decisions to buy and sell: turnover of its stocks is twice that at the mainstream fund. So there will be at least four commission opportunities for any bank dealing with the hedge fund, compared with two for the conventional fund. However, it does not stop there. The hedge fund will probably 'hedge' its long-only position by going short. So there will be a further four commission opportunities for the bank that services it – or eight commission opportunities in total. There is more. Since it has long and short positions, the hedge fund may have eliminated too much market risk – which means the potential to make a decent return has fallen excessively. To improve prospects, it may 'gear up': it may borrow in order to double its long and short positions. In other words, from an identical sum raised from clients, the hedge fund would create 16 commission opportunities for investment banks compared with just two from the mainstream long-only fund.

And that's just the trading commission. The hedge fund will pay a fee to a bank for borrowing and will pay interest on the loan. It will also handsomely remunerate its bank's prime broker, the administration unit that deals exclusively with hedge funds. Or, to put it another way, the fee-generating potential of a hedge fund is perhaps 20 times that of a traditional fund. The consequence is that between 30 per cent and 40 per cent of large investment banks' income comes from hedge funds in some form or other, compared with almost none ten years ago (an analyst at Morgan Stanley, which owns the world's largest prime broker, estimated that investment banks' prime brokerage services alone – excluding all the other fees from hedge funds – generated $5bn of revenues in 2005).

Today, hedge funds are supporting the vast global infrastructure of the largest investment banks. Or, to put it in the words of a leading prime broker at a US bank, whom I interviewed for the *Sunday Telegraph* in December 2005: 'If you are a retail store, you love the family with 12 kids. Hedge funds have 12 kids for us.' So this 'family' tends to boss around a Morgan Stanley or a Goldman Sachs. One illustration is that these banks have devoted more time, effort and money to wooing hedge funds as clients over the past few years than to persuading big companies to employ them for advice on takeovers and fund-raising (the investment banks' more traditional activity). And when there is a bid in progress, the corporate client (a company) may well wonder whether his or her interests are being best served by a bank which is simultaneously servicing hedge funds that may be doing their damnedest to destabilize said client. Such paranoia is not misplaced. During a recent cross-border battle for control of a well-known company, I talked regularly to a banker at a leading Wall Street firm advising the bidding company and to one of his colleagues who provided services to a hedge fund that was trying to frustrate the bid: consistently, the hedge-fund banker was the more confident and optimistic of the two, and conveyed greater authority; and it was the hedge fund that won the day.

HEDGE FUNDS TOUCH EVERYONE

The hedge funds don't just boss the investment banks. Their behaviour is increasingly affecting millions of people. One example was the way that Polygon prevented Telent – the rump of the famous British telecommunications-equipment maker, Marconi – from being taken over in the summer of 2006. This was of particular relevance to the 65,000 active and retired workers dependent on Telent's pension scheme. The company trying to buy Telent was a US private-equity house, Fortress Investment Group.

Another example was how two hedge funds, the Children's Investment Fund (TCI) and Atticus, completely altered the balance of power between Europe's leading stock markets in 2004–5 and set in train events that changed the ownership and structure of those markets. They frustrated the attempts of the leading continental European stock markets, the Deutsche Börse and Euronext (based in Paris), to buy the London Stock Exchange. Having acquired shares in Deutsche Börse and Euronext, TCI campaigned assiduously against their respective takeover attempts, on the grounds that the London Stock Exchange was too expensive. They castrated the directors of all three stock-market companies – who traditionally would have been regarded as very powerful individuals and would have expected to decide whether their respective companies could or should merge. What is more, the flamboyant chief executive of Deutsche Börse, Werner Seifert – a former McKinsey consultant – resigned in 2005 after trying and failing to ignore the wishes of his shareholders, led by the hedge funds.

The power of hedge funds over a company, whether big or small, is directly related to whether its share price is 'correct' – in the sense of properly reflecting the value of its assets and prospects. To state the obvious, hedge funds tend to intervene and to be effective when there is money to be made. For example, if a company wants to buy another one – such as when Deutsche Börse and Euronext wanted to buy the London Stock Exchange – an event-driven hedge fund such as TCI calculates whether there is profit to be had in supporting the relevant takeover, or in doing the opposite, attempting to prevent it. In this case, TCI astutely worked out that Deutsche Börse's share price would be considerably higher if it were blocked from buying the London Stock Exchange.

By contrast, if a hedge fund thinks that a bidder is offering too little to buy a company, it will buy shares in the target and indicate a reluctance to sell at the offer price (which happens in almost every takeover bid). And when a company is in financial distress and needs to convert some of its loans into shares, a hedge fund will frequently exert great influence by buying up the company's debt at a knockdown price and then refusing to back the rescue terms unless they're improved. In cases like this, hedge funds literally have the power of life or death over very substantial businesses. Recent examples include the financial reconstruction carried out between 2002 and 2004 of British Energy, owner of the UK's nuclear power generators, and the struggle for survival of Eurotunnel, where most of its €6.4bn debt had been bought by hedge funds or similar investors (the banks which originally lent to the operator of the Channel tunnel gradually and steadily sold off their loans). In the coming economic downturn, as and when companies find it hard to keep up the payments on their debts, it is highly likely that hedge funds will adopt a racy new strategy, of simultaneously going 'long' and 'short' of the borrowings of a troubled company. The big bet would be on the short side, on the prospect of the company going bust. And the long position would be exploited to obtain a seat in negotiations on the future of the business, in order to hurry the company along towards bankruptcy. Such behaviour would not be pretty and could cause a stink. But it would be highly profitable. All hail the creative ruthlessness of naked capitalism.

Among the agent provocateur class of hedge-fund managers, Chris Hohn of the Children's Investment Fund is the most intriguing. Dour and aggressive in conversation, this graduate of Southampton University and Harvard Business School – who spent seven years in New York and London at a hedge-fund pioneer, Perry Capital, before setting up TCI – has a crusader's zeal when his fund buys a stake in a business like Deutsche Börse or Euronext. As an owner of these businesses, he would not be swayed from putting pressure on their managements to take actions designed to have only one outcome: the maximization of their respective share prices.

In 2007, along with his equally hard-nosed colleague Patrick Degorce, he's been at it again, although this time reshaping the European banking industry. TCI took a relatively small stake in ABN, the leading Dutch bank, and instructed it to stop making expensive acquisitions and to sell either some of its businesses or the whole of itself. Its intervention worked because of the quality of its analysis, which persuaded other shareholders that what TCI proposed would probably lead ABN's share price to rise. In the face of this pressure from shareholders, ABN entered merger talks with Barclays of the UK, which then precipitated a battle between Barclays and a rival consortium led by Royal Bank of Scotland for control of ABN. TCI preferred the Royal Bank offer. And guess what? Royal Bank – in partnership with Santander of Spain and Fortis of Belgium – won the contest. In other words, an investment in ABN by TCI that was probably less than £1bn has totally changed the future of ABN, which was worth almost £50bn and was one of Europe's biggest banks. Even so, all that really matters to TCI is that ABN's share price soared, generating big profits for TCI.

In many ways, Hohn has been importing the techniques of activist investors in the US. But that is not to belittle the significance of his actions: his impact on Europe's economic and political discourse has been profound. His actions sparked a noisy debate among Germany's political class about whether the country was right to have liberalized its markets. Passions ran high: in April 2005, Franz Müntefering, the SPD chairman – who was then the country's Deputy Chancellor – told the German tabloid *Bild*: 'Some financial investors spare no thought for the people whose jobs they destroy. They remain anonymous, have no face, fall like a plague of locusts over our companies, devour everything, then fly on to the next one.' Hohn consistently insisted that he would be a long-term shareholder whose only motive was to prevent Deutsche Börse from damaging the financial interests of its shareholders. And the evidence does indeed suggest that, unlike most conventional institutional investors, he isn't a cut-and-run investor and engages with the companies in which TCI invests – although the respective boards of those companies don't seem to welcome his intervention. Seifert, whom he dethroned at Deutsche Börse, described him in his autobiography as a 'shark who smells blood in the water'. But to hedge-fund peers he is a hero:

I'm surprised Chris is being demonized, given all that he's done for this company [Deutsche Börse]. These guys should be erecting a statue of him for creating a billion and a half euros of value for this company and setting it on the right course and bringing a measure of capitalism to Germany. [Daniel Loeb, chief executive of Third Point, *Wall Street Journal*, 13 May 2005]

BETTER TO RECEIVE THAN TO GIVE

What really stands out about the 41-year-old Hohn – the son of a white Jamaican car mechanic who emigrated to the UK in 1960 – is that there is a point to TCI beyond the desire to accumulate money for money's sake. Hohn has created a charity called the Children's Investment Fund Foundation, which defines itself as 'dedicated to improving the lives of children living in poverty in developing countries by supporting strategies that will have lasting impact on their lives and on their communities and will also influence others'. Hohn and his wife, Jamie Cooper-Hohn, who runs the charity with him, say it is pouring millions of pounds into projects to combat AIDS, sexual exploitation and extreme poverty in Africa and Asia. The charity works with children who have been orphaned by Aids – or are at risk of being orphaned – in Kenya, Uganda, Malawi, Ethiopia and India. It is also helping with agriculture, training mentors, and supporting educational initiatives. Like most things that Hohn does, the aim is to effect long-term change, rather than simply avert a short-term disaster. 'He's very businesslike about it,' says a banker who knows him well. 'The projects he runs, if they don't work he cuts them off.'

The amount he gives to charity is not subject to the vagaries of his whims at any particular time. His hedge fund is contractually obliged to give 0.5 per cent of all its assets under management to charity every year. And it gives a further 0.5 per cent if the return on its fund exceeds 11 per cent. He says that the return he made on his funds was 43 per cent in 2004 and 51 per cent in 2005 [Chris Hohn interview, 27 June 2006]. At the time of writing he had about $7bn under management – which means he is obliged to make charitable contributions of $70m per year, so long as his investment performance does not deteriorate sharply. However, it does not stop there: 'I put some money in personally, but I don't give out the number,' he says [Chris Hohn interview, 16 November 2005]. As it happens, as of 31 August 2005, his two charitable foundations had received £96m – £63m in a UK one and about $60m (£33m) in a US one. A year later, the British charity had funds of £362m, a staggering increase (of which £30.9m looks to have been transferred from the US in a tidying-up operation). This is a stunning achievement, given that Hohn set up his businesses and charities only in 2002.

Hohn may now be the most generous charitable donor based in the UK – although Sir Tom Hunter, the retailing entrepreneur and another new-money magnate, announced in the summer of 2007 that his intention was to donate at least a billion pounds to his philanthropic ventures in the coming years. Understandably, Hohn is unimpressed at the absence of a giving culture in most of the rest of the hedge-fund industry:

> It is correct that there is almost an irrelevant amount of money that goes from the industry into philanthropy. And I would actually argue that it is bigger in the US but it is still small . . . There isn't as much philanthropy as could happen in the City . . . We certainly would like to see more done. [Chris Hohn interview, 16 November 2005]

Hedge-fund managers do engage in a frenzy of wad-waving for 'charidy' at least once a year, at the ARK Ball. ARK, the brainchild of a hedge-fund veteran, Arpad 'Arkie' Busson – who split in 2005 from Elle Macpherson, his girlfriend of nine years – stands for Absolute Return for Kids. It is a charity that helps sick and poverty-stricken children in Eastern Europe and Africa, and is building seven new schools or Government-backed academies in the UK too. It raised a record £18.4m from the 2006 ball, which was held at Marlborough House in the Mall. That was £1m more than its US equivalent, the Robin Hood Ball, but is still less than TCI contributes to charity on its own. However, the 2007 shindig – attended by President Bill Clinton and for which Prince provided the entertainment – raised just under £27m, which may make it the most successful single fund-raising event ever in the UK.

Much of the ARK Ball proceeds come from an auction. In 2006, a guest paid £150,000 for tennis with Elton John and 35 people contributed £35,000 each to close down horrific orphanages in Romania. At the 2005 ball, which was held at Battersea Power Station, one hedge-fund executive paid £230,000 for a ticket on the first space flight of Sir Richard Branson's Virgin Galactic. Some 1,000 guests were also invited to bid for a dancing lesson with Richard Gere and a spot of art tuition with Anish Kapoor. The previous year, a Goldman banker paid £90,000 to play tennis with Tony Blair. A banker whose own self-generated fortune is worth an estimated £0.5bn describes the Ball as: 'sheer adrenalin-pumped, money-fuelled high jinx.'

BUT HEDGE FUNDS ARE BETTER PROPRIETORS

ARK's name is a play on one characteristic of hedge funds and private-equity funds that differentiate them from conventional investment funds: the point of this younger generation of financial firms is to generate an 'absolute return', as opposed to a relative one, such as doing better than the FTSE 100 index. Their popularity has been boosted by a growing disillusionment with so-called benchmarking, following the collapse in share prices in 2000, at the end of the internet bubble. Benchmarking is the process of defining success by reference to – obviously enough – a benchmark, such as a stock-market index. Thus, if an investor makes a return of 10 per cent on an investment, the absolute return – again, obviously enough – is 10 per cent. But if that 10 per cent return compares with a 5 per cent return on the FTSE 100 index, then the positive return relative to the FTSE 100 index would be 5 percentage points.

Disillusionment with benchmarking really set in after global stock markets went into a slump in 2000. Investors, especially wealthier ones, started to question why it made sense to place funds with a money manager who promised to do better than a stock market, if that simply meant that the manager would lose 29 per cent of their money rather than the 30 per cent they would have lost if their investments simply tracked the relevant index or benchmark. Far better to provide incentives to a manager to earn an absolute positive return, irrespective of whether markets in London, New York or Japan are falling or rising.

In 2000, hedge funds on average generated a 4.85 per cent return (according to the Credit Suisse/Tremont Hedge Fund Index). That was not spectacular, in the sense that anyone who had simply put their cash on deposit would have done as well without taking any of the risk of putting money in a hedge fund. But it looks pretty good compared with the 10 per cent fall in the FTSE 100 index that year. Similarly, the average hedge-fund return of 3 per cent in 2002 may look paltry, but it is magnificent compared with a 24 per cent stock-market drop. What is more important, the variation between individual hedge funds is vast: every year, some generate flat or negative returns, while others produce 50 per cent plus. In 2006, the average return in the industry was 13.86 per cent on the Credit Suisse/Tremont index, almost double the 7.61 per cent performance of 2005. It is a Darwinian industry. The decent performers are offered more cash than they can possibly invest. The mediocre ones see their investors flee almost overnight, forcing them to close:

> Hundreds of funds fail every year. You never hear about them, maybe 20 per cent of funds a year; they don't lose much money for their clients, they just wind up . . . Those that survive will probably get bigger, and the industry will appear to be consolidating. [Interview with owner of hedge-fund management firm, November 2005]

As I have made clear, one of my concerns about hedge funds is that they are over-rewarded for what they do – and where there are such riches to be had, impetuous behaviour and fraud aren't usually far behind. That said, there is much to be said for hedge funds' approach to investment, especially when it comes to the ownership of companies. The hedge funds who seek an absolute return are often better owners than the conventional active-fund managers who seek to beat a benchmark (albeit for a fraction of hedge funds' remuneration). Doing better than the index, or than the stock market as a whole, sounds like a laudable aim. But it's a bit like old-fashioned redistributive socialism: it tends to be 'a leveller down', a promoter of mediocre performance rather than an encourager of exceptional performance.

Here is why (what follows is complicated, but please bear with me). The managers of benchmarked funds frequently hold the directors of certain companies in contempt. They may also view the strategies of those companies as lousy. But they still hold shares in those companies because there would be too great a risk that their funds would perform worse than their benchmark indices if they held none at all. About a third of the entire British stock market by value is held by such funds, according to Paul Myners (see Chapter 4), who spent years running the fund-management company Gartmore before becoming a serial non-executive director and habitual adviser to the Treasury. The implication is that a startling proportion of shares in substantial British companies is controlled by managers who really don't like those companies.

The benchmarked funds manifest their dislike of supposedly sub-standard companies by being 'underweight' in them, or owning less than the companies' value relative to the whole market. So what the system of benchmarking has created is a paradoxical world in which companies are owned by funds that regard them as stinkers. And, what's worse, those funds have no incentive to put pressure on the stinkers to mend their ways. The monstrous explanation is that if the stinkers' shares soared, the relevant fund manager would be deemed to be a failure. Why so? Because the value of the index would rise by more than that of the benchmarked fund (remember that the fund manager owns proportionately fewer of the relevant shares).

Or, to put it another way, the system of benchmarking creates fund managers who, by definition, are unfit owners. They control swathes of equity in inferior businesses but have an economic incentive to leave those businesses to rot. One example was Marks & Spencer, which fell into the category of a once-great company where many of the British shareholders were negligent absentee landlords in the few years preceding Philip Green's attempt to buy it in 2004.

But if this poisonous consequence of benchmarking were not bad enough, there is a corresponding evil when a benchmarked fund owns a slug of a company that is bigger than its index weighting. On these occasions, a fund has a massive incentive to accept a takeover bid, to 'lock in' performance superior to the index. This probably means that many more takeovers take place than is healthy for the economy: many studies over the years have indicated that mergers and acquisitions tend to damage corporate health in the long term and destroy shareholder value (although a recent report by McKinsey concluded that the return on takeovers for the acquirers had been improving recently).

The behaviour of these benchmarked funds is bad for companies, bad for the economy and bad for the millions of us whose pensions are invested in such funds, whether we know it and will it or not. So, for all the arguments that will rage and rage about whether hedge funds are a global toxin or the efficient distributors of capital to the most deserving businesses and markets, there is an honest simplicity in their greed that shames the conventional fund managers who manage most of our retirement savings.

CHAPTER 7

WHO STOLE OUR PENSIONS?

The British system of occupational pensions was held up as a model for the world only ten years ago. They supposedly provided a comfortable and financially secure retirement at minimal cost to the taxpayer and the state. Millions of employees were confident that they would receive a pension guaranteed to be a specified proportion of their earnings. It was old-fashioned paternalism – and for years it worked. But, in today's United Kingdom, barely any of these 'final-salary' or 'defined-benefit' pension plans remain open to new members. Some are even refusing to take contributions from their existing members. These plans will survive only as long as their existing members are alive. The demise of these schemes represents the abandonment of the interests of ordinary working people, those in middling jobs on middling incomes. Their grinding-down is the flip side of a reactionary, regressive counter-revolution in global financial markets: for much of the post-war era, the main point of stock markets was to provide decent pensions for the majority; now those same markets best serve the canny individual seeking a personal fortune.

Predictably, there is even an opportunity for the entrepreneur and financial trader to profit from the anxiety and needs of those still dependent on these pension funds. Special new insurance companies have been created to swallow up the assets and obligations of closed pension funds by taking them over from the companies that originally set them up. Even Goldman Sachs is trying to get into this pension buyout business, to assume responsibility for spurned schemes. The motivation is not charity. The new controllers gain access to massive pools of shares, bonds and cash, which give them serious clout in financial markets. What they are mostly after are the economies of scale from crunching lots of pension funds together. The proportionate costs of managing and protecting £10bn of other people's money should be much less than for looking after £500m. So, with any luck, surpluses will be generated. Or, to state the obvious, the financial engineers amalgamating these funds hope to generate substantial rewards. We should be relieved if, in doing so, the prospects for the relevant pensioners are also improved. But there is something intrinsically tawdry about pension funds, which were designed to reward employees for a lifetime of service to a business, becoming classified as just a bothersome liability for their corporate founders, to be offloaded if at all possible.

How did it come to this? How could there have been such a comprehensive failure of one of the great examples of stock-market capitalism serving the interests of the many? Was it part of the natural order that final-salary pension schemes should wither and die? Were they killed by incompetence and neglect? Or were they murdered – and if so, by whom? If you were to apply the forensic analysis of a crime-scene investigator, this is what you would conclude: there was a mob of guilty parties. Actuaries were incompetent in the exercise of their duty to properly monitor the health of pension schemes. Trustees charged with representing the interests of pensioners lacked the technical expertise and confidence to do so effectively. Successive Governments raided the funds for billions of pounds in extra tax. And the chief executives of the funds' parent companies stopped putting cash into them at just the wrong time. The death of so benign an institution is a scandal – and although the victims are legion, those responsible for what went wrong have fled the scene and have largely got away with it.

The charges that stick against these participants in the great pensions wipe-out are that most of them were ignorant and negligent. They just did not see the risks, through either blind stupidity or self-glorifying complacency. The benighted claim of ministers and City in the early years of Tony Blair's Government was that Britain's pension system was the envy of the world. It insisted that we had a private-sector retirement savings system that was as safe as houses, whereas most other European countries had unaffordable state-funded pension systems. Such was the analysis in a Green Paper published in December 1998 by the Department for Social Security (now absorbed into the Department for Work and Pensions):

> This country already has a well-developed framework of funded pensions. Occupational pension schemes sponsored by employers are one of the great welfare success stories. The growth of occupational provision is one of the main reasons for the improvement in pensioner incomes over recent decades. Nearly half of all current employees are in an occupational scheme. The market value of the funds held in occupational schemes is £640bn. Personal pensions, and their predecessors, also hold an increasingly significant amount of retirement savings. The value of personal pension funds stands at about £190bn. Taken together, funded pension rights in the UK represent around 40 per cent of all pension rights. This balance of funded and unfunded provision is a key strength of the UK pension system. It is one of the reasons we face less severe public finance pressures than many other industrialized countries which are also experiencing an ageing of their population. We are determined to build on this sound framework by supporting and strengthening funded pensions. The key to this is an effective partnership between the public and private sectors. [*A New Contract for Welfare: Partnership in Pensions*, 1998]

In the annals of British political history, this must rank as one of the most hopelessly misguided departmental assessments ever made. And the Green Paper's forecasts of the financial implications of Government policy towards pensions were cringe-makingly naive:

> Public spending on pensions will decline as a share of GDP, from 5.4 per cent today to 4.5 per cent in 2050. By 2050, the proportion of pensioner incomes coming from the State, now 60 per cent, will have fallen to 40 per cent, and the proportion coming from private pension provision will have increased from 40 to 60 per cent. This will ensure that the pension system remains both fair and affordable. [ibid.]

The scale of the error here is quite something. Just seven years later, the Treasury was projecting that public spending on pensions would have to be the much higher figure of 7.6 per cent of GDP – almost 70 per cent more than it had originally projected. Or, to put it another way, it acknowledged that by 2050 state spending on pensions would have to be £40bn a year more (in today's money) than had been expected. Even if 2050 seems a long way off, that is a vast amount of money to find. There are entire Government departments which receive significantly less from the Exchequer than £40bn a year. If the pensions increment were funded by taxation, all taxes would have to rise by around 7.5 per cent – which is a political impossibility.

The error was in large part due to foolish optimism about the strength of occupational pensions. Within a period of just a few years, the entire final-salary pension system was collapsing, gradually at first and then in a great whoosh. And although it is arguable that they were hit by the perfect storm, most of the factors that generated the storm were foreseeable.

Occupational-funded pension schemes had been one of the great twentieth-century institutions. They were provided, mainly, by private-sector companies, encouraged by the state through tax breaks. Typically, these final-salary schemes pay up to two-thirds of an individual's final salary as a pension until he or she dies, and therefore (in theory) eliminate much of the anxiety and insecurity associated with retirement. They were fairly well established by 1900 and had 2.5m members by 1936. Their growth was fuelled by the introduction of tax relief on contributions and on investments in the 1920s. But they really took off in the decades following the Second World War: they had 12m members in 1967, which was to be the peak. It was the tax advantage that really accounts for their popularity in this period. Income tax for those on higher earnings and corporation tax were both punitive. This meant there were seductive tax savings for any senior manager who put generous amounts into a pension plan. Pension schemes therefore took off as a tax-efficient way of providing substantial deferred remuneration for senior managers. However, companies were sensitive to the accusation that such schemes were an unfair perk for bosses, so they opened them up to all their employees.

Then the rot set in. From the 1970s onwards, growing Government regulation of the schemes – and changes in the way they were taxed – made them increasingly costly for companies to provide. Successive British Governments legislated to force corporate schemes to become more generous, in an attempt to offset miserly state provision for the elderly (British state pensions were significantly worse than those in France, Germany and much of the Continent). Assorted Prime Ministers and Chancellors endeavoured – and still do – to achieve social engineering through the imposition of obligations on the private sector. Thus it became mandatory for company pension schemes to increase pensions in line with inflation, to provide a transferable pension pot or a deferred pension to any scheme member who left the company, and to give pension rights to the spouse of a contributing employee. Which all sounds like a good idea. That said, these reforms were expensive for pension funds, much more so than the funds realized at the time. Also, the cumulative effect of legislation was to undermine the basic 'trust' status of the schemes and the power of trustees to decide how much to pay pensioners. The autonomous power of trustees to vary commitments to future pensioners had been an important bulwark against those commitments becoming prohibitively expensive. So when it was eroded, and companies woke up to the devastatingly costly promises that had been made to current and future pensioners, their respective boards would come to loathe and fear their own pension funds.

But self-delusion about pensions was the order of the day in boardrooms and at the Treasury during the 1980s and 1990s. Companies and ministers did not see them as a liability at all. Instead, they regarded them as a giant asset, an enormous piggy bank, which could be periodically raided when cash was needed. The first such raider was Nigel Lawson. As Chancellor under Margaret Thatcher, he was concerned that companies were actually putting too much into their pension funds in an attempt to artificially reduce their tax bills. So in his 1988 Budget he stipulated that no fund could accumulate assets whose value was greater than 5 per cent more than the value of its liabilities (the aggregate value in today's money of its future obligations to pay pensions). The reform was a nice little earner for him. Tax revenues rose by more than £1bn a year, as many companies and their employees strove to reduce pension-fund surpluses by ceasing to make tax-deductible pension contributions. In fact, it looked as though companies and pensioners were winners too: when a company cut the expense of making pension contributions its profits would rise, which tended to boost its share price; and when lots of companies did this, all their share prices would rise, which had the paradoxical effect of appearing to increase the financial strength of pension schemes that held shares in those companies.

However, in practice, Lawson had established a pattern of behaviour that would turn out to be disastrous. It would have been far better for pensioners if these companies had never taken their 'holidays' from contributions. As the stock market surged during the 1990s, pension funds appeared to be in rude health. They all seemed to be in surplus whenever they were revalued. So companies acquired the habit of never paying into them. Taking contribution holidays became the norm. Final-salary pension schemes were increasingly regarded as a free lunch – and the trustees of the funds, who are supposed to verify on behalf of pensioners that enough money is going into their respective funds, lacked both the confidence and the knowledge to make a proper assessment of whether the cessation of contributions was genuinely prudent.

The Treasury too fooled itself that the funds were stronger than they really were. It dipped into them when the public finances were in a mess – as they were in the early 1990s following a sharp recession. In his Budget of 16 March 2003, Norman Lamont raised cash by reducing the value of a tax credit on dividend payments received by charities and pension funds, in parallel with a linked reduction in Advance Corporation Tax (ACT) paid by companies. Lamont claimed he was trying to provide some relief to international companies with large overseas earnings. He explains:

> We devised a new way of taxing dividends paid out of overseas profits and at the same time also decided to reduce the rate of tax on dividends. This had the added advantage of giving industry, still suffering from the recession, a cash-flow benefit of about £2bn. And paradoxically the reduction in the rate of tax on dividends also raised money for the Treasury because those who paid no tax on dividends, like pension funds, were able to claim back the Advance Corporation Tax which was paid out on their behalf by companies. It is one of the curiosities of taxation that sometimes reducing a tax or even abolishing one can bring in more revenue. This is because of those who reclaim a tax, or claim a deduction against a tax. In this case, reducing the tax on dividends brought us in £1.2bn a year in a way that also was going to delight manufacturing industry, though not pension funds. [Norman Lamont, *In Office*, 1999]

In fact, any erosion of the financial strength of occupational pension funds would ultimately rebound on the manufacturers and other companies that supported them. But they, like the politicians, remained blind to the crisis being engineered. Even four years later, when Brown extracted several billions per year from pension funds, most of the City, industry and Westminster foolishly seemed to believe that this was a windfall that would damage no one.

The logical extension of Lamont's cut in the tax credit on dividends into total abolition had been planned by Gordon Brown as Shadow Chancellor for months before the May 1997 general election. He and his colleagues – notably Ed Balls, his special adviser, and Geoffrey Robinson, a wealthy MP who funded much of Brown's research while in opposition – hoped that the reform would be seen as part of a long overdue modernization and streamlining of the corporate tax system. However, Robinson makes explicit in his memoirs (*The Unconventional Minister*, 2000) that the main motive was to raise cash and eliminate what Brown perceived as a 'structural deficit' in the public finances. The many billions they thought were available to be taken from the pension funds were just the ticket.

Even before the general election, Brown, Balls and Robinson were aware they were taking a risk with the health of the pension-fund system. Secret papers written for them by Arthur Andersen, the now defunct accountancy firm, just a few months before the election (Robinson commissioned this work), spelled out dangers – although Andersen argued that the impact on the funds might not be severe. The Andersen work was code-named Cascade and was overseen by a tax expert from the firm, Chris Wales. He later joined the Treasury to work for Brown. These days he works at Lucida, one of those new insurers to which I have already referred that are trying to make a mint by taking control of company pension schemes. Lucida – which is owned by a private-equity firm, Cerberus Capital Management – is a resonant place for him to land, since, arguably, these pension schemes would not have been in such a mess and therefore available for Lucida and its ilk to capture were it not for the change to the tax system pushed through by Brown after he received advice from Arthur Andersen. Here is Cascade's assessment:

The exempt funds [mostly pension funds] would be most affected by the changes. Their income from UK equities would fall by the amount of the ACT lost [i.e. by 20 per cent compared to today's levels]. This could adversely affect actuarial valuations, leading to a reduction in Stock Market prices and requiring companies to increase the level of their contributions into defined-benefit pension schemes . . . However, there is a view, within the fund-management business, that even a change of this magnitude in the ACT system could have a negligible impact on Stock Market prices.

Once Brown became Chancellor on 2 May 1997, the trio worked with Treasury officials to flesh out the tax changes. As papers obtained by *The Times* in March 2007 show, these officials gave him stronger and more detailed warnings than Andersen about the possible undermining of the financial strength of pension funds that might stem from the abolition of the dividend tax credit. But as Robinson makes clear, the Treasury needed the cash and that's what mattered most. It is notable that what particularly concerned him as Paymaster General was that the Inland Revenue did not believe the proceeds would be as great as Andersen had thought:

I reflected that perhaps there was a touch of the 'not invented here' syndrome in the IR reaction . . . I insisted that Andersen's work be evaluated and that we reconvene within a week for a review meeting. I have never known such a change of atmosphere. Michael Cayley [an official at the Revenue] came to the next meeting beaming. The Andersen numbers were right. We might expect even more, since corporate profits were expected to remain high – provided, as always, we avoided a recession. He then confessed: 'This is something I have wanted to do all my life!' and pronounced his blessing: 'Brilliant Chancellor! Brilliant Paymaster!' [*Unconventional Minister*, Geoffrey Robinson, 2000]

The plan was to announce the tax change in Brown's first Budget on 2 July. That Budget would also abolish so-called

Advance Corporation Tax, reduce the rate of Corporation Tax and introduce a system of paying that tax in instalments. This package in the round was welcomed by the employers' lobby group, the Confederation of British Industry (CBI), whose director general, Adair Turner, led no noisy campaign against the plundering of occupational pension schemes – although he has latterly pointed out that his members did not want the end of the tax credit and that he wrote to the Treasury disagreeing with its abolition. Some five years later, as Lord Turner, he would head the Pensions Commission that would try to rebuild a pensions system from the wreckage of occupational schemes bashed by Brown's tax grab.

But what of the stock market? Did it collapse at the prospect of all that cash being siphoned from pension schemes? Not in the slightest. Investors were gripped by 'irrational exuberance', to adopt the resonant contemporaneous diagnosis of Alan Greenspan, who was then chairman of the Federal Reserve Board, the US central bank. Shareholders' reaction to almost any news was that all was for the best in the best of all possible worlds: so the FTSE 100 index closed up 23.1 points on the day of the Budget and rose a further 43 points to a new record of 4,795.1 on the following day.

But the market's reaction was wrong. Damage had been done. According to the Inland Revenue, the tax relief on pension-fund investment income fell from £7.1bn in 1996–97 to £3.3bn in 2001–02 – a massive reduction in their annual cash resources. Even so, Brown and Balls have always refused to accept any responsibility for the weakening of pension funds. They claim that their decision to cut the rate of Corporation Tax boosted the profitability of companies and their ability to increase dividends – thus offsetting, in part at least, the direct reduction in pension funds' cash flows from the abolition of the tax refund. There is, indeed, some evidence that has happened – since in recent years big British companies have been paying out unprecedented sums to shareholders in the form of special dividends and the repurchase of shares. But there is also a contradiction in the position taken by Brown and Balls, in that they have also argued at various times that they were right to abolish the tax break on dividends for the pension funds precisely because it created a culture in which executives tended to pay bigger dividends to shareholders rather than investing in their businesses to enhance productivity and growth. On this analysis, they actually wanted companies to make cuts in dividend payments, thereby compounding the woes of pension funds. In practice, Brown and Balls would probably be better off acknowledging that they needed money and – like Lawson and Lamont before them – they mistakenly viewed the pension funds as a bottomless purse. However, their mistake was shared by the Tory opposition: I had written an exclusive report before the 1997 Budget for the *Financial Times* about Brown's decision to abolish the tax credit and was staggered that few Conservative MPs seemed exercised by the Treasury's plan – although they would eventually wake up to the economic reality as the months and years rolled by.

What is Lord Turner's considered verdict, now that the dust has settled? 'At the very least, the bit of the City which says defined-benefit schemes would still be here if it were not for Gordon is hugely overstating,' he says. 'When I say that, Ed [Balls] always says "overstating" is not enough. But I say: "No, what I am saying is it is hugely overstated." ' The truth is that Brown in this Budget was not single-handedly responsible for the ultimate destruction of defined-benefit pension schemes – but he played his part.

A further – and probably more important – contributor to the demise of the funds was that the funds themselves did not realize how sick they were. One enormous forecasting failure was that the actuaries completely misjudged how long pension-scheme members would live – their longevity. According to Stephen Yeo, of the actuaries Watson Wyatt, more than 80 per cent of today's deficits in pension funds stem from past mistakes in predicting when pensioners were likely to die, together with the collapse in the yield on UK index-linked Government bonds between 1997 and 1998. The significance of the fall in the bond yield is that it is the benchmark for estimating future returns from investments in pension funds and it is used to determine whether the prospective return on assets will be sufficient to cover aggregrated future liabilities – so a fall in the yield automatically increases deficits in pension funds.

Turner elucidates how pension schemes were misled about mortality:

> The Government's Actuary Department, on the best analysis it could do in 1980, estimated that the life expectancy of a 65-year-old man in 2004 would be 14.8 years, and that was the advice going to defined-benefit funds at that time. The present estimate is 19 years. So . . . we got it wrong by about a third. ['Too Little, Too Late? The Risky Business of Pensions', *New Statesman*, February 2005]

Pension funds were seriously underestimating the number of years over which they would have to pay pensions to their members – which meant that their respective assessments of liabilities were far too low. Schemes showing a surplus were almost certainly in deficit. One consequence was that many companies made zero contributions to the funds at just the moment they ought to have been making substantial injections. As we have seen, contributions to occupational pension schemes fell, especially after 1986, when Lawson ordered them to reduce their surpluses. In 1979, companies' average contributions to self-administered pension schemes were more than 11 per cent of their wage bill but this dropped to just 6 per cent by 1991 and remained far too low on average until the new century; those schemes that still exist are now receiving corporate contributions nearer 20 per cent or more.

To compound the illusion about the robustness of the funds, share prices were absurdly overvalued towards the tail end of a bull market that had begun in 1974 and did not end until 2000. During this 26-year period the average annual real return on British equities was 13 per cent – and because it went on for so long, fund managers, bankers and trustees began to regard that magnitude of return as normal. Final-salary schemes were heavily invested in equities, which created a false sense of comfort that the increasingly expensive promises they had made to members were easily affordable.

There was an epidemic of false confidence and lousy statistics. It extended into the heart of Government and distorted policymaking. The most egregious example was uncovered by David Willetts, then Shadow Work and Pensions Secretary, in the early summer of 2001. In May of that year, the Department for Work and Pensions (DWP) published figures showing that private-sector contributions to pensions were £86bn in 2001, equivalent to 9 per cent of national income and representing a 54 per cent inflation-adjusted or real increase since 1997. The numbers were described by the Pensions Minister of the time, Ian McCartney, as evidence 'that our policies to encourage higher levels of private saving are having a positive effect'. If only. As Willetts pointed out, it just did not tally with anecdotal evidence that Britons were simply not saving enough for retirement. Willetts was right. On 1 July 2001, the DWP announced that the Office of National Statistics (ONS) had supplied it with erroneous figures. What had gone wrong was that the ONS was double counting: it classified as new saving monies that had in fact been invested as much as years earlier and were simply being switched from one pension provider to another. At the time there were massive flows between funds, as savers moved away from life insurers they thought might be in trouble, so the overstatement of genuine net new saving was considerable.

Using Inland Revenue data, Willetts estimated that the true savings figure was nearer £51bn. The DWP did not yet have a correct number, but it stupidly insisted that Willetts was being unduly pessimistic. In fact, even £51bn turned out to be far too much – which became clear in 2004 when Lord Turner's Pensions Commission pronounced. 'It took us till early 2004 to work out what was going on,' says Turner. 'We said it was £40bn. And ONS and Inland Revenue then agreed with us.' [Adair Turner interview, 29 September 2005]

Turner is scathing of how the civil servants dealt with the statistical disaster:

It is a classic example of how power works and the misuse of civil servants. The extent to which civil servants apply their intelligence to supporting their minister rather than actually thinking is quite distressing. The Treasury/DWP reaction to the David Willetts stuff was damage limitation . . . I am a great admirer in many ways of the civil service. There are a lot of very intelligent people. But they are heavily politicized, not in a left or right sense, but politicized in loyalty to the Government of the day. [ibid.]

Turner perceives a pattern of behaviour:

When I first went in to the DWP and I said, 'Look, defined-benefit schemes are closing,' they said, 'People are overstating this, Adair, the latest figures from the Government Actuary's Department show that only 10 per cent of all schemes are closed to new members.' And I said: 'Look, guys, I work in business and I read the *FT*. The HSBC scheme is closed, and the British Airways scheme is closed, and the Sainsbury scheme is closed. It may be only 10 per cent of schemes, but I am already running at a million people.' It was just bloody obvious. It was a really interesting example of bits of the civil service where you just thought: 'Do they actually read the *FT*?' [ibid.]

Contrary to DWP wishful thinking, there was a stampede of companies announcing that new employees would be excluded from joining final-salary pension schemes. By February 2002, 10 of the 20 biggest listed British companies had barred new employees from joining their defined-benefit plans. If these younger staff were saving at all, they were putting money into so-called defined-contribution schemes whose ultimate returns were uncertain – and which received far smaller corporate contributions than the final-salary arrangements.

Companies were moving with alarming speed from blissful ignorance about the true cost of their pension commitments to information overload. There were two immediate causes: first was the downward lurch of share prices in 2000 and 2001; the other was the introduction of Financial Reporting Standard 17, an accounting rule that would force companies to disclose on their balance sheets a rigorous and regularly updated valuation of their pension funds. But the Government, especially the Treasury, was even then insufficiently concerned about how the weakness of pension schemes was undermining the robustness of the entire pensions system. As far as the Treasury was concerned, the problems with private pensions could be put in a box and – for the time being at least – put to one side. Here is what a senior Treasury official told me while all around him pension schemes were falling down:

> We have a private pensions problem. It is a problem for people in the upper/middle bracket. It is to do with expectations and incentives. It is not a trivial problem. But if your problem is that you have made massive state commitments that you can't afford, then you've got a real problem. That isn't the Government's position.
>
> What we have got is all across the country employers reneging against the implicit contract that the employees thought they had with the employer – and the employees not really knowing what to do in the face of that but not really wanting to save themselves. It's not really clear they want to pay a huge amount more tax either. All of the supposedly bold and radical solutions basically end up with a very substantial tax rise of 2 to 3 percentage points of GDP in order to finance an expanded state safety net which still won't meet the expectations of people in the upper and middle income brackets. [Interview with Treasury official, 29 July 2004]

From time to time the Treasury could be shaken out of its complacency. One such occasion was when a clique of influential business people pressed the case of a minority of well-heeled future pensioners. Their intervention was precipitated by one of the more rational pensions initiatives taken by the Government, which was to simplify the ferociously complicated tax system for pensions. In

a Green Paper published in December 2002, Andrew Smith, then
Secretary of State for Work and Pensions, proposed replacing the
eight tax regimes covering the contribution and benefit levels for
different types of pensions with just one. It included the suggestion
that anyone should be able to enjoy the tax benefits of saving for a
pension until the value of his or her accumulated savings – the
pension 'pot' – reached £1.4m. There would be a tax surcharge on
savings above £1.4m. And up to £200,000 could be put into a
pension free of tax in any one year.

For most savers, £1.4m was a substantial sum and seemed a fair
limit. The Treasury calculated this as being broadly equivalent to
the existing ceiling on how much could be saved tax-free for
retirement. The Inland Revenue calculated that the new system
would allow 99 per cent of people to pay more into their pensions
than previously was possible, and to pay into as many different
schemes as they chose. At the time, £1.4m would have provided
an annual retirement income estimated at between £60,000 and
£65,000, well above the average.

However, the proposal upset many employers, even though
anyone who had already accumulated £1.4m or more would have
been exempted from the surcharge on their net savings to date. But
rational debate was again made more difficult by the unreliability
of statistics, this time about the numbers of people likely to be
affected. Employers pointed to estimates by the actuaries Mercer
that the new ceiling on savings would ultimately hurt up to
600,000 people, compared with an Inland Revenue estimate that
just 5,000 would be disadvantaged. In November 2003, Digby
Jones, who was then director general of the CBI, warned: 'The
people hit by this will be aspirational middle managers. It says to
them: "We are going to tax you out of existence."'

The tone of business opposition had been set by Niall FitzGerald, who at the time was chief executive and joint chairman of
Unilever, the multinational food manufacturer. FitzGerald – currently chairman of Reuters, the financial data company – is an
effective lobbyist and a brilliant schmoozer, whose has precious
contacts at the heart of many governments and businesses. He was

aware that the best way to overturn a tax reform of this sort was to tell the Prime Minister that it would be viewed as anti-business, since this would dent Blair's self-image as the friend of wealth creators. On Tuesday, 3 September 2003, FitzGerald made his views known to Blair very forcefully when he and seven other heads of leading British companies – including Martin Broughton, then at BAT, Sir Christopher Hogg, then chairman of GlaxoSmithKline, Lord Browne, then chief executive of BP, Arun Sarin, chief executive of Vodafone, and Sir John Bond, then chairman of HSBC – met the Prime Minister in 10 Downing Street.

'We told him that unless Government policy in vital areas was changed, vast numbers of highly paid staff – especially those performing central functions – would be transferred to Switzerland, the Netherlands or New York. A headquarters employing thousands could be reduced to 50 over a decade,' says one of the business leaders at the meeting. 'It was not a threat, not blackmail, but a dire prediction.' The business leaders talked about the inadequate transport system in London and complained that the Government's massive investment in health and education was failing to yield sufficient benefits because of an apparent unwillingness to commit to substantial public-sector reform. Then FitzGerald launched into pensions. He described the £1.4m ceiling as 'a disaster' and insisted that the Inland Revenue's assessment that just 5,000 executives would be penalized was wildly wrong – the eight companies represented at that meeting could identify more than 5,000 who would be hurt just from within their own ranks. 'We told him [Blair] that unitary company pension schemes would be destroyed,' says a business leader, 'and that companies would find other ways of beefing up the long-term savings of their top people.' There was a coded warning that if top executives no longer benefited personally from their occupational pension schemes, they would be closed down – and less well-paid members of those schemes would be hurt most. FitzGerald was laying at the door of the Prime Minister personal responsibility for the future destruction of what remained of the UK's system of final-salary occupational pensions.

Blair became anxious, according to Treasury officials, but Brown showed no sign of being prepared to lift the savings ceiling. FitzGerald then made his argument in a public arena by writing an article published by the *Financial Times* on 8 September 2003. In it he said:

> The Government's attitude to pensions is . . . troubling. We need to rebuild the position of strength the UK once enjoyed in company pension provision. Some of what the Government is doing should be welcomed, but the plan for a £1.4m limit on the accumulated value of individual pensions is another example of a failure to see the arguments through to their conclusions. This surtax on saving will add further cost and complexity to business. It will also be divisive, as companies will be forced to set up alternative arrangements. Equally dangerous is the inevitably greater pressure it will place on the diminishing band of occupational pension funds. None of this will help in attracting and retaining essential senior talent. Surely this is not what the Government intended. [*FT*, 8 September 2003]

FitzGerald knew Blair well enough to be able to press all the right buttons. His campaign was directed at Blair's almost neurotic determination never to be associated with the anti-business image of the old Labour Party. Brown was harder to move – although the then Chancellor eventually asked the National Audit Office (NAO), the auditor of the public sector, to assess the competing claims about how many people would be penalized by the imposition of the £1.4m ceiling. On 9 March 2004, the NAO reported that about 10,000 people rather than the Inland Revenue's estimate of 5,000 would be affected on the day of implementation. But the pain would be felt by hundreds of thousands fewer than claimed by FitzGerald and the CBI. Even so, the Chancellor surrendered in his Budget of the following week, on 17 March. He raised the limit on savings to £1.5m and said it would rise to £1.8m by 2010. He also delayed implementation of the new regime by a year until April 2006 to allow more time for those affected to take whatever financial measures they needed. It was a remarkable victory for FitzGerald. 'I thought it was outrageous,' says Turner. 'I told one of Brown's advisers that he had changed public policy unnecessarily because ten rich people came and moaned. It was disgraceful. Some of the figures they put out were ridiculous – it was never was more than 10,000 people affected. But it was a classic example of power.'

But if executives on relatively high pay were bailed out, there was no such luck for Britons at the bottom of the income scale. Probably the most fatuous initiative in the history of New Labour was developed to alleviate their plight: the creation of the 'stakeholder' pension. The idea behind stakeholder pensions was to spread the savings habit and wealth to those on below-average incomes. They were designed as low-cost, easy-to-purchase pension schemes for those unable to obtain access to a decent company fund. The process of turning them into a practical proposition took up vast amounts of time for civil servants and insurance company employees. But all the brainpower, analysis and marketing that went into their creation were for nought. They have been an unmitigated flop.

The basic concept of the stakeholder pension was developed while Labour was in opposition, and it expropriated the fashionable 'stakeholder' concept popularized by Will Hutton, who at the time was a left-leaning journalist and is now chief executive of the Work Foundation, a not-for-profit employment consultancy. In fact, there was a hint of the initiative's fatal flaw in the name itself. The word 'stakeholder' is normally associated with theories about the rights of individuals or institutions over an enterprise in which they have 'a stake', either as employees, as customers or – more obviously – as shareholders. In the New Labour formulation, all it meant was 'anybody can have one of these' but there was no associated philosophy of governance. It was a bit of branding with no intellectual substance.

Worse still, the failure of the stakeholder-pensions scheme was built into its design. The Government wanted to cap the charges levied by the financial firms selling the stakeholder pensions at 1 per cent so that the investments of poorer people would not be eaten up in commissions; but few insurers or financial firms were prepared to market stakeholder pensions in a proper systematic way because the costs of doing so would eat up too much of the 1 per cent annual fee. The concept may have been attractive to policymakers, but it was doomed by a lack of enthusiasm for it in the private sector. If that was not bad enough, a 1 per cent charge would probably have been too great for savers on the lowest incomes, or those who needed pensions the most: most of any gains they would have made on the tiny investments they could afford would have been wiped out by even that small annual deduction.

It took years for the penny to drop at the Treasury and the Department for Work and Pensions. In fact, they were so in love with the 'stakeholder' label that they tried to attach it to a whole range of financial products that were supposed to be cheap and simple to understand. In June 2001, the Government asked Ron Sandler, a former chief executive of Lloyd's of London, the insurance market, to review 'medium and long-term retail savings' in the UK and advise it whether consumers were being well served by existing institutions and products. A little more than a year later, in July 2002, Sandler unveiled his big idea, which was to create a 'suite' of basic, simple, 'stakeholder' investment products, including a pension. They would be so simple and reliable that purchasers would not have to be given detailed explanation and advice by those selling them. They would be the financial equivalent of a tin of baked beans, and capable of being sold by Tesco or other supermarkets trusted by the great unpensioned.

Sandler's supposed breakthrough was to eliminate the expensive requirement on an insurer or other financial firm to verify that a particular product was really suitable for any specific customer. That innovation would surely make them profitable to sell, even at a maximum fee-rate of 1 per cent. Not so. In the event, they were another exercise in futility, although they were endlessly debated in the press (there were almost 7,000 articles in national newspapers about stakeholder pensions between 2000 and 2005) and they precipitated countless meetings between insurers, regulators, civil servants and ministers. Again, the failure was in the design. The plan to reduce investor protection procedures to the minimum raised serious concerns among consumer groups and the financial watchdog, the Financial Services Authority (FSA), who feared that unsophisticated individuals would be ripped off or would buy inappropriate products; and even if there were some reduction in regulatory costs, insurers and other financial firms still had little appetite for selling the products for maximum annual fees of 1 per cent of the funds invested. The FSA tried and tried to come up with a simplified set of consumer protection rules for those who wanted to sell the stakeholder products, but what the watchdog imposed in April 2005 was not significantly simpler than normal conduct-of-business regulations. In the face of a sustained lobbying campaign by the Association of British Insurers, the Treasury eventually showed some flexibility on charges. The relevant minister was Ruth Kelly, who was then Financial Secretary to the Treasury. In 2004, the Treasury raised the price cap to 1.5 per cent for the first 10 years of a policy. It would fall to 1 per cent after 10 years, but since few policies are held for more than 10 years the effective cap would be 1.5 per cent.

This was a significant U-turn by the Treasury. For years, it had argued with almost religious fervour that 1 per cent was quite enough for the City's supposedly bloated insurers. But even the Treasury's U-turn could not make a success of stakeholder products – as is explained by Lord Turner:

> The problem is that the industry was right. It could not sell personal pensions on an individual basis to someone on £15,000 or £20,000 per year at a price cap of below 1.5 per cent. And even then, the profitability was marginal. But if that's the case, why bother? Why try to push water uphill by having a process selling personal pensions to people on such low incomes? [Adair Turner interview, 25 October 2005]

The extent of the stakeholder failure was almost total. Here is the verdict of the Government-sponsored Pensions Commission which Turner chaired:

A primary policy initiative that focused on increasing participation, the Stakeholder Pension, while achieving some reduction in costs, has not achieved any measurable increase in participation. Eighty per cent of all employer-designated Stakeholder schemes are 'empty shells': nominated schemes with no members. [*A New Pension Settlement for the Twenty-First Century*, November 2005]

Turner puts it more starkly:

Frankly, what happens for something like five years is that an entire slice of policy went nowhere. And at the end of the day, the level of under-penetration of private pensions in the small and medium enterprises, which was meant to be the gap and was meant to be what this stuff was supposed to fill, slowly got bigger . . . The problem was not dealt with, was getting bigger, policies hadn't worked. They were literally policies in which in the [official] figures you can see almost no trace. It isn't that they didn't have much effect; they just had zero effect. [Adair Turner interview, 25 October 2005]

As for Brown's relationship with those actually drawing a pension, as opposed to saving for one, that has been complicated and troubled too. He has frequently been accused of letting down the poorest pensioners. Both he and they bear the scars of a titanic battle in the mid-1990s over what kind of commitment Labour should make about future increases in the basic state pension, which culminated in a showdown at the party conference in October 1996, the final one before the 1997 general election. Brown's determination to contain the growth of public spending and thus avoid a financial crisis for a New Labour administration meant he was determined to stand by the Tory Government's system of raising the basic pension in line with retail prices. This approach had been introduced by Margaret Thatcher in 1980 and still riled much of Labour's left wing, which wanted a return to increasing the pension at the generally faster rate at which salaries and wages rise: the rate of increase in average earnings. With only months to run before the most important general election of Brown's and Blair's careers, the doyenne of Labour traditionalists, the late Barbara Castle – who had been a minister when Brown and Blair were still in school – tried to persuade Labour delegates in Blackpool to back her motion for what was known as a return to the 'earnings link'. It was the culmination of a campaign she had been waging in partnership with Jack Jones, the retired trade union baron, and Peter Townsend, the distinguished academic. The 86-year-old firebrand's opponent on the conference platform was Harriet Harman, then Shadow Social Security minister and now deputy leader of the Labour Party. On this occasion, Harman was little more than a cipher for the Shadow Chancellor. On reading Harman's words now, the accent that resonates is Scottish, booming and male:

> These composites make substantial spending promises but they are only paper promises if we do not have the power. As we found out and as the country found out to its cost in 1983, 1987 and 1992, all the promises in the world will be worth nothing if we lack the discipline on spending that threatens our chances at the election. And you know who in the country is most concerned about prudence – not only for themselves but for the Government: it's pensioners. And you also know who has most to lose from a fifth Tory term: it's pensioners.

Baroness Castle's argument was that the basic state pension was worth 20 per cent of average male earnings in the late 1970s but had fallen to the equivalent of just 14 per cent because of the abandonment of the peg to earnings. She urged that a single person's basic state pension should be boosted by £5 per week and a married couple's by £8. That, said Harman, could cost £5.5bn, which was unaffordable. It would be the equivalent of a 3p increase in the standard rate of income tax and would provide the Tories with lethal propaganda material on Labour's alleged profligate ways. Although Castle won the battle for the hearts of

Labour members, minds were focused by the proximity of power. Harman won the vote – at some personal cost to Brown, as he became widely seen as insensitive to the plight of the elderly.

The apotheosis of granny-basher Brown was the autumn of 1999. The annual rate of inflation was a mere 1.1 per cent and his purist's obsession with raising the basic pension in line with prices rather than earnings meant that the basic pension would increase by just 75p. The pensioner lobby was outraged. However, Brown had by then established a broader approach to helping the poorest pensioners that he hoped would ultimately placate Castle and her supporters. He tried to direct resources at those who needed help most. What he was doing looked like means-testing, though he dared not use that label since it was associated in the minds of Labour members with humiliating the poorest by obliging them to admit their poverty. Brown said he was providing every pensioner with a Minimum Income Guarantee (MIG): the poorest pensioners would receive an increment above the basic pension, and this increment would be raised in line with earnings. Brown also resorted to fairly crude bribes to stifle the protests of pensioners at the almost invisible rise in the basic pension: in his pre-Budget announcement on 9 November 1999, he offered free television licences to those aged 75 and above and said that a flat-rate winter fuel allowance of £100 for the elderly would become an annual fixture. At a time when his priority was to establish his reputation as a prudent Chancellor, this so-called targeting was understandable, although it would have unfortunate long-term consequences.

One disadvantage with the MIG was that it was a disincentive to save because the additional state payments were not given to anyone who had accumulated modest savings. So in the autumn of 2000, Brown announced plans to reform it by creating a Savings Credit. This would allow someone with small savings to enjoy a higher net income than someone with none. He claimed that the entire approach was based on 'progressive universalism', which is his semi-coherent intellectual framework for a whole range of social policies whose centrepiece is the Tax Credit system of payments to employed people on lowish incomes. When the whole Brownite state-pensions edifice was at last unveiled in its final form in the autumn of 2003, the Savings Credit became the Pension Credit, which guaranteed a minimum income and rewarded limited savings. Some 3m pension households have benefited from it, which means that 3m households have suffered the indignity of *de facto* means-testing – which is not exactly a retirement fit for heroes.

But even after removing some of the more conspicuous disincentives to save, the direction of resources to the poorest pensioners through the Pension Credit was inconsistent with the Treasury's desire to promote its stakeholder products. The relevant point is that the majority of independent financial advisers believed, rightly or wrongly, that low-earners would be better off saving nothing and then falling into the safety net of the Pension Credit. So they were reluctant to offer stakeholder products to anyone on below-average earnings, because of the fear that they would be accused of mis-selling. And they were hardly reassured by a note issued by the Financial Services Authority:

> Pension Credit means that, for most people, most of the time, it will pay to save. For a limited group of people, however, the decision will not be so clear-cut, and these people will have to think carefully about their personal circumstances. In particular, people in their fifties and over who have not been able to save much and have only a limited ability to save as they approach retirement should seek expert advice before they take out a stakeholder pension. [Notes on Decision Trees, FSA website]

The Pension Credit was another nail in the coffin of stakeholder pensions. The Pensions Commission carried out market research which confirmed the anecdotal evidence that one of Brown's flagship creations, the Pension Credit, was killing off another one, the Stakeholder Pension.

By the end of 2002, the evidence of grotesque failure in a pensions system that had only recently been lauded as among the world's best was too conspicuous to ignore. And the Prime Minister had lost confidence that a solution could be found by a

Treasury and a Department for Work and Pensions whose preference was to muddle through. The great debate among pension experts was whether or not everybody should be compelled to make greater contributions to pension schemes (there was already a degree of compulsion in the system in the sense that payments for the State Second Pension, S2P, were and are obligatory). But Blair was wary of forcing people to contribute to a pension. He feared that such an obligation would be seen as a tax, whether the funds were injected into a private-sector scheme or went to the Exchequer. On the other hand, there was a great clamour for the Government to do something to stem what was increasingly perceived as a pensions crisis, as a Treasury official recalls:

> Number 10 were very keen on having a Pensions Commission. They originally talked about having a Royal Commission and then a cross-party commission chaired by a Tory. And we said none of those things make sense because it'll just become a forum for disagreement. We proposed Adair Turner. And we also said: 'You've got to be clear what he is looking at, what his remit is.' We said to Andrew Smith [then Secretary of State for Work and Pensions]: 'If this works, it may avoid the compulsion thing [more compulsory saving], but, on the other hand, it is on the table and it will now be examined.' But Number 10 didn't want it that way because they did not really want an explicit remit and certainly not one that raised compulsion. Were we committed to compulsion? No. Did we know we needed compulsion? No. Did we fear that the non-compulsion solutions may turn out to be insufficient? Yes. Did we really need to know what the truth is? Yes.
>
> So we set this group up and we said to them: 'If, in the end, you recommend compulsion, maybe that's okay, but we know you won't be recommending that as a first resort.' [Interview with Treasury official, 29 July 2004]

In other words, Brown believed that a small commission under Turner was more likely to come up with palatable solutions than the kind of grandiose Royal Commission favoured by Blair. He was wrong. Although Turner's Commission ultimately came up with clear and practical policies, the minister who found them most obnoxious turned out not to be Blair but the then Chancellor.

Turner says he was known to Blair and trusted by him because he had already done some confidential work for him on whether and how the National Health Service should be reformed:

> I first heard about this [possible job] from Geoff Mulgan [who was then in charge of the Government's Strategy Unit, based in the Cabinet Office]. After I had done the health thing, Geoff said: 'We are talking about whether we can get you to do something else and there are two ideas: could we get you involved in doing a big thing on the future of drugs policy or pensions?' I said: 'If you are going to do drugs policy you have to read a footnote in the paperback edition of my book, which basically says "I believe in the liberalization of all drugs." I think it describes the war against drugs as a fatuous, unwinnable war, which simply destroys other societies, etc.' And Geoff looked at that and said: 'Yes, I have a lot of sympathy with that, but hmmm . . .' So we moved on to pensions. [Adair Turner interview, 29 September 2005]

The creation of the Commission was announced on 17 December 2002. There were to be two other members: Jeannie Drake, deputy general secretary of the Communication Workers Union, and John Hills, professor of social policy at the London School of Economics and a world authority on social exclusion. Its explicit terms of reference were that it would review the provision of occupational and personal pensions in order 'to make recommendations to the Secretary of State for Work and Pensions on whether there is a case for moving beyond the current voluntarist approach'. But in practice the scope of the Pensions Commission's work turned out to be much broader. The Treasury tried to keep it away from any examination of the state-pensions system because Brown did not want any criticism of the Pension Credit or interference in his control of public expenditure – but Turner felt it was impossible not to review all elements of the state system, because he could not make recommendations about private savings without taking account of the impact of state provision. 'Eventually the Treasury gave up,' says Turner. 'But for quite a long time the Treasury was saying [each time Turner strayed into state-pension questions], "Oh, Adair, where's your terms of reference?"'

Even if Turner had wanted to be a patsy for the Government, that would have been impossible because there was no coherent view coming from Government as a whole. 'The Prime Minister . . . thought there must be something big to do in pensions. He was not sure what that was but instinctively felt it could not be duck and weave, muddle through, a bit here and a bit there,' Turner says. 'Meanwhile, the Treasury said: "We don't need a big reform, we can just muddle through." That split is an amazingly fixed part of the political constellation.' [Adair Turner interview, 25 October 2005].

However, one factor working in Turner's favour was the bad news about pensions that exploded on to the front pages week after week (which began when Equitable Life – a life insurance company which had been widely regarded as one of the superior providers of personal pensions – ran into serious financial difficulties in 2000). Most companies were banning new employees from joining their final-salary schemes. Some decided that even existing staff would no longer contribute to these defined-benefit pension plans (such as Rentokil Initial, the business services group, in late 2005, and Debenhams in 2006). Worse still, pension funds backed by weak companies collapsed, causing hardship and anxiety to their members. And, yet again, a Government initiative, the Pensions Act 2004, was having a perverse effect in that it accelerated pension-scheme closures. This legislation created a Pensions Regulator to police the industry and a Pension Protection Fund (PPF) to provide limited compensation to victims of collapsed funds. The Pensions Regulator and the PPF put pressure on companies to inject more cash into their funds in order to meet their obligations to current and future pensioners. This additional cost was the final straw for many businesses, which decided they could no longer afford to support the relevant schemes. The number of private-sector members of open defined-benefit schemes, which was more than 5m in 1995, is now heading towards zero.

By contrast, the public sector was still offering very generous final-salary pension arrangements. However, the cost of these to the Government was beginning to seem prohibitive. So in the run-up to the 2005 general election, Alan Johnson, then Work and Pensions Secretary, undertook the delicate task of trying to reduce pension benefits for public-sector workers. When talks began in March 2005, he tried to persuade the unions to agree to an increase in the normal pension age from 60 to 65. This was doing no more than following the trend of the private sector. But it was bitterly opposed by the unions, who wielded great clout as pay-masters to the Labour Party – and this power was always at its greatest in the weeks running up to a general election.

The election came and went with no deal being reached. But such was the sensitivity of the issue that Blair asked Johnson to stay on as lead negotiator for the Government even though he was moved from the Department for Work and Pensions to become Secretary of State for Trade and Industry. Strikes were threatened if Johnson refused to compromise and, on 18 October 2005, he formally signalled the Government's surrender on a central element in the negotiations. The deal was that existing employees could still retire at 60, but new ones would have to wait until they were 65 before drawing a pension. Johnson – a former postman and erstwhile joint general secretary of the Communication Workers Union before entering Parliament in 1997 – had not engaged in a freelance operation. Before the proposal was formalized, he had asked Blair whether he was happy with it. 'Blair did not go through the fine print,' concedes a minister. 'He never does. His eyes glaze over. But he approved it.'

The deal prompted a stink, especially among private-sector employers. They felt that a disastrous precedent had been set that would make it harder for them to adjust pension benefits in an optimal way. 'Even if you don't expect the Government to lead by example, you don't want it to actively set a terrible example of employment practices,' says the chairman of a major international company based in London. Apart from anything else, Johnson's compromise was bound to foster a less cohesive culture within the public sector: if two people of the same age were sitting next to each other doing identical jobs for identical salaries but one happened to join after the retirement age was raised, he or she would in practice be much worse off than the neighbour. What's more, the policy would be discriminatory against women and those on lower incomes, who tended to give up work or change jobs on a more frequent basis. For the best paid, such as older, senior civil servants, it was marvellous: they rarely left Whitehall for gainful employment outside, so they were the most likely to stay till 60 and then draw a very substantial pension. 'It's amazing that the unions basically defended the interests of the mandarin class, who have no time for them,' says an official. 'It is an odd form of social justice.'

Turner was livid about Johnson's deal. He already knew that one of his central recommendations would be that the state-pension age would have to rise and that people in general would have to work until they were older to acquire adequate pension rights. But arguing that case was now much harder. However, there was a much more serious crisis looming for the Pensions Commission – which was that the Chancellor became determined to bury its central recommendation: that the basic state pension should once again be increased in line with earnings rather than prices.

The Chancellor had learned, from private meetings with Turner, that the Commission would recommend a reinstatement from 2010 of the system of uprating the basic state pension in line with increases in average earnings. This was infuriating to Brown for three reasons: he took it as a personal affront, after all his self-harming toil to persuade his party in the 1990s to abandon the link between pensions and earnings; it was a reform blessed by Blair, and therefore – by definition – anathema to Brown (for the Treasury, Turner's ideas were uncomfortably similar to those of Blair's chief adviser on strategy, Matthew Taylor); finally, it might well lead to a rise in public spending shortly after the next general election, which would provide ammunition for the Tories to argue that taxes would increase at a time when Brown expected to be Prime Minister.

This is an account by a former official of conversations between Turner and Brown in the first half of November:

> Gordon kept saying to him: 'Don't go hard on this, set out some options.' Gordon had a huge row with him. He said: 'I want to be able to implement your report. You must do this in a way which makes it possible to get to the point of implementation.' But Turner is too arrogant. He is egged on by Number 10. He ignored Gordon . . . Turner was being very 'my independence cannot be compromised'.

On 24 November 2005, six days before the Pensions Commission was due to publish its report, the *Financial Times* printed leaked extracts from a letter written on 17 November by Gordon Brown to Turner. The letter seemed dry and technical; its most important section said that 'you should not assume' that the Pension Credit's link to average earnings 'will continue beyond 2008'. This was an explosive sentence because the Commission had assessed the affordability of its recommendations in the light of what the Government was proposing to spend on its existing pension initiatives. But what Brown was saying in the letter was that there might be less money available for pensions than the Commission had thought. It was an explicit threat by Brown to rubbish the Commission's proposals as unaffordable at the very moment they were made public.

Gordon Brown writes official letters only on rare and special occasions. Such a letter can, for example, be the underpinning of a campaign to do in a colleague (three years earlier, Brown wrote to every member of the Cabinet in a ploy to destroy the plans of the then Health Secretary, Alan Milburn, to give financial autonomy to Foundation Hospitals). This latest missive would direct discussion of Turner's proposals towards whether taxes would have to rise to pay for it all, which would generate a black aura around the Commission's ideas. But Turner, convinced that he would be protected by the Prime Minister and by Matthew Taylor, with whom he was in regular contact, refused to soften his proposal to restore the earnings link. So after the Chancellor's letter to him was made public, a vitriolic battle ensued over the normally tedious issue of public-spending projections for the next decade.

Who leaked the letter? For a day or so, the rumour around Westminster was that Matthew Taylor was the leaker, although this was denied by him and by Number 10. Such was the febrile mood that the head of the Home Civil Service, Sir Gus O'Donnell, asked the new head of the Treasury, Nick Macpherson, to write a letter to Taylor reassuring him that there was no Treasury vendetta against him. This Macpherson duly did, under the impression that it was a private letter. But it was immediately published by 10 Downing Street. Macpherson's letter says: 'I wish to put on record that the Treasury is not accusing you [Taylor] of leaking these letters, and I am discounting any press speculation about named individuals. As with any enquiry, the Treasury will not prejudge the outcome. The Treasury press office continues to make this absolutely clear to anyone who enquires.' Taylor immediately put out his own response: 'I welcome this letter. I hope it will correct and end the damaging and entirely unfounded speculation linking me with the leak of correspondence between the Chancellor and Lord Turner. I will, of course, cooperate with any enquiry seeking to establish the real source of the leaked correspondence.'

Emotions in Government were running high: 'The whole thing has gone mad,' a senior official said to me at the time. Turner himself felt that he was caught in the middle of a vicious war between the Treasury and 10 Downing Street. 'I understand that politics can be a brutal business where people brutally pursue their own self-interest,' he told me. 'But there seems to be a group of people who brutally pursue the opposite of their self-interest. It's such a mess.' [Adair Turner interview, 26 November 2005]

The Pensions Commission published its report on 30 November, the last possible date before it would have been overdue on Turner's own schedule. Its 460 pages of A4 contained a series of interrelated prescriptions to provide a respectable income for those retiring in the subsequent 45 years. Its main recommendations were as follows. First, as a minimum, the typical earner in the economy ought to receive retirement income equivalent to 45 per cent of typical earnings. A third of this would be provided by a new private-sector contributory savings scheme, called the National Pension Savings Scheme, or an equivalent occupational pension scheme, and the rest by state provision. The great advantage of this National Scheme is that it would have the sheer size required to secure enormous economies of scale, such that management charges would be equivalent to just 0.3 per cent of the funds invested, a fraction of the supposedly low charges levied on the flopped stakeholder products. All employees would be automatically enrolled into it, unless they were already a member of a comparable or better scheme, and they would automatically contribute 4 per cent of their post-tax earnings to the scheme unless they explicitly opted out. By dint of its prospective size and importance to the economy, it would probably become one of the great British institutions created since the Second World War. This so-called 'soft compulsion' was proposed because of international evidence that individuals are more likely to save if confronted by a decision to withdraw from a scheme rather than a decision to sign up for one (there is a whole branch of economics called 'behavioural economics' devoted to infusing the modelling of the economy with such psychological insights).

In addition – and controversially – companies would be obliged to pay the equivalent of at least 3 per cent of an employee's earnings into the scheme if that employee contributed. This was pretty 'hard compulsion' on companies and has – predictably – been criticized by the CBI. Equally predictably, Blair was initially uncomfortable about it.

As for state provision, the Commission recommended a gradual phasing out of means-testing. It wanted the basic pension to become a universal and individual payment based on residency in the UK rather than on contributions, which would be fairer to women and the disabled. It also proposed that the basic pension should be increased significantly and raised in line with earnings from 2010 or 2011 onwards. Meanwhile, it suggested that the second state pension, S2P, should gradually be transformed into a flat-rate payment.

So far, so elegant. But there are also significant costs associated with such a system: public spending on state pensions and pension benefits would rise from 6.2 per cent of national income to between 7.5 per cent and 8 per cent by 2045. And the increase would only be capped at that level if the state-pension age were to rise to 66 by 2030, to 67 by 2040 and to 68 by 2050.

The Treasury's private horror at elements of this package burst into the open on publication. In particular, officials started to brief explicitly against the Commission's recommended timescale of 2010 or 2011 for implementing a move to restore the earnings link to the basic state pension. Its tactics were cynical and ruthless: it repeated the point made in the leaked letter that it might well decide to cease increasing the Pension Credit in line with average earnings, which meant that it could present the Commission's plans as representing a much bigger increase in public spending than would otherwise have been the case. It was classic scare tactics. At the time, Turner was horrified:

> The bit [of what they are doing] which I think is completely absurd is when they say: 'Yes, but we could link the guaranteed credit [the Pension Credit] for 12 years to prices', which they have never said they would do. There is not a single published forecast which ever said they would do it, and if they did it would be a complete reversal of all their commitments on pensioner poverty, which is just not practical politics. And, frankly, it has only been created in order to give them a base line to say this thing is unaffordable. It is the whole purpose of it: it has no other purpose. [Adair Turner interview, 2 December 2005]

In a public-relations battle between the Treasury and the Pensions Commission, there was claim and counter-claim about what it would cost – and whether it was affordable – to increase the basic state pension in line with earnings. The picture was confused by the widely differing views taken by both sides about how increments to spending should be measured. The Treasury said the net rise in spending would be more than £16bn by 2020, equivalent to a substantial increase in the basic rate of income tax, but Turner claimed it was less than £2bn. They were comparing apples with pears. And on this occasion, Turner was probably more in touch with statistical commonsense than the Treasury.

One manifestation that the Treasury had lost the basic argument was a waspish assessment by a former head of the Treasury, Lord Turnbull, who had also been head of the Home Civil Service. He compared what he saw as the relatively small increase in public spending proposed by Turner with the massive increases in expenditure on the National Health Service that had been announced by the Prime Minister in an unconventional way only a few years earlier.

The first recommendation of the noble Lord, Lord Turner, is that if excessive dependence on means-testing is to be avoided, the state pension needs to be raised in line with earnings. I confess that in my time at the Treasury I enthusiastically supported breaking the earnings link. One reason why I have now come to support the link is that we are now going to spend much longer in retirement – often 25 to 30 years, occasionally even more. An economy that grows at 2.5 per cent per year over 25 years will be nearly twice as rich. Will those who have retired not share a bean of that extra prosperity? This leads to the next step in the noble Lord's argument, which is that to make this affordable the retirement age should rise over time to around 68 – an increase close to that projected in life expectancy. The net increase in public expenditure beyond that already projected is about 0.5 per cent of GDP, spread over 40 years. A Government that committed themselves on breakfast television to raising the proportion of GDP spent on health by 3 per cent over 8 years cannot plausibly argue that this is unaffordable. [*Hansard*, 4 May 2006]

Even so, as winter turned to spring in 2006, the Treasury was still trying to put obstacles in the way of a restoration of the earnings link. In the end, the argument was reduced to one over whether its implementation should be delayed significantly from Turner's proposed date of 2010 (or 2011), whether it should apply only to much older pensioners, or whether the basic pension should instead be increased by a flat rate that would be higher than price inflation but lower than earnings inflation. Throughout the internal Government battle over all this, the relatively new Secretary of State for Work and Pensions, John Hutton, made the dangerous decision to side with Blair and Turner against Brown and the Treasury. Amazingly, he kept his place in Cabinet even after Gordon Brown became Prime Minister.

As this argument progressed, the dog that hardly barked was compulsory saving, which from the outset had been expected to be the most explosive issue of all. In the end, Turner did not recommend additional enforced saving by individuals. But his proposal that companies should be obliged to put money into their employees' retirement savings accounts was a comparable policy which infuriated libertarians and those who objected to anything that looked like a *de facto* tax on business. It was opposed by the CBI. But although Blair had qualms about it, Turner secured victory when the Tories – and the Treasury – backed the new charge on companies.

After months of agonizing, the Government finally published its definitive pensions reform package in a White Paper on 25 May 2006. Its pillars were essentially those recommended by Turner. One difference was that it did not opt to transform the basic state pension into a universal one payable to anyone who passed a residency test, as suggested by the Pensions Commission. The principle was retained that the full pension should be received only by those who made sufficient financial contributions through the National Insurance system. However, it would be easier for women and carers to earn the right to a full pension because there would be a reduction in the number of years of contributions that were required and notional contributions would be attributed to those looking after children or the infirm at home. Also, Brown and the Treasury achieved a small victory that would allow them to claim they had not been humiliated. The Government would aim to restore the earnings link in 2012, subject to 'affordability and the fiscal position', and by the end of the next Parliament at the very latest. This was later than Turner had wanted. But the delay was hardly a disaster and the Government's commitment to make the change was unambiguous. In all other important respects, the future of the British pensions system would be that prescribed by Turner and his two colleagues.

These painfully agreed reforms offer hope of tolerable income in retirement for millions of younger employees. But what of those who have saved for years in pension schemes that are now closed or closing? The sheer weight of pension-fund liabilities on British companies is still quite something, even after the rises in global stock markets of the past few years. The Pensions Regulator calculated in 2006 that the deficit in 5,800 UK final-salary pension schemes would be £440bn in aggregate, if the schemes were valued on what is called a 'buyout' basis. This is a valuation that assumes continuous increases in the life-expectancy of fund members – their 'longevity' – and also values the respective funds on the very cautious basis that investment performance will be in line with the low but certain return on index-linked gilt-edged stock or Government bonds. It is a genuine liability for companies, because it in effect measures the cash that they would have to put into their respective funds if they wanted to cease having any responsibility for them (since 2003, the only companies that can escape making such a payment are those that become insolvent). On this measure, the aggregate deficit on all 7,000 UK final-salary occupational pension schemes is £518bn, according to the actuaries Watson Wyatt – which is about the same size as the British national debt, so not a small number.

For many managers of British companies, the potentially large and seemingly unpredictable claims on their businesses from their respective pension schemes are a scary distraction from the day job. They want to sell hi-tech gizmos to the Chinese or insurance to the Americans, not worry about whether the deficit in their pension funds could overwhelm them. So increasing numbers of them want to get shot of what they perceive as the whole ghastly business of guaranteeing their employees a comfortable retirement – and such is the creativity of capitalism that a new industry has been created to relieve them of this burden.

Companies can transfer their pension-fund liabilities to insurance companies – some old, like Legal & General, some new, like Paternoster and Lucida – but only if they are prepared to inject sufficient cash into them to cover the liabilities on the basis of a conservative 'buyout' valuation of the sort I have described. The good news, in this instance, is that pensioners in such transferred funds should be no worse off than they were before – and they may even be better off, because these European Union insurance companies are very tightly regulated by the Financial Services Authority. However there is some grounds for anxiety in that overseas insurers from less well-regulated jurisdictions are also trying to gain control of British pension schemes.

Another development is that a private-equity veteran, Ed Truell, has been muscling in on the action. His business, Pension Corporation, buys whole companies where he sees an opportunity to make money from their pension funds. At the time of writing, he had responsibility for the Thresher and Thorn pension funds and was attempting to buy Telent, the rump of GEC Marconi, for its substantial fund. Truell's aim is to generate and pocket a surplus from these funds over the long term, after all the respective funds' obligations to pensioners are met.

There has been a stampede of financial institutions trying to relieve companies of their pension schemes. Billions of pounds of pensioners' savings are coming under new stewardship – and the transfers may eventually run to hundreds of billions. Regulatory oversight of these deals is strict. And there may be little reason to assume that there will be more failures of pension funds under their new stewards than there were in the past. Even so, there is something troubling about the way that the link between an employee's income in retirement and his or her company is being broken, without the consent of the employee. These pension savings represent the most important financial assets of millions of people. It is surely inappropriate that the savers themselves – current and future pensioners – have so little say in the choice of who will nurture and protect their savings and how it will be done.

Another disturbing new trend – which, fortunately, is not yet desperately prevalent – is for companies to persuade non-retired members of final-salary pension schemes to transfer out of those schemes in return for a cash lump sum. The motive for the companies is simple: they would be reducing substantial long-term obligations to pensioners. But what makes it attractive for businesses ought to deter employees from accepting. Future hardship could be the consequence of surrendering a specified future pension entitlement. However, for cash-strapped employees on lowish incomes, the offer of a few thousand pounds in cash can be too seductive to turn down.

What has happened to corporate pension funds reflects a change in the culture of the United Kingdom, the abandonment of the notion that companies have a moral obligation to promote the welfare of their employees after a lifetime of service. It is part and parcel of the death of paternalism and the rise of individualism. Company directors are no longer asking what it will cost them to provide a comfortable retirement for staff. Instead, the majority of big companies are investigating the price of ridding themselves of any liability for the retired workforce. This is a less conspicuous but hugely important example of how the wealth of the many is being eroded, while that of the super-rich has soared.

CHAPTER 8
DEMOCRACY FOR SALE

For the children of émigré Jews living in the East End of London, the Worshipful Company of Grocers Hackney Downs Boys' School was a route to prosperity, academic and artistic success, and even to membership of the British establishment during much of the twentieth century. My father, Maurice Harry Peston, now Lord Peston of Mile End, attended Hackney Downs in the 1940s, and went on to become an academic economist and adviser to assorted Labour politicians. One of his classmates was Harold Pinter. A few years later, another distinguished playwright Steven Berkoff went to the school. And in the late 1950s, Michael Abraham Levy, now Lord Levy of Mill Hill, was a pupil at Hackney Downs.

What Lord Levy and my dad had in common as young men was a determination to escape the East End – and they succeeded triumphantly, like so many from assorted émigré communities in that part of London, both before and since. The Lords Peston and Levy still share a belief in the duty of us all to help build the good society. They have a strong sense of their Jewish cultural identity – although my father is an atheist who is contemptuous of organized religion – and they have powerful bonds to the Labour Party (arguably, Levy's bonds are first and foremost personal bonds to Tony Blair, but there's no doubting the passion he showed in raising money for Labour).

But their paths have diverged in ways that say a great deal about the evolution of Labour since 1994, when Tony Blair became leader of the party. In the 1970s, my father (and mother) championed what New Labour would denigrate as 'bog-standard' comprehensives. Lord Levy is the leading fund-raiser and cheerleader for the institutions designed by New Labour to replace failing comprehensives: Blair's beloved city academies – those new schools which try to harness the drive and focus of the private sector and give considerable independent power to their respective head teachers and financial sponsors.

City academies are anathema to my dad. But for him there is a cruel parallel history here. Hackney Downs became a comprehensive in 1974, in a victory for my parents' cherished Campaign for Comprehensive Education. Then the rot set in. By the mid-1990s Hackney Downs had become a byword for the shortcomings of urban comprehensives, as attainment levels collapsed. Hackney Downs (probably unfairly) was given the appalling tag by the media of 'worst school in Britain' and in 1995 was closed by the Conservative Government. It is moot whether this ignominy was an indictment of the comprehensive concept – or of a lethal combination of lousy school management, inappropriate teaching methods and under-motivated pupils (many of whom spoke English as a second language).

On the ashes of Hackney Downs has risen a city academy that appears to be the kind of beacon of excellence in an area of deprivation that Levy's and my father's school once was. Called the Mossbourne Community Academy – and sponsored to the tune of £2.15m by the late Sir Clive Bourne, a transport entrepreneur who was born in Hackney – it is described by the standards watchdog, Ofsted, as 'outstanding', 'exceptional' and 'dynamic'. The school expects some 80 per cent of its pupils, way above the national average, to achieve the five A* to

C grades at GCSE (including English and maths) which represents a basic standard of academic achievement. Perhaps
more importantly, there is a hunger among the kids to go on to
university. The school, under its knighted head, Sir Michael
Wilshaw, appears once again to be showing what can be
achieved by the ambitious children of immigrants, but this time
black and Asian ones, rather than the Jews of the mid-twentieth
century. That said, my dad will never be persuaded that
Mossbourne is a good thing. For him, city academies represent
a dangerous step on the path back to the kind of academic
elitism in schools that he regards as highly damaging to the least
able (my own view is that he's a bit too ideological in his
opposition to schools like Mossbourne).

There's another parable of the diverging experiences of the
Lords Peston and Levy that speaks to the essence of New Labour.
My father became a senior adviser to Labour ministers in the
1960s and 1970s from a background as an academic economist at
the London School of Economics and Queen Mary College
(where he founded the economics department). Lord Levy became a close adviser to the Prime Minister after a successful career
as an entrepreneur in the entertainment industry. And when my
father was nominated by the then Labour leader, Neil Kinnock, for
a peerage in 1996, Kinnock's chief of staff, Charles Clarke, asked
him if he had ever made a substantial donation to the Labour Party
– because if he had, that had the potential to embarrass the party
and would disqualify him from becoming a Labour peer. Fortunately, my dad never earned quite enough to make a transforma-
tive contribution to Labour's coffers and he was deemed fit to put
on the ermine.

By contrast, Levy entered the House of Lords in 1997,
having raised a fortune from wealthy individuals for Blair's
office and for Labour (although it's not known what personal
financial contributions he has made). He then went on to raise
millions more, largely from business people, plenty of whom
famously went on to sit with him on Labour's benches in the
Lords. Unlike Kinnock, Tony Blair was not squeamish about

giving peerages to those who had donated to Labour. Although he must have been aware that selling peerages and honours is a crime, and therefore took care not to do so, he wanted to reward service to Labour – and he'd have been crackers to view donations as a disservice to Labour. From the moment he became Prime Minister he eagerly nominated party donors, and latterly lenders too, for peerages.

The innocent explanation I'm prone to put on all this is that from the outset Blair had a touching faith that only good could come from infusing his party and Government with the ethos of the private sector and from surrounding himself with putative entrepreneurs. The first conspicuous manifestation of his infatuation with business was at Labour's 1995 annual conference, when he struck a deal with British Telecommunications that BT would connect up schools, hospitals and libraries to the internet in return for a Labour Government allowing BT to become a broadcaster. Blair loved the short-term headlines it generated about his imaginative entente with a business colossus – but the deal was never executed, partly because the party eventually worked out that extending the reach of a near-monopolist (as BT was at the time) would be harmful to consumers.

A naive and touching faith in the ability of business and business people to get the job done well, coupled with contempt for much of the public sector, was a characteristic of Blair from the moment he became party leader – and it's also been responsible for periodic embarrassments, from which he never seemed to learn. Many would say it was a good thing to have a Prime Minister who celebrated wealth creation and was sympathetic towards the private sector (well, I would, anyway). But judgement is required about which business people are first-rate and which are less than that. That said, initially at least, a lack of discrimination in Labour's business relationships was deliberate. That was the message given to me in 1996 by Alastair Campbell, who was then main spokesman and media adviser to Blair as opposition leader. At the time, Campbell and his team had been boasting of the financial and moral support they had been receiving from a colourful businessman. It showed, they said, that Labour was no longer perceived by successful capitalists as hostile. That's all well and good, I told Campbell, but he ought to be aware that this particular capitalist didn't have a spotless reputation in the City. Campbell neither knew nor cared about that. He glibly pointed out that the party's polling showed it was perceived as anti-business – which was damaging to its electoral prospects. On that basis, it was good for Labour to be seen as good friends with a cowboy, if that's what this individual was, because it showed that the party loved business, warts and all.

Almost any businessman would therefore do. In that context, my second favourite anecdote of the late 1990s – which I believe to be true, though I cannot prove it, so I won't name the relevant business executive – is that Blair once put a businessman in the Lords by accident. He'd thought he was ennobling a more distinguished business leader, and only found out he had the wrong man after the peerage had been awarded. Even if the nobleman in question has been traduced, the story contains an inner truth, which is that Blair and his inner circle were utterly desperate to woo and win business to their side. He and his close colleagues chased business leaders like over-eager lovers, and rewarded quite a number of them with places in the Lords.

But even ennobling prominent industrialists could go wrong. For example, the peerage list in 1997 that made lords of Michael Levy and of David Sainsbury, the billionaire scion of the grocery family, also gave a barony to George Simpson, who was then chief executive of the defence and electronics conglomerate GEC, which was to rename itself Marconi. Simpson, who was not particularly famous for his support of Labour, was a bit surprised to be offered the peerage. He rang a mutual friend, a leading industrialist, for advice on whether he should take it. This other business eminence told him he would be crazy to turn it down. So Simpson became a so-called working peer, but that turned out to be a misnomer. Lord Simpson became a minor national celebrity for his unblemished record of never turning up to the House to vote. After that, he became a byword for the mad deal-making of the dotcom era and was ousted from Marconi in September 2001, when the once-proud electronics company was engulfed in a financial crisis of Simpson's own making. Curiously, Blair and Labour were henceforth not quite so keen to tout Simpson as one of theirs.

My favourite story of all regarding a peerage nomination is about how one businessman somehow hijacked a peerage which another businessman thought had been earmarked for him. What happened, I am told, is that a prominent entrepreneur assumed he would be ennobled after he had made a very big gift to Labour. But it transpired that a chum of his, whom he thought was squaring it all with the Prime Minister, got the peerage and he got none. Which is really just to say that the process of making appointments to the Upper House was a bit of a messy one.

The business leader who consistently played Blair the most astutely – and seems now to have hooked his successor, Gordon Brown – is Sir Richard Branson. In the run-up to the 1997 general election, Labour was desperate to win the endorsement of the Virgin boss. Jonathan Powell, the adviser who stayed with Blair from more or less the beginning to the end, told me in 1996 that backing from Branson would be more valuable than support from anyone else he or Blair could imagine. Why? Because Branson was a real entrepreneur – and, unlike most entrepreneurs at the time, he was both famous and loved by the public. But Branson refused to be seduced. He was cognizant of his own value and for months refused to come out for Labour. However, just five days before the election, he deigned to allow Blair to travel with him on one of his Virgin trains. The media was encouraged to report this as a *de facto* endorsement, since Branson said he backed some Labour policies and admired Blair. But Branson still refused to say how he would actually vote. So it wasn't a product endorsement of the sort that Virgin would ever run in an advert. It was rather less effusive than Uma Thurman's recent adverts for Virgin Media, the cable and mobile-phone group. And in retrospect, given that Labour was on the verge of a landslide that Branson could not influence one way or the other, it's astonishing how grateful Labour was at the time for these few crumbs from Branson's plate. But grateful Labour most certainly was – and Branson milked it as only he can, by turning up at Labour's celebration party on the morning after the tectonic plates of British politics had shifted, and behaving for all the world as if he was Blair's oldest friend.

In fact, Blair's best and closest friend from the business world has consistently been Michael Levy. He raised funds for the blind trust which paid much of the substantial staff and research costs of Blair's office as opposition leader. And in the 1990s, he worked with the first ever finance director of the Labour Party, a former City executive called Paul Blagbrough, to reduce Labour's dependence on trade union funding by tapping what are known as high net-worth individuals. But of Blagbrough and Levy, there can be no doubt which of them was the fund-raising genius. The consistent theme of hard-nosed business people to whom I've spoken is that they have emptied their wallets for Levy's Jewish charitable causes, or his beloved city academies, or Labour, even when they've entered a conversation with him determined to hang on to their cash.

He began his career as a chartered accountant working for assorted entertainment clients. Then he evolved into a suited pop-music mogul in the 1970s and 1980s, managing, promoting or recording a series of acts, none of them megastars but many of them pretty commercial. Levy's roster of talent has at various times included the unlikeliest glam-rock star ever, Alvin Stardust, middle-of-the-road Chris Rea, the 1980s dance group Kissing the Pink, and the pop ska band Bad Manners. He inspired loyalty in those he backed. And he turned those relationships into hard cash in 1988, when he sold the record label he had created, Magnet Records, for a reported £10m to Warner Bros.

Another substantial part of Levy's life is organized religion. He is an observant orthodox Jew, who spends an hour every Friday discussing Jewish philosophy with Rabbi Yitzchak Schochet, who runs his local synagogue in Mill Hill in north London. That synagogue complex contains a substantial building paid for by Levy to honour his parents and he's been the leading force in raising funds to rebuild the temple. There are, in fact, few more active members of Anglo-Jewry than Michael Levy. What puts him at top table at most Jewish functions are the innumerable millions he's raised for a whole range of Jewish causes and charities, notably his beloved Jewish Care, the largest health and social care charity for Jews in the UK. When in 2006 he become mired in the controversy of the failed police investigation into whether he had sold peerages on behalf of Labour, he received strong public and private support from much of the Jewish community.

What drew Levy and Blair together in the 1990s – after they were introduced to each other by Eldred Tabachnik, the barrister and former president of the Board of Deputies of British Jews – was tennis and fund-raising. Blair loved playing tennis in the privacy and tranquillity of Levy's private court. Also, Levy offered a way to realize Blair's ambition of reducing Labour's financial dependence on the trade unions: cash from the wealthy.

Levy's growing power in the court of Tony Blair was a function of the electoral conditions of the 1990s. The cost of fighting general elections was rising fast, as both Labour and the Tories lavished expenditure on marketing campaigns involving advertising, mailshots, market research, computerized databases, call centres, and so on. And neither Labour nor the Tories could rely on contributions from their traditional donors. In the case of the Tories, donations from public companies were shrinking fast, because shareholders increasingly told listed businesses that such donations were a waste of money and even a potential embarrassment (it was bad publicity for a company to be accused of trying to buy influence over Government). As for Blair, he feared that the perception of Labour as being owned by its trade union founders was damaging to its electoral prospects, so he wanted to be less reliant on union contributions. It was also a case of 'needs must': membership of the trade unions was dwindling, in part due to Margaret Thatcher's onslaught against them, which meant they had diminished financial resources to put Labour's way.

So both Labour and the Tories had only one place to turn: wealthy individuals who could do what they liked with their own money. And Levy had a genius for extracting cheques from them. It was he – almost single-handedly – who weaned Labour off its traditional dependence on the trade unions. Levy raised extraordinary sums from private donors for a party that was traditionally seen as hostile to the interests of capital. And he did it through a combination of charm, persistence, chutzpah and ruthless exploitation of his proximity to the Prime Minister. 'I'll put you down for a million' was his refrain to donors and potential donors – who were softened up at dinners held at Levy's lavish north London home, where the guest of honour was frequently Tony Blair.

He lives in a hacienda-style mansion tucked away down a leafy private lane and at the end of a gravel drive behind daunting security gates. It feels like a little bit of LA transplanted to north London. Inside, it's wall-to-wall deep-pile white shag carpet. First-time visitors are typically shown his private tennis court, his outdoor swimming pool and his indoor swimming pool. He invites the powerful, well-connected and well-heeled for cosy Friday-night suppers, when gentiles are gently instructed in the traditional Jewish ritual. And there are also grander, more formal, catered affairs.

The more lavish dinners take place around an enormous glass table on marble pillars. A friend of mine recalls one such event when the other guests included eight Middle East ambassadors. Another acquaintance attended a dinner whose purpose appeared to be to persuade a couple of successful business people that they would get a nice warm feeling if they put a few million pounds behind city academies. On that occasion, Ruth Kelly, the former education secretary, and Andrew Adonis – probably the greatest Government champion of city academies, first as an adviser to Blair in Downing Street, latterly as an education minister – were both in attendance. Characteristically, there was a strong media contingent among the guests: present were Sly Bailey, chief executive of Mirror Group, Alan Rusbridger, editor of the *Guardian*, and Murdoch Maclennan, chief executive of Telegraph Group. Levy's journalistic and political guests were often rounded up by Sir Nick Lloyd, former editor of the *Daily Express* and now co-proprietor of a public-relations firm, Brown Lloyd James.

One of Levy's party pieces is to walk around the huge table pointing to the places where so and so 'handed over 200 grand, Lord Sainsbury handed over a million' and so on, his tone varying between Hackney wide boy and hoity-toity grandee.

Another illustrative story is that of a Jewish entrepreneur who once told Levy that he never gives money to Jewish charities, and found himself writing out a cheque for £30,000 to Jewish Care ten minutes later. And Levy's rabbi, Yitzchak Schochet, gave me another example of his fund-raising prowess when I interviewed him for the BBC:

> A couple of years ago on Rosh Hashanah, the Jewish New Year, I asked him if he would be willing to help me to encourage people to contribute to the rebuilding of this synagogue, which we're looking to do, and he readily agreed, if only because he was keen to help me and to help the community. And within the two hours that he was here, he raised somewhere in the region of one to one-and-a-half million pounds in pledges from people, because everyone who gets to know him understands the sincerity of the man, knows and appreciates how he's looking to help the cause, and wants to come on board and be a part of it. [Rabbi Yitzchak Schochet interview, 6 March 2007]

When raising money – for Labour, or charities, or the city academies – he taps into a vast number of acquaintances and friends, who are connected through the astonishing number of positions he holds in charitable and voluntary-sector bodies and through his other appointments. The following are just a few of the hats he has worn. From 1999 to 2007, he was Tony Blair's personal envoy to the Middle East. He is president of the Jews' Free School, which traces its origins back to 1732 and claims to be 'Europe's largest and most successful Jewish secondary school'. Its new campus in Kingsbury in the far north of London cost £42m, of which Levy raised £10m. He is also president of the Jewish Lads' and Girls' Brigade, president of Community Service Volunteers, president of the Specialist Schools and Academies Trust, president of Jewish Care, honorary president of the United Jewish Israel Appeal, a member of the advisory council of the Foreign Policy Centre think tank, chairman of the Chief Rabbinate Awards for Excellence, and a trustee and member of the Executive Committee of the Jewish Leadership Council, among other positions. He raises money for some of these organizations. And those people whom he persuades to help one of these bodies seem often to end up supporting other causes of his as well. Thus, at Community Service Volunteers, the UK's largest volunteering organization, nine of Labour's most generous recent donors or lenders have been patrons: Lord Bhattacharyya, Gordon Crawford, Sir David Garrard, William Haughey, Sir Christopher Ondaatje, Chai Patel, Derek Tullett, Isaac Kaye and Lord Bernstein.

What's more, those who have given generously to Labour or to other organizations with which he's associated, including city academies, often ended up receiving honours of various sorts. There is no suggestion that these honours were unmerited or that they were awarded in an improper way. And obviously, Levy didn't have the actual power to bestow gongs and titles. But when it came to the allocation of them, especially the creation of working peers, Levy had a loud and influential voice in 10 Downing Street.

These days, most nominees for honours other than peerages go through a complex vetting procedure involving specialist White-hall committees. In the case of non-party-political peerages, choice and scrutiny is by the Lords Appointments Commission. That said, Tony Blair as Prime Minister retained more or less absolute power over the decision about who became a so-called Labour working peer. In his latter period of office, it was the task of Ruth Turner, director of Government Relations, and John McTernan, director of Political Operations, to sift through all the possible candidates for working peerages. 'It's a nightmare job,' said one of their former colleagues, before they and Blair resigned in 2007. 'They've got MPs lobbying them for a place in the Lords as a reward for years of loyal service, they've got pressures on behalf of trade union leaders who want to be peers and then there are the demands from Lord Levy that this or that loyal supporter should go to the Upper House.'

In Lord Levy's case, the sheer number of his roles, all the different hats he wore, made it very difficult for officials to decide precisely why he was lobbying for this or that individual to receive an honour, as a former senior civil servant who worked closely with Blair explained to me:

> The problem with Levy was that he had too many fund-raising roles: raising money for Labour, raising money for academies, raising money for charities. So when he recommends someone for an honour, it's never clear what the honour is for. I never knew whether he was pushing someone because he had given money to an academy or to Labour. It was all deeply unsatisfactory. And he was always frantically lobbying for honours. He got the lists of who was put forward and pushed for those he wanted to reward. And when the various committees excluded some or delayed them till another list, he would try to get the Prime Minister to intervene to reinstate some or speed up others. [interview, 6 February 2007]

The measure of Levy's clout was his 60th birthday party in June 2004, which was held in the majestic and elegant Banqueting Hall opposite Downing Street in Whitehall. More than 300 were entertained at a sit-down dinner, including three-quarters of the Cabinet. 'There was a three-line whip from Number 10,' said one of the guests. 'I've been to some fancy dinners in my time, but this was astonishing.' At the dinner, Blair lauded Levy's 'extraordinary energy and ability' and his 'wisdom, compassion and humanity'. Britain's influence in the Middle East was largely down to Levy, Blair claimed.

Blair was also convinced that the connections Levy made for Labour with successful business people were good for his party. He was keen to disclose the names of its new wealthy donors, because such disclosure would challenge the perception of Labour as hostile to wealth creators and wealth creation. Blair also believed – somewhat hubristically, as it turned out – that the Tories had much guiltier secrets when it came to party funding and that it was good party politics to taunt them about their failure to publish the names of donors. But right from the outset there were risks for Blair in preaching transparency for donations. Labour's practices could not be described as saintly, and Blair would be baited by the Tories for years about the anonymity of donors to the blind trust that funded his office in opposition.

At the end of August 1996, Labour published the names of all donors who contributed more than £5,000 to the party during 1995, though it did not reveal the actual amounts given by such 'high value' donors. This was really the end of the ante-Levy era. The annual report to Labour's ruling National Executive Committee showed that just five individuals had given more than £5,000 each. They included the late Paul Hamlyn, the publisher, and Geoffrey Robinson, the Labour MP and former industrialist who would go on to become Paymaster General at the Treasury in Blair's Government. But little more than two months later, Labour was swaggering that it had raised £6m from what it described as 'business' to help fund the looming general election. Donors in 1996 included Matthew Harding, a prominent insurance entrepreneur, who gave £1m. Harding looked like a particularly sexy donor for Labour because he was a bit of a lad and owned 27 per cent of Chelsea Football Club. Only months after making the gift, Harding died in a helicopter accident. Others who donated that year included Greg Dyke – the television executive who was subsequently appointed by Blair's Government as director general of the BBC and then fell out in spectacular fashion with the Prime Minister – and (again) Hamlyn, who gave a further £500,000. Blair also lit the fuse on the petard that would ultimately blow up in his face, when he called for a review by the Committee on Standards in Public Life of how parties are funded.

But while Blair was taking the high moral ground in his public utterances, Levy and Labour's finance director, Blagbrough, were exploiting the existing party-funding rules as effectively as they could. Blair was convinced that there was a strong correlation between campaign spending and election outcomes and he was terrified of being outspent by the Tories. In the event, the 1997 general election cost Labour £13.7m during the weeks of the formal campaign and £26m over three years. Of this, Levy raised just under half, or £12m, according to sources at the time – and he'd already raised £7m for the blind trust that funded Blair's opposition office. Among the individuals in the engine room of the operation which brought New Labour to power in 1997 and sustained it there, Levy was a serious player. In the creation of New Labour, his importance doesn't rank far behind Blair, Brown, Campbell, Mandelson, Powell and Philip Gould (the focus-group guru).

The long-term importance of Levy's expert fund-raising was that it ultimately reinforced the influence of the wealthy over Labour. To be clear, I'm not arguing that there was the crude, systematic sale of individual policies. But much of this book is about how New Labour in Government has never flinched from the view that economic disaster for the UK and electoral disaster for Labour would be inevitable if the super-wealthy ever felt their interests were under attack in the UK. Blair and Brown are true believers in one of the main commandments of the Book of Globalization: 'Thou shalt not be seen to use the tax system to take from the well-heeled, for fear of driving them and all their valuable capital into exile.' Even Brown – who has a much stronger emotional attachment than Blair does to Labour's traditional values – believes that it would be self-defeating to take conspicuously from the haves to help the have-nots. But it's also perfectly natural for Blair and Brown to feel well-disposed towards the plutocratic benefactors who helped to fund their three general election victories. In Brown's case, for example, his instinct as both Chancellor and Prime Minister has been to defend the private-equity industry in the face of growing criticism that it benefited from excessive tax breaks to massively enrich its leading executives, with little tangible benefit for the British economy. It is striking that two of the founders of this industry, Sir Ronnie Cohen and Nigel Doughty, have respectively given £1.8m and just over £1m to Labour over the past few years.

That said, Blair learned early the damage wreaked on his reputation when there was a perception of murky deals being struck. In November 1997, there was a massive media outcry when the journalist Tom Baldwin at the *Sunday Telegraph* disclosed that the Formula 1 motor-racing billionaire Bernie Ecclestone had given £1m to Labour shortly before the young Government decided to exempt F1 from a European Union ban on tobacco advertising in sports. Labour was humiliated and gave the money back to Ecclestone, on advice from Sir Patrick Neill, chairman of the Committee on Standards in Public Life. Shortly afterwards, Levy issued a statement that he'd met Ecclestone to discuss funding and that a cheque had subsequently arrived at Labour's headquarters. But the incident didn't undermine Levy's role and power. Blair could have put in place a new system of funding political parties that reduced their reliance on wealthy individuals. There was much talk of it. But although there were reforms to the system of financing the parties, if anything their dependence on the largesse of the wealthy increased.

From the moment he had the power, Blair gave peerages to a series of individuals who had donated to Labour. These included the printing magnate Bob Gavron, Paul Hamlyn (who died in

2001), the food manufacturer Chris Haskins, the author Ruth Rendell, the businessman Michael Montague (who died in 1999), the broadcaster Melvyn Bragg, the film producer David Puttnam, among others. A couple of very generous business donors, David Sainsbury and Paul Drayson, became lords and ministers in Blair's Government. Other contributors from the business world, such as Christopher Ondaatje, Gulam Noon, Christopher Evans and Ronald Cohen, were knighted. And thus, through media coverage of the awarding of these honours, a connection was established, in the public mind at least, of peerages and knighthoods being linked to financial support for Labour. All the donors believed they had been knighted and ennobled for their services to Labour or to the wider community. And Labour has consistently and vigorously denied that it was in the business of flogging seats in the Upper House or titles of any sort. There may be a statistically significant correlation between donations and honours, but it is plausible that contributing money was just one of the services to Labour performed by those in receipt of honours.

To be clear, this correlation between donations and honours applies just as much to the Tories as to Labour. In fact, Levy always argues that fewer of Blair's peers are significant political donors than recent Tory peers. And what is striking is that the Lords Appointments Commission, which vets nominees for peerages to assess whether they are fit and proper for the Upper House, has signalled unease at the way that Tory peerages have been created. It was uncomfortable about the preponderance of donors on a list of nominees for peerages drawn up by Iain Duncan-Smith shortly before he was replaced as Conservative leader by Michael Howard. The peerages were announced in April 2004. At least three of the new Tory peers – Leonard Steinberg, Stanley Kalms and Irvine Laidlaw – had been very generous donors to the Tories. According to a senior Tory official, the Appointments Commission was so unhappy at what it saw as too close a connection between the nominations and donations that it sent a warning to Michael Howard:

Almost as soon as Michael Howard was elected leader, Douglas Hurd [a former Conservative Foreign Secretary who is on the Lords Appointments Commission] went to see him. He warned Howard to be less blatant about nominating donors for peerages. Three out of Duncan-Smith's five peerages were big donors – and the Commission wanted it to stop. [Interview with Tory official, 26 February 2007]

What's more, Laidlaw, a Scottish tycoon who in 2005 pocketed an estimated £700m after selling a conferences business he created, wasn't even resident in the UK for tax purposes. But, on 2 April 2004, the Commission secured his agreement that he would move back to the UK from Monaco as a condition of becoming a peer. One of the Commission's rules is that peers should pay their taxes here. To demand that legislators should pay their subscription to the British club in this way is no more than common sense. If they didn't pay taxes, what authority would peers (or MPs) have when speaking about public services, for example? Lord Stevenson, chairman of the Commission, is in no doubt that he secured Lord Laidlaw's acquiescence that he would move onshore for tax purposes. A civil servant's note of the 2 April meeting confirms this agreement. Understandably, the Commission then became furious with Laidlaw in 2007 having learned that he had still not become resident in the UK for tax purposes.

Many years earlier, the growing stench surrounding the funding system for parties had already led Blair to legislate in an attempt to clean up the system. In 1999, the Government published a draft Political Parties, Elections and Referendums bill, based on recommendations from the Committee on Standards in Public Life, and passed it into law in 2000. With effect from 30 November 2000, new ceilings were introduced on party spending in elections. There was to be a ban on donations from overseas, which was expected to be damaging for the Conservatives. A new requirement was introduced to publish details of donations greater than £5,000 to party headquarters and more than £1,000 to local accounting units (the constituency organizations). The new system was to be overseen by an Electoral Commission. And there was also a formal obligation imposed on each registered political party for the first time to appoint a registered treasurer, who would take responsibility for submitting annual audited accounts to the Commission. The overall effect was to make it far easier for voters to see how much the parties were spending and who was financing them. However, there was a significant loophole. Parties did not have to disclose loans they had received, as opposed to donations, so long as those loans were made on 'commercial terms'. If parties chose, they could still be funded in a secret way.

Labour initially decided that its commitment to openness in party funding meant that it would not take secret loans from individuals. But there were no such qualms for the Tories. It had been financing itself from loans provided by the wealthy for more than a decade, according to a past treasurer of the Conservatives – who says that after the 1992 general election the party had debts to supporters of £19m. He says some of the loans had a life of up to 25 years. The treasurer's method of ensuring the party did not over-extend itself was to make sure that no more than £7.5m of borrowings was repayable within a year. The ceiling on callable debt was set at that level because he estimated that property owned by Conservative Central Office was worth £8m (though it turned out to be worth about twice that). Further checks on the Tories borrowing too much were that the 16 members of the board of Central Office were personally liable for all the debt, and details of borrowings were known by every board member and other party officers. 'The idea that we'd all be in the poo if the party ran into serious financial difficulties was a powerful discipline,' says a senior Tory.

There was a certain logic to the notion embodied in the new legislation that donations should be disclosed and loans on 'commercial terms' did not need to be (what the Act actually says is that 'any money lent to the party *otherwise* than on commercial terms' has to be disclosed). The logic is that a genuinely commercial loan

doesn't represent special favours or help for a party. It's a service
purchased by the party, like a telephone line or a rented building –
and if parties don't need to disclose who provides their respective
phone services, why should they disclose the providers of a
financial service? There is, however, a problem with this phrase
'commercial terms'. It is intrinsically imprecise and the legislation
makes no attempt to define it. Arguably, no loan to a party can ever
be 'commercial', in that parties are not proper businesses. They
have volatile and variable income of a sort that would normally
prompt banks to run a mile and not extend any credit. As a result,
pretty much any loan to a party represents something of a favour
and ought to be disclosable.

But the Tories took advice from City solicitors that if they
charged their lenders a smidgeon more than the Bank of England's
base lending rate, their loans would count as 'commercial' and
therefore would not have to be published. What's more, a former
Tory treasurer tells me that he and his colleagues routinely
checked with the Electoral Commission that the loans they were
receiving did conform to the spirit of the law when it comes to
disclosure obligations. 'The Commission knew precisely what we
were doing,' he says. The Commission has implied to me that the
Tories have rather overstated their case when claiming that their
borrowing arrangements had received its consent, though it refused to elaborate.

For the Tory lenders, secrecy was apparently hugely important.
Some had confidentiality clauses in lending agreements lasting for
15 years. Within the Tory party, consideration was given to
disclosing the identity of the lenders anyway – when the furore
over borrowing from the wealthy was at its peak in 2006. But the
party's leadership was advised by its treasurer that some lenders
would be furious if their names were made public and it would
become much harder (probably impossible) for the Tories to raise
serious money from the wealthy ever again.

Labour and Levy were aware that the Tories were raising money
in this way. But they decided not to emulate their great rivals
because Blair's rhetoric had been so strongly in favour of trans-

parency in party funding. However, the balance between principle and necessity started to alter as the 2005 general election loomed ever closer. Levy moved into serious fund-raising mode from the summer of 2004 onwards, according to one of Labour's financial backers. The party courted controversy by accepting £505,000 in a donation from Paul Drayson, a healthcare entrepreneur, on 17 June 2004, just six weeks after he had been appointed to the Lords by Blair. Drayson was already a controversial character, having handed Labour £100,000 before his company won a lucrative £32m public-sector contract to provide a smallpox vaccine. Then on 21 December 2004, Drayson made a further £500,000 donation – and in May 2005, he was given a Government job as a junior defence minister.

Drayson was, however, an exceptional character, in that 2004 was something of a barren year for donations from wealthy individuals – even though it was to be the year before a general election. A couple of long-standing City supporters, Sir Ronald Cohen and Derek Tullett, gave £250,000 and £200,000 respectively. A trio of habitual donors from the business world, Sir Sigmund Sternberg, Sir Christopher Ondaatje and William Haughey, provided £101,384, £500,000 and £330,000. There was £50,000 from the gambling magnate Peter Coates and £100,000 from Patrick Stewart, the Hollywood actor. And that was more or less it. Total donations from high-value donors in this crucial period were a miserly £3m – which was little short of a disaster for Labour. The funding drought was easy to explain. Blair's personal popularity had slumped, due mostly to a backlash against his decision to join with the US in invading Iraq. And many potential donors hated the way that the media rounded on those who gave money to both Labour and the Tories. What's more, many of the unions felt estranged from Blair and had become more reluctant to dig deep for the party in its hour of need than would have been the case a decade earlier. Blair was so desperate that he made an accommodation with the unions in what became known as the Warwick Agreement, which provided them with assorted policy promises – such as that Royal Mail would not be privatized.

It looked like a straight deal for cash by a party in dire financial circumstances.

Quite how dire only became apparent after the general election, when Labour published its 2004 accounts. These showed that at the end of December 2004, just four months before the general election, Labour had a deficit on reserves of £6.4m and an £11m excess of current liabilities over current assets. This deficit also took no account of a £5.2m hole in its pension scheme. Had it been a normal company faced with the huge financial demands of a looming general election, it would probably have been filing for bankruptcy protection. Blair was becoming frantic about the risk of Labour being significantly outspent by the Tories, who were enjoying a modest revival in their popularity under Michael Howard. No thought was given to finding other ways to promote Labour's cause than spending the normal fortune on advertising, no imagination was shown about how to reduce election expenditure to a level that would be affordable. Blair's belief was that it was spend or bust. So Levy, ever the optimist, continued to try to tap more or less anyone who had shown themselves willing to help in the past.

One wealthy individual with a history of support for Labour was Sir Christopher Evans, a flamboyant biotech entrepreneur whose father had been a steelworker in the South Wales town of Port Talbot. Out of swish offices in London's St James's – all deep carpet and glass walls – he has raised €2.5bn (£1.8bn) for between 30 and 35 companies in just the past two years. And companies he is funding currently have 85 medicines undergoing clinical tests on humans. He was a natural lifelong Labour supporter, who had been making relatively modest contributions to the party, of between £5,000 and £25,000, for a decade or so. Evans had been making his donations before he met Levy, and had no desire to pay any more, because – in words he uses of himself – he's a 'tight-fisted Port Talbot boy'. But he got to know Levy in the 1990s, came across him a fair amount at assorted functions, and got on with him well. They're both garrulous and have a tendency to show off. Their similarities are such that they would either have hit it off, or annoyed each other. As it turned out, they warmed to one another.

On one occasion, thought by Evans to have taken place at the beginning of 2000, they chatted at a do in front of other people about Evans's longer-term ambitions. Levy said to Evans that a successful businessman like him should have a knighthood or a peerage. But Evans – who years earlier had been given an OBE for services to biotechnology by the then Tory Government – thought he didn't have the time just at that moment to serve as a working peer. However, after the meeting he made a note of their chat, which is his habitual way of remembering things: he makes thousands of such notes and lists, as a memory jogger. His shorthand was to refer to a 'K' and a 'P', to stand for a knighthood and a peerage. More than six years later, the Metropolitan Police would get hold of this note and attach significance to it, in their investigation of whether Levy had in fact been in the business of selling honours. But Evans insists it was an innocent conversation, detached from any chat about donations. It turned out that Levy had been prescient: Evans was awarded a knighthood in the New Year Honours list announced on 31 December 2000, a list which also saw a knighthood going to a more generous Labour donor, Ronald Cohen.

In subsequent years, Evans had other conversations with senior Labour figures, including Levy, about whether he wanted to work for Labour as a peer in the Lords and whether he would be interested in being a minister. The idea that he might replace David Sainsbury as Science Minister was floated several times, by Levy and others. In 2004, Evans recalls having a tantalizing conversation with the then Chancellor, Gordon Brown, after he had given a talk at a meeting of the Smith Institute, a think tank which has close links to Brown. After having requested a private tête-à-tête with Evans, Brown said to him, 'You know, you are really well thought of round here.' Evans concluded that a role in Government might be his, if that's what he desired.

In the words of a businessman, Levy started to put serious pressure on 'his people' for desperately needed cash from the summer of 2004 onwards. Levy told Evans that the 'small change' he had given Labour in the past wouldn't be enough this time. The party needed 'a big one'. But Evans was unpersuadable, and told him he never had and never would give a mega-donation. However, towards the end of the year, Evans put a proposition to Levy: he said that if Labour's cash-flow crisis was so severe, he could have a £1m loan. Evans was adamant that he wanted the money back, it would not be a gift. I'm told Levy was not happy about this, presumably because at this juncture Labour was still opposed to taking loans. Levy has said to me that his personal position was that Labour should not take loans. It would certainly look odd for Labour to take secret loans from supporters after all its years of attacking the Tories for the secrecy of their funding arrangements.

The decision on whether to take loans was so momentous that it could only be taken by the Prime Minister. Blair gave his authorization. But although Levy agreed to take Evans's loan, the biotech entrepreneur did not hand it over immediately. He had been told that Labour's cash-flow need would be greatest after the election, so Evans did not provide the £1m until 31 May 2005. The interest rate was 6.75 per cent and the agreed duration of the loan was a year.

Levy now had a new method of raising cash, through loans. And in April, with just weeks to go before the general election, he set about persuading other friends of the party to follow Evans's example. One person he telephoned was one of the founders of the supermarket ready-meals industry, the Curry King, Sir Gulam Noon.

Noon is a remarkable example of intrepid entrepreneurialism. He grew up in Mumbai where he lived, slept and ate with his mother and siblings in a single room smaller than his current office. The tragedy of his life, which he still feels acutely, was the death of his older brother and his father within six months of each other in 1946, when he was six. The dates are noted in a little pocket book he carries around with him. After leaving school, he turned a single shop into a sweets business, Royal Sweets – and then came to the UK in 1971 at the age of 35, to expand the Indian sweets operation. From one shop in Southall in the far west of London, he set about supplying a big new market created by the arrival of thousands of Indian immigrants from east Africa. One of his claims to greatness is that he more or less invented one of the towering staples of British snacks: Bombay Mix. Then, in the 1980s, he set about transforming Britain's ready-made Indian food business – by lobbying Unilever to buy frozen curries from him before he even had a proper factory. It paid off and he subsequently did as much as anyone to add variety to the British diet. These days, his chilled, prepared Indian meals are a fixture in almost every supermarket.

He's had his share of setbacks. A fire in 1994 destroyed his main factory, almost putting him out of business. But he refused to sack the 250 workers and with help from friends was back cooking meals by the thousand remarkably quickly. His latest factory, also in Southall, amazed me when I visited it. The giant, industrial-size kitchen cooks traditional Indian dishes in the proper way, albeit the quantities are enough to feed an army. And hygiene standards would put a typical hospital to shame. The sheer number of meals loaded on to supermarket trucks – not just Indian food, but Moroccan, Mexican, French – is mind-boggling (around 120,000 meals go every day just to J Sainsbury). Something like a ton of garlic and chilli per day is consumed by Noon Products. Noon has bought and sold Noon Products a couple of times (it is now part of Ireland's Kerry Foods) and he personally is probably worth more than £50m. He retains a business supplying food to airlines and the original sweets operation.

A Moslem, he showed gumption after the London bombings of 7 July 2005 by attacking those who preach 'sedition and treason' in mosques. His passion is cricket and his main office in Westminster is filled with cricket bats. The walls of that office and one in Southall are covered with photographs of him standing next to Tony Blair, Gordon Brown and assorted notables. Noon became close to Blair when as an entrepreneur he raised concerns after Labour's landslide in 1997 that a new limit on working hours, which Labour had said it would introduce, could damage a business like his. Blair asked to see him because it was plainly not helpful to the Government to be attacked by someone who had created a significant number of jobs. Noon was impressed that Blair wanted to consult him on this, the implementation in Britain of the European Union's Working Time Directive. He dropped his allegiance to the Liberal Democrats and switched to Labour. In 1998, he gave Labour £25,000, followed by £100,000 in 1999, and two gifts of £50,000 in June 2001. A year later, on 15 June 2002, it was announced that he had been awarded a knighthood in the Queen's Jubilee Birthday Honours list. And on 3 December that year, he gave a further £100,000.

So for Levy, Noon had an encouraging history of supporting Labour with his wallet. Which is why, with the 2005 general election just days away, Levy rang him and said he wanted them to meet. Noon agreed to go Levy's house in Mill Hill, which he did a couple of days later. Alone, Levy said that Labour was short of money to fight the election. Noon said he was prepared to give between £30,000 and £50,000. But Levy then said, 'Not a donation, a loan,' and asked for £1m. Noon said that was too much and offered £200,000. They settled on £250,000. A couple of days later, on 20 April, Matt Carter, who was then Labour's general secretary, wrote Noon a letter, which was the loan agreement. Carter was also Labour's registered treasurer, or the individual responsible for ensuring that Labour's accounts were filed to the Electoral Commission on time and that these accounts gave a true and fair view of its state of health and activities (Carter these days runs the London office of Penn, Schoen & Berland Associates, the US political and corporate strategy group brought in by Blair to help run the 2005 general election campaign).

The letter from Carter to Noon described Noon as having made a 'kind offer to provide the Party with an unsecured loan to help finance the forthcoming General Election'. It said Noon was to provide £250,000 in a single advance, payable by 30 April 2005, and the initial duration of the loan was to be just 180 days. The interest rate would be '6.75 per cent per annum for the initial term, being equivalent to the current Bank of England base rate plus 2 per cent'. If the loan were to be rolled over the rate would continue to be the Bank's base rate plus 2 per cent – and interest would be payable on the last business day of the initial term of the loan, and subsequently every 180 days till repaid.

Here was the clause in the loan that was subsequently to cause Noon, Labour and Levy considerable grief:

> The agreed interest rate is broadly equivalent to the Party's normal cost of funds and therefore can be considered as a commercial rate of interest. Accordingly, the loan will not give rise to any reportable donation within the meaning of the Political Parties, Elections and Referendums Act 2000. [Letter from Matt Carter to Sir Gulam Noon, dated 20 April 2005]

In other words, Carter was explicitly saying that the loan could be kept secret because in his view this loan had been made on commercial terms. That said, the letter was explicit about how valuable the finance was. Carter concluded by saying: 'Finally, may I take this opportunity to thank you on behalf of the Party for your valuable support.'

Levy was at the same time extracting loans – rather bigger ones – from two other wealthy business people. One was Barry Townsley, a stockbroker, who had made donations to Labour of around £500,000 prior to 2001, which is when the law requiring disclosure of substantial donations came into effect. This is the account of how he came to make his loan, which is contained in a letter he wrote to the Commons Public Administration Committee on 21 March 2006:

> Shortly before the May 2005 General Election, I was informed by the Labour Party that it urgently needed to raise money in order to mount its campaign. After having discussed this with Lord Levy, who I knew not only as a leading Labour fund-raiser but also in other charitable contexts, I agreed to make a loan of £1m.
>
> Thereafter, I signed a loan agreement which took the form of a

letter dated 13 April from Matt Carter, then General Secretary of the Labour Party. The loan was on commercial terms. The payment was effected by transfer from my bank to the Labour Party current account on 25 April 2005.

I believe the loan was not a reportable donation for the purposes of the Political Parties, Elections and Referendums Act 2000. The letter of agreement makes this point . . . There was no agreement or discussion of any kind whatsoever that I would or might be 'rewarded' with any honour. I was willing to make the loan because I was and continue to be a Labour supporter. [Letter from Barry Townsley to the Public Administration Committee, dated 21 March 2006]

Townsley has also been a great supporter of city academies. He has pledged £2m for the Stockley Academy in Hillingdon, London. The honorary president of the Specialist Schools and Academies Trust, a body which helps to raise funds for city academies and provides other support to academies and specialist schools, is Lord Levy. Townsley received a CBE in the New Year Honours list of 2004, which was announced on 31 December 2003, for 'charitable services, especially to education and to arts'.

Levy approached two other businessmen for loans in April 2005. One was Gordon Crawford, a computer software entrepreneur who pocketed just under £75m in 2004 when his firm, London Bridge Software, was bought by a US rival, Fair Isaac. On 13 April, he lent £500,000 at an interest rate of 6.75 per cent. The other was the property tycoon Sir David Garrard, who is also a generous backer of a city academy. Garrard had contributed £2.4m to the Bexley Business Academy in south-east London. On 31 December 2002 – not long after Garrard had opened the £20m school – it was announced in the New Year Honours that he was being knighted 'for charitable services'.

Garrard, the chairman of a stock-market-quoted property company, Minerva, was a passionate fan of Margaret Thatcher and for years he had been a Tory supporter. In the 1980s and 1990s, he gave irregular donations to the Tories of between £5,000 and £10,000, before providing the Conservatives with £70,000 in the run-up to the 1997 election (or so the *Mail on Sunday* reported in May 2006 as part of the only substantial interview Garrard has given about how he came to give a loan to Labour). It was his interest in city academies that established links with Downing Street and in 2002 he attended one of Levy's private dinners, where Mr and Mrs Blair were the star attractions. Garrard became increasingly impressed with Blair, largely because he was a strong supporter of the decision to go to war against Saddam. So on 23 May 2003, he gave a £200,000 gift to the Labour Party. This is what he told the *Mail on Sunday* was his reason for making the donation:

> I was in Israel during the first Gulf war with the Scuds raining down and the gas masks. We were disappointed that the coalition alliance did not then take out Saddam Hussein. When Blair determined to join America in the second Gulf war, he was doing absolutely the right thing.

A second invitation to dine with the Blairs at Levy's home followed in 2004. And then in April 2005, Levy asked Garrard for help with Labour's general election campaign. According to the *Mail on Sunday*, Garrard was only prepared to give £20,000 or £30,000. Levy then asked him for a loan. Garrard couldn't pretend he was short of a bob or two, since he had just cashed in his £40m stake in Minerva (he's said by the *Sunday Times* to be worth £105m in total). So he offered to lend £2m and eventually had his arm twisted by Levy to lend a total of £2.3m. Garrard said in this interview – and his spokesman, Lord Bell, has consistently made the same point – that the loan was not intended as support for Labour as a party, but rather it was intended to be helpful to Blair personally. He wanted Blair kept in office so that momentum could be maintained behind the development of city academies. This question of whether Garrard was a Labour supporter was to become resonant.

Garrard made his loan on 19 April. The previous day, Lord Sainsbury – the billionaire former chairman of J Sainsbury, and a long-standing member of Blair's Government as Science Minister – lent £2m to Labour, having already given the party an identical sum in March. In fact, Sainsbury's gifts to Labour in aggregate are thought to have totalled around £17m during the previous decade (it's difficult to be more precise because some of his gifts preceded the legislation that requires disclosure of large party donations). Sainsbury was certainly more important to Labour's financial health than any individual and has probably been a more generous and reliable donor than any single trade union.

Labour made effective use of Sainsbury's, Garrard's, Noon's and Townsley's loans and won its third successive general election victory. However, its share of the vote fell and its majority in the Commons was cut to 66. The victory had also come at quite a price. It spent £17.93m on the campaign – just a whisker below the maximum permitted, and about £90,000 more than the Tories. This was greater than it could afford, so Levy had to press on with seeking funds. Initially, he didn't go far from those who had already lent: on 18 May, he received a £1m loan from Andrew Rosenfeld, Sir David Garrard's business partner, who had co-founded Minerva with Garrard and is estimated to be worth £80m by the *Sunday Times*. Since June of the previous year, Rosenfeld had been a trustee of Jewish Care, the Jewish social-care charity for which Levy had raised a fortune over many years. Levy is president of Jewish Care, though served in an *ex officio* capacity from 23 June 2004. Another intriguing link with other Labour lenders is that in 2005 Rosenfeld also became a backer of a city academy to be built in Wembley in the London Borough of Brent. On 15 November 2005, Brent announced that Rosenfeld had pledged £2m towards the capital costs of the proposed academy.

Levy was accumulating very substantial debts for the Labour Party. In theory, the Labour Party would have had to repay them over the course of the next year: its 2005 accounts say that all these initial loans were repayable either after 180 days or after 365 days.

But where would the cash come from to make these repayments? It's always harder to raise money after a general election. But this time it would be harder than ever: membership of the Labour Party was in steep long-term decline and the trade unions were neither flush with cash nor particularly enthusiastic to help a Prime Minister who always made it clear that he didn't like them much. Which is why what Levy did next seems particularly strange.

In July, Levy was trying to arrange a financial contribution from Chai Patel, a healthcare entrepreneur who at the time was chief executive of the Priory Group, owner of mental-health hospitals and clinics that are famous as refuges for tired and emotional celebrities. Patel was a well-known business supporter of Labour. He had given formal and informal advice to Labour ministers over many years on health policy and is an enthusiastic proponent of the increasing use of private services by the NHS. Patel has told me on a number of occasions that he was happy to give Labour a very substantial donation, of £1.5m. And he made this clear to Levy. But what surprised him was that Levy didn't want the donation, he wanted a loan. Patel says that it took him literally seconds to conclude that a loan was preferable, in that he might have got his money back with interest – although he never banked on getting his money back. In fact, Patel has described the loan to me as a 'soft loan', one that would probably never be repaid and would therefore be converted into a donation at some point in the future. But although it might have turned into a gift one day, for the Labour Party, when it received the £1.5m in August, it was a genuine and substantial liability, which in theory had to be repaid. So what advantage was there for Labour in a loan rather than a donation? Well, a loan, of course, could be kept secret, whereas a £1.5m donation would have been disclosed. Patel says he wasn't bothered one way or another whether his Labour contribution was made public or not. After all there was no great secret about his support for Labour. So the secrecy attaching to a loan as opposed to a donation appears to have been for the benefit of the party.

The narrative of Labour's fund-raising in 2005 is – so far – a story about Michael Levy's remarkable ability to raise money from a circle of contacts. It is a slightly puzzling story, in that Michael Levy had been a successful businessman and would therefore have been acutely aware of the financial risks being taken on by Labour with all these loans. What is also striking is not just the size of the sums these wealthy individuals loaned to Labour, but also that Townsley, Garrard and Rosenfeld are supporters of city academies and they also have charitable interests in common with Levy. What gave greater resonance to this fund-raising was that most of these lenders were about to find themselves nominated by the Prime Minister for peerages. In early October, Townsley, Garrard, Noon and Patel were all contacted by Ruth Turner, director of Government Relations who was based in 10 Downing Street, and were told that Tony Blair wanted them in the House of Lords.

Evans did not receive such a call. However, he was informed by the police that he too was on an internal Downing Street list of individuals being considered for a place in the Upper House – though Evans says he was never notified by any Government official that he was being put forward for ennoblement. Apart from anything else, it would not have been an ideal moment for Evans to be nominated. On 26 September 2005, following weeks of rumours, Merlin Biosciences, the biotech venture-capital firm founded and run by Evans, confirmed that it was being investigated by the Serious Fraud Office (SFO). The SFO was reportedly examining a complaint from Andrew Greene, a former banker who became Merlin's managing director for 18 months in 2002, about a £2.5m investment made by a Merlin fund (Evans denies any wrongdoing).

Other wealthy individuals, Derek Tullett, Rod Aldridge and Nigel Morris, would shortly also lend money to Labour. The earliest of these loans, £400,000 from Derek Tullett, was agreed on 5 September and paid at the end of that month. Tullett, who built an international financial brokerage firm that is now part of Tullett Prebon, the substantial City firm, has been a generous Labour donor for many years. He donated £900,000 between

March 2002 and October 2005. Then on 25 September 2005, Nigel Morris agreed to advance £1m. Morris had accumulated a fortune estimated at £300m as a former senior executive of the US credit card business, Capital One. As for Rod Aldridge, he was well known to Labour ministers and officials as the founder and chairman of Capita, the out-sourcing business which does a huge amount of work for the public sector. On 4 October 2005, Aldridge lent Labour £1m. Because of Capita's commercial relationship with central and local government, there was a stink when his loan was disclosed in March 2006, and he quit as chairman of Capita. However, he insisted that his decision to lend to Labour was 'entirely my own . . . made in good faith as a long-standing supporter of the party'. And he added that allegations that the loan had 'resulted in the Group being awarded Government contracts' were 'entirely spurious'. Since then, he has concentrated on charitable projects aimed at helping disadvantaged young people, and on pursuing public-sector reform, which is one of his great passions. Like Garrard, Rosenfeld and Townsley, he has also pledged substantial funds – through his foundation – for a city academy. As long ago as 2004, he promised £2m for a £34m academy in the Lancashire borough of Blackburn with Darwen.

Here is a striking fact: according to an official, Tullett, Aldridge and Morris were on an internal Downing Street list of possible peers, along with Garrard, Townsley, Noon and Evans. In other words, there is a striking correlation between those who gave loans and those who were either nominated for a peerage or considered for one (although, to be clear, there is no suggestion any of the lenders asked for a peerage, or that they even knew they were on this list). There were three names from the initial lenders not on the Number 10 list for possible peerages: Sainsbury, Rosenfeld and Crawford. But they would have been unlikely candidates for a variety of reasons. Sainsbury was already in the House of Lords. Rosenfeld was Garrard's business partner and it would have looked odd if they had been nominated at the same time. And Gordon Crawford lives in Monaco.

Labour was to receive one more substantial loan from a business supporter. In early 2006, Richard Caring lent £2m. Caring is an immensely wealthy supplier of clothing to major retailers, and has more recently become a leading restaurateur as owner of several fashionable London restaurants, including the Ivy and the Caprice. One of his oldest and closest friends is the billionaire Sir Philip Green, and it is intriguing that he has not shared Green's wariness of party politics.

Those who made it on to the final peerage nomination list – Noon, Patel, Garrard and Townsley – were told on 4 October 2005 of the honour they were to receive. When Ruth Turner rang Sir Gulam Noon that morning to give him the news that the Prime Minister wanted him to sit on Labour's benches in the Lords, Noon was surprised, delighted and excited. He enthusiastically said he would be pleased to accept the offer. Soon after, the relevant forms to be filled in and forwarded to the House of Lords Appointments Commission were faxed to him in his elegant Westminster office, which is on the ground floor of a Georgian townhouse on the south side of St James's Palace.

Since 2000, all nominees for the House of Lords have been vetted by the Lords Appointments Commission. It was set up by Tony Blair to increase confidence in the system of creating peers and is chaired by the distinguished businessman Lord Stevenson, who is also chairman of the leading bank HBOS, and governor of the Bank of Scotland. The Commission has two distinct roles. It selects and nominates to the Queen non-party-political peers, or those thought worthy to be lords because of their expertise or history of service to the community. Its second role is scrutinizing the nominees of party leaders. Here is Lord Stevenson's account, given to the Commons Public Administration Committee, of the Commission's fairly limited evaluation of these political appointees:

> We are vetting them for propriety; we are not playing a part in the selection . . . We need to satisfy ourselves that a given nominee is of good standing in the community, both in general

and with regard to the regulatory agencies in our society. Second, we want to satisfy ourselves that a given nominee is credible. Again, credibility is a matter of judgement, and these are judgements. The broad test we work to is to convince ourselves that a given nominee will not diminish, demean, but will enhance the House of Lords and its workings and the workings of the honours system.

With donors who are nominees for party-political peerages, we also address the question of whether that person would be a credible nominee if he or she had not made a donation or a loan . . .

Our process starts with a bundle of papers from Number 10 and ends when we advise the Prime Minister. So we receive a list from the Prime Minister, coordinated through the parties, and for each nominee we have . . . a declaration and consent form signed by each nominee covering quite a lot of subjects which are all set out in the documents, a citation from the party explaining why the nominee is being put forward, and a certificate from the party chairman which sets out the details of any donations, links to the party, etc. They are all set out.

We then carry out whatever checks we judge are necessary along the lines that are indicated in the papers, we collate our findings, and we sit and talk about nominees. We will go back and make further checks, follow particular questions if it is necessary. We will then form our opinions, and we will give our advice to the Prime Minister. And I think it is important to stress, because it is something of which there has been a certain amount of understandable public misunderstanding, we do not have a right of veto. We give the Prime Minister advice, and he is the final decision-taker. [Lord Stevenson to Public Administration Committee, 16 May 2006]

All nominees have to complete and sign a form for the Commission on their financial interests. At the top of this form, it states: 'I am resident in the United Kingdom and intend to remain so. I am also resident for tax purposes.' As it happens, Sir David

Garrard and his wife were in the throes of becoming tax exiles in Switzerland, basing themselves in a suite at the Mandarin Oriental in Geneva. But after the offer of the peerage was made, he proposed to resume paying UK tax. Patel too is not domiciled in the UK for tax purposes and, like Garrard, would probably have had to become a conventional UK taxpayer in order to take up a seat in the Lords – though in the end he didn't need to, because the Commission recommended against him becoming a peer for another reason. Each nominee also has to disclose 'donations to a political party which are declarable to the Electoral Commission or would have been if it had been in existence'.

On receipt of this form, Noon passed it to his accountant and told him to list all his contributions to the Labour Party, for forwarding to Downing Street, which was supposed to then send it to the Appointments Commission. The accountant listed £220,250 of donations made by Noon since May 2001. And he also put the £250,000 loan on the form, because it never occurred to either Noon or his accountant that he shouldn't disclose it. Before that same morning of 4 October was over, Noon had the completed forms walked around to Richard Roscoe, an official in charge of coordinating the honours process at 10 Downing Street, which is ten minutes on foot from Noon's office. Roscoe described his role to Noon as a sort of postbox, since he simply collected the forms and then gave them to the Commission.

It was, for Noon, a great moment, the kind of recognition from the British establishment that he never dreamed would be his. But the following morning, around 11, he had a surprise: Lord Levy telephoned him on his mobile phone. It was unusual for Levy to ring him, because they are not 'bum chums', in Noon's words. They hadn't spoken on the phone for months, according to Noon. The Indian businessman was keen to share his joy and blurted out that he was to become a lord. Levy then said that he hoped that Noon had not disclosed the £250,000 loan on the form for the Commission, because there was no reason to do so. Noon regards it as odd both that Levy should have phoned him then and that he should have pointedly advised him not to disclose the loan. Anyway, following the conversation Noon feared he had done something wrong by supplying details of his loan to the Commission. And in something of a panic he rang Richard Roscoe at 10 Downing Street to find out if he still had the papers. Roscoe hadn't yet given them to the Commission. So Noon asked him to throw away the version in his possession, and wait for an amended one to arrive. Noon then re-sent the relevant document, this time excluding mention of the loan – which is an action he now bitterly regrets.

On the face of it, Levy was going to considerable lengths to keep the loan secret. He, however, disputes that he rang Noon, claiming that Noon telephoned him. Noon has checked all his phone records and can find no trace of having placed a call to Levy. He gave all his phone numbers to the police, so that they could independently check who rang whom.

By contrast with Noon, Chai Patel was simply unsure whether to disclose the loan to the Appointments Commission. He is clear that he rang Levy to ask his advice. In a way, that's a slightly odd thing to do, because Levy has no formal role in the creation of peerages. However, Patel's explanation is that he knew Levy and he didn't really know anyone else with the relevant knowledge. Levy didn't answer immediately and went off to take advice in 10 Downing Street. He then rang Patel back and told him not to disclose the loan.

As for the Appointments Commission itself, one of its senior members has told me that Noon's initial instincts were correct, that the Commission would have regarded information about the loans as highly relevant to its deliberations. There's no doubt that the loans were helpful to Labour in its hour of need. And this Commission member says that some nominees have in the past disclosed party loans. But he also concedes that the advice the Commission gave to nominees on its forms and on its website perhaps did not make that clear enough. So it is not the case that Noon, Patel and the others were conspicuously breaching the rules by withholding the information. What is relevant, however, is that

Levy should have taken pains to prevent the Commission from knowing about the loans.

There is a related question about whether the loans really were made on 'commercial terms' and were therefore not disclosable according to the 2000 Political Parties, Elections and Referendums Act. Both Labour and the Tories were advised by lawyers that the kind of interest rates they were charging were 'commercial' in the relevant sense. But there is a further common-sense test. Could Labour have borrowed all those millions at those rates – or at all – from conventional banks or other financial institutions? The answer is no, since Labour didn't and doesn't have the income to make the relevant repayments in a comfortable and orderly way. So in a basic sense these were not loans made to Labour on 'commercial terms' in the way that most of us would understand. Apart from anything else, Levy only sought to borrow from these wealthy individuals after banks refused to extend it sufficient further credit. What is more, the interest on many of the loans was not paid by Labour but was simply rolled into the principal, for repayment if the loan was ever paid off – which was also jolly helpful for a party with a cash-flow shortage.

Anyway, when the completed forms were passed to the Commission, it took a very unusual step: it judged that three of the lenders, Garrard, Townsley and Patel, were unfit to be peers. Here's what I see as highly significant: it assessed them as unsuitable without even knowing about the loans. What disqualified them, for the Commission, were other facts about their respective careers and activities.

Patel was rejected because of a stink about the management of a care home in Twickenham, Lynde House, which was Patel's responsibility when he ran Westminster Healthcare from 1999 to 2002. There was a very effective campaign by friends and relatives of Lynde House's residents to highlight what they perceived as negligent treatment of the elderly people in the home. An independent review of conditions in Lynde House was damaging to Patel and Westminster Healthcare. Patel believes that many of the allegations were exaggerated and based on hearsay. He also points out that Westminster Healthcare operated 140 facilities in 92 locations, that there were next-to-no complaints about other homes, and that he takes his duty of care to residents and patients extremely seriously. But the mud stuck – and what galls Patel is that he had no opportunity to discuss the charges against him with the Commission. However, a Commission member points out that it isn't a court. It is not in the business of trying nominees for the Lords, merely in assessing whether the presence in the Lords of an individual would enhance or diminish the reputation of the Upper House. And it was persuaded that the passions about what went wrong at Lynde House were held so strongly and sincerely by campaigners that they could not be ignored.

Garrard too was given the thumbs down because of perceptions of his behaviour, in his case over the fate of a pension fund. In February 2003, the property business he founded with Andrew Rosenfeld, Minerva, took a 60 per cent stake in a company, Scarlett Retail, which in turn controlled Allders, the department-store group. Minerva's motivation, according to its 2004 annual report, was 'to secure the key land holding [in Croydon] that was represented by the existing Allders store which we have now therefore successfully completed'. Or to put it another way, Minerva gained control of Allders' plum asset, which it needed because of its ambitious plans for a massive retail development in Croydon, called Park Place. But Allders itself, which employed 7,000 people in 44 stores, was in a mess – and the management of Scarlett could do nothing to reverse it. Allders went into administration under bankruptcy procedures in January 2005, prompting particularly acute anxiety for the 3,500 members of Allders' pension fund who learned that there was a £70m hole in the fund. Minerva argued it had no responsibility to make good the deficit in the fund, because it was not involved in the actual running of Allders, having left that to the management of Scarlett Retail. But Allders' bruised employees and media commentators took a different view. Patience Wheatcroft, who was then business editor of *The Times*, wrote:

Minerva will contend that they are not asset strippers and independent advisers set a fair value for the Croydon store. But there is a moral issue. The prospectus for Bexley's Business Academy, whose sponsor is Minerva chairman Sir David Garrard, spells out how lessons include 'ethically difficult decisions people are faced with in the world today'. Whether to ditch the pensioners in search of profit should not be a tough one to answer.

Minerva's behaviour was examined by the Pension Regulator, which in March 2006 cleared it of any liability for Allders' pension fund. But the Lords Appointments Commission sided with Wheatcroft. Its members took the view that Garrard's behaviour in deserting the members of the pension fund was not appropriate for a member of the House of Lords.

As for Townsley, it was his fairly distant past that did for him. Townsley is well connected and widely liked in business circles. In fact, the chairman of the Appointments Commission, Stevenson, counts him as a friend, and therefore stood to one side when his nomination was examined. But the other members of the Commission decided that he was unfit to be a lord because he had been seriously rebuked by the Stock Exchange in the early 1980s (he and a business partner were found guilty of 'gross misconduct' for the way their firm dealt with a notorious fund manager who was enriching himself at the expense of clients). There was a separate problem for Townsley, which was that a company to which he had been an adviser, Langbar, was being investigated by the Serious Fraud Office – and Townsley was damaged by association, even if there was no implication that he had done anything wrong in the Langbar case.

To be clear, it was not difficult for the Commission to determine that Townsley, Garrard and Patel were not appropriate candidates for the Upper House. There had been negative media reports about the contentious aspects of their careers. In fact, what astonished Commission members was that Downing Street officials had not apparently carried out even a cursory check on them before putting their names forward: 'It would have taken an official ten minutes using Google to work out they weren't right for the Lords,' says a member of the Appointments Commission.

Once again, elementary statistical analysis is damning for Blair as the individual who had total personal responsibility for creating Labour's peers, subject to the advice of the Commission. Based purely on their personal histories and with no knowledge of their loans to Labour, the Commission deemed that three out of the four Labour lenders were unsuitable to be peers. It is highly relevant that Blair nominated seven other individuals to be peers at precisely the same time, none of whom had a financial relationship with his party. They were Colin Boyd (Lord Advocate of Scotland), Keith Bradley (a former Labour minister), Margaret Ford (chair of English Partnerships), Maggie Jones (a trade unionist from Unison), Denise Kingsmill (a former solicitor and regulator), Bill Morris (the former union leader) and Joyce Quin (another erstwhile minister). The Commission advised that they were all suitable. So the question for Blair is whether the financial help given by the four lenders had made him and his officials less scrupulous and meticulous in assessing their suitability to be lords than would normally have been the case. Or, to put it in cruder terms, were the loans at least a part of the entry price for the House of Lords?

However, it was not just Labour's choice of peer that was denigrated by the Commission. A Tory nominee, Robert Edmiston, was also deemed unfit to be a peer by the Commission after it became aware that the Inland Revenue was carrying out a major investigation of his tax affairs (which has subsequently been satisfactorily settled by Edmiston). He is a multi-millionaire who made a fortune as an importer of cars manufactured in the Far East and is one of the UK's most generous charitable donors. Edmiston also chairs the Midlands Industrial Council which gives the Tories a six-figure donation each year. And he is a personal donor to the party: he donated £250,000 to the Conservatives on 10 September 2004. But here is the striking thing: he lent £2m to the Tories through his private company, IM Group (it was converted into a donation in early 2006). In a statement on 31 March 2006, the Conservatives said that Edmiston's loan had been notified to the House of Lords Appointments Commission, though they did not specify whether they had done this before or after there was a public furore over loans to parties.

The Commission's deliberations were rather more exposed to external scrutiny on this occasion than is normally the case. Typically, there is complete secrecy about who has been nominated for a peerage – and therefore the Commission can rule a nominee as fit and proper or not without fear of embarrassing the nominee. But on this occasion, there was a breach of the normal rules of confidentiality. Literally within days of the Commission receiving the list of Blair's choices for the Lords, there was a disclosure in the *Independent on Sunday* of 23 October 2005 that Chai Patel, Gulam Noon, David Garrard and Barry Townsley had all been recommended for peerages. The report by the *IoS*'s political editor, Marie Woolf, did not mention they had made loans to Labour. It simply stated that their nominations would be controversial because of their history of donating to Labour and – in the case of Townsley and Garrard – of donating to city academies. Another leak took place on 11 November 2005. The entire list of nominees being considered by the Commission – including Tories, Liberal Democrats and Northern Ireland's Democratic Unionist Party – was published by *The Times*.

The Prime Minister was in a hugely embarrassing position. His selection for the Lords was now in the public domain. So if he accepted the Commission's advice that Garrard, Patel and Townsley were inappropriate choices, he would have been humiliated. It took months for this issue to be settled. In the meantime, the nominees were becoming restless and irked by all the media attention.

Eventually, Townsley decided to take the initiative. On 10 February 2006, he wrote to Blair saying he no longer wanted to be a peer and was withdrawing from the list. And less than a month later, on 5 March, the *Sunday Times* disclosed that the Commission had recommended to Blair that Townsley, Garrard and Patel were all unsuitable.

Shortly afterwards, rumours started to circulate about the loans to Labour. On 9 March, *The Times* suggested Garrard may have made a loan to Labour. There was near hysteria in the media, to which the then Lord Chancellor, Lord Falconer – who at the time was the oldest and closest of Blair's friends still in the Government – responded on BBC Radio 4 on 10 March. He was asked about the links between donations and honours. 'I don't take the view that making a contribution to a political party in which you believe debars you from any honour,' he said. 'If you accept that, then what you need is some body to ensure that there is propriety in the honour or the appointment to the Lords. But you should not be prevented because you, for example, believe that Labour should have been supported over the years it was in the wilderness. That should not debar you in any way at all from being a peer. You have a choice. You either say people who give money to political parties can't get an honour and I don't think that would be right or sensible.' Challenged over a report in the *Sunday Times* that claimed (not quite accurately) that every donor who had given more than £1m to Labour had received either a knighthood or a peerage, Lord Falconer insisted that did not mean people could buy peerages. 'Absolutely not, no. You are not guaranteed a peerage,' he said.

But rumour about Labour's fund-raising was turning into embarrassing fact. On 12 March, the *Sunday Times* said there were £10m of secret loans to Labour, which prompted the Public Administration Committee of the House of Commons to announce on 14 March that it would probe lending to parties and the awarding of peerages. The following day, Garrard withdrew his acceptance of a nomination for a peerage. A spokesman said Garrard had been told that he had been nominated for his 'lifelong commitment' to child welfare and education and his support for the city academies programme. According to Lord Bell, Garrard's public-relations adviser, Garrard sincerely believed they were the reasons his name had been put forward for a peerage. And Bell reiterated that Garrard had always thought of himself as a Blair supporter rather than a Labour supporter. Which is why, months later, he was shocked when he heard that in response to questioning by the police on 14 December 2006, Blair had given a different account of why he had nominated the individuals for peerages. Blair's account was given by the official spokesman for the Prime Minister in a briefing to political journalists. The official spokesman said:

> The Prime Minister explained why he nominated each individual. He did so as party leader in respect of those peerages reserved for party supporters, as other party leaders do. The nominations were therefore not honours for public service but expressly given for party service. In those circumstances, the fact that they had supported the party financially could not conceivably be a barrier to their nomination. [Prime Minister's official spokesman, 14 December 2006]

However, this explanation given by Blair to the police begged a really important question. Precisely what were the important party services provided by any of the nominees, other than giving and lending money? Patel had given formal and informal advice to ministers on health policy. And Noon, Patel and Townsley had all been Labour supporters for a while. But that hardly made them better qualified to be lords than a vast number of other loyal Labour supporters. As for Garrard, he had until recently been a staunch Tory – and even after being nominated for a peerage he didn't pretend to be a passionate Labour Party man. He couldn't possibly have been rewarded for party service, as Blair claimed, because he had never given any.

The total amount Labour ended up borrowing from wealthy individuals was £13.95m. And it finally published the names of the lenders and how much each had given on 20 March 2007. After Sir Gulam Noon's loan was confirmed, he concluded that the controversy made it impossible for him to take up his peerage. So he wrote to the Prime Minister withdrawing his acceptance of the honour. To be clear, the Commission never actually recommended that he should not go to the House of Lords. However, a Commission member has told me that had it known about the loan, it would probably have recommended that it was not an appropriate time for Noon to become a peer, because it looked unseemly for anyone to go to the Upper House so soon after providing financial help to Labour. That said, Lord Stevenson is an admirer of Noon and wrote to thank him for the way he conducted himself during that difficult period. Noon was also invited in to see the Prime Minister within hours of the withdrawal of his nomination. Blair told him he was devastated that he would not be sitting on Labour benches and was sorry for all the fuss.

Meanwhile, there was mayhem at the top of the Labour Party. The trade unionist Jack Dromey – who is married to Harriet Harman, the long-standing ally of Gordon Brown and current deputy leader of the Labour Party – is the treasurer of the Labour Party and co-signs its accounts. He announced that neither he nor most of the other senior officers of the party knew anything about the loans from wealthy individuals. Dromey told Channel 4 News on 15 March that 'I do not think it is right that loans should be secured from wealthy individuals behind the backs of the elected officers of the Labour Party . . . To be absolutely frank, I don't think the Labour Party has been sufficiently respected by Number 10.' And on 21 March he told a meeting of Labour's National Executive Committee (NEC) – the governing body of the party, broadly the equivalent of its board of directors, had it been a company – that no elected member of the NEC had been kept in the picture about the borrowings.

The unarguable implication of what Dromey had said was that Labour had been run like a cowboy business, without proper checks and balances or oversight from the *de facto* non-executives. Vast borrowings had been incurred in its name by the activities of Lord Levy, who was neither a member of the National Executive Committee nor a registered party officer. One of the two individuals who sign its annual accounts, Dromey, had no idea about the loans. However, Dromey isn't Labour's 'registered' treasurer, or the individual responsible to the Electoral Commission for the accuracy of its accounts. At the relevant time, that was Matt Carter – and it was Carter who signed all the loan agreements in 2005 with the lenders and also co-signed Labour's annual accounts (till he was replaced in January 2006 by Peter Watt, who signed off the 2005 accounts). Nonetheless, the law would almost certainly have been broken if Labour had been a company, subject to the strictures of the Companies Act, and the National Executive Committee had been its board: it's illegal for one or two members of a board to take on potentially crippling liabilities in a company's name without consulting or even informing other board members. But the Labour Party is not a company, and the governance standards imposed on it by the Electoral Commission are not as onerous as those of the Companies Act.

Also, in an important respect Labour's 2004 accounts give a less complete view of Labour's financial health than the comparable accounts would normally do for a business. The accounts were not signed off until 30 June 2005, by which time Labour had accumulated £7.05m of additional debt from six lenders, all of which was repayable within a year. This was greater than all its other short-term loans and overdraft as shown in its 2004 accounts. The point is that if Labour had been a normal business, it probably would have printed the £7.05m of new debt as a 'post-balance-sheet event' in a note to the accounts: the existence of the loans had weakened Labour, which was something that its other creditors would have wanted to know. But there was no such disclosure in Labour's 2004 accounts.

When the 2005 accounts were finally published in the summer of 2006, they actually showed that Labour's total indebtedness from banks and individual lenders had exploded from £11.2m at the end of 2004 to £25.7m at the end of 2005. Its deficit on reserves had ballooned to a staggering £27m. Although Labour has since taken steps to put itself on a more secure financial footing, at the time of writing it was still uncertain how it was ever going to be able to repay all that debt. The interest charges alone are roughly half what it receives from members' subscriptions. To revert to the analogy between Labour and a business, Labour has just under 200,000 members, who are the equivalent of its shareholders. They obviously have two interests, which ought to be compatible: achieving electoral success for their party and maintaining the long-term health of their party. Arguably that second interest was well and truly trampled by the way in which Blair, Levy and Carter went on a frenzied and clandestine borrowing binge.

But it was the wider electorate which has been let down. The impression was created that places in the legislature, in the Upper House of Parliament, could be bought. There isn't quite the 100 per cent correlation claimed by the *Sunday Times* between those who give more than £1m to Labour and those who receive knighthoods or peerages. For example, William Haughey, a Scottish philanthropist and refrigeration entrepreneur, has donated £1.03m to Labour since the end of 2003 and he is neither knight nor lord. But there is still a statistically significant correlation.

So although it was a bit of a shock to the political system, it was altogether healthy that Scotland Yard announced on 21 March 2006 that it would investigate whether honours had been sold. However, I never believed it likely that the police would be able to amass sufficient evidence for a criminal prosecution to take place. This is no reflection on the talent, commitment or impartiality of the Metropolitan Police team working on the case. It is simply that the corruption of the honours system was general and systematic. Which is very different to saying that the conferring of any one honour to any single lender or donor was provably corrupt. It would always be possible to argue that any specific peerage given to a lender or a donor had been awarded for reasons other than the relevant loan or donation. Just imagine the challenge for a prosecutor of demonstrating beyond reasonable doubt that Horatio Bloggins became Lord Bloggins only because of his £1m loan to the Stinky Party. Bloggins's clever barrister would always be able to cite Bloggins's other many services to the party.

The extraordinary thing is that it was not till 16 months after the police opened the file that the Crown Prosecution Service (CPS) finally concluded there was no basis on which to prosecute anyone. And the statement it put out made it clear that the burden of proof required for a successful prosecution was almost impossibly high. This is what the CPS said on 20 July:

> If one person grants . . . an honour to another in recognition of [in effect, as a reward for] the fact that the other has made a gift . . . that does not of itself constitute an offence. For a case to proceed, the prosecution must have a realistic prospect of being able to prove that the two people agreed that the gift, etc., was in exchange for an honour. [Crown Prosecution Service official statement, 20 July 2007]

To translate, the CPS was saying that it was perfectly all right for the Stinky Party to give Bloggins a peerage as a reward for his £1m loan, just so long as Bloggins never had a conversation with the leader or treasurer of the Stinky Party in which they agreed that the peerage would be the reward for the loan. Or, to put it another way, it is fine to sell honours so long as you are not explicit about what you are doing.

The CPS added that circumstantial evidence would almost never be able to provide sufficient proof of a crime in this kind of case – because there would almost always be a plausibly legitimate reason for giving an honour to a lender or donor.

All of which raises the question why the Metropolitan Police were allowed to waste so much of their own time and taxpayers' money in pursuing this case for quite so long. We should all probably cheer that we live in the kind of stable and open polity where the police are able to exercise the power to interview the Prime Minister – which they did on several occasions – in a criminal investigation of this sort. But the wild goose chase of the police inquiry went on too long.

But let's not take comfort from the conclusion that neither Levy, nor Blair, nor Downing Street officials broke the law. Blair offered places in Parliament to individuals whose main qualification was that they were wealthy enough to bail out Labour in its hour of greatest financial need. He was contemptuous of the idea that a place representing his party in the Upper House should only go to those of unblemished record and with a long history of service to Labour. The leader of a party created to give voice to the neediest and most oppressed was attempting to confer political power on the wealthy for no other conspicuous reason than that they had the financial means to keep him in power. And it is no excuse that for years the Tories too showed a careless disregard for the principles of democracy by routinely giving peerages to donors. That democracy was for sale degrades and humiliates all of us.

CHAPTER 9

ALLAN LEIGHTON: A DIFFERENT KIND OF PUBLIC SERVANT

The chairman of Royal Mail has his own characteristic way of keeping the owners of the business, the Government, at arm's length:

> They [in Whitehall and Westminster] hate our independence. Because what is their job if they are not interfering or anything? When the Treasury rang up to ask us the reason for doing something, I would say, 'Phone them back and say, "Allan says you can fuck off; it's nothing to do with you."' And for a while, that was how it worked . . . You have to be extreme to get the message down the organization. [Allan Leighton interview, 12 June 2006]

Leighton is a new breed of public servant. In some ways, he is a new breed of one, because there is no one quite like him – though what he originally represented was a determination on the part of the Labour administration to transplant those with private-sector experience and skills into the public sector. But even within the private sector he is hardly run-of-the-mill. If you met him, you would think he was a showbiz magnate or a Premier-League football manager: he fizzes with energy; he is always fixing a problem or doing a deal; and he talks non-stop, at breathtaking pace. And quite a lot of what he says is a hair's-breadth away from nonsense. However, it's fair to say that Royal Mail – which, depending on your prejudice, is either an enormous public service or a vast nationalized industry – would be in a much bigger mess if he hadn't been at its apex for the past six years. And although he has been disappointed in his ambition for Royal Mail to be wholly or partially privatized on his watch, he has made it more competitive, more commercial, almost viable.

In some ways, he should be seen as a hit man for the super-rich – and for the Government – in that he's worked for and alongside the entrepreneurial giants of our age: Rupert Murdoch at British Sky Broadcasting, Philip Green at Bhs, James Dyson at the consumer electricals firm of the same name, the Canadian plutocratic dynasty, the Westons, the the mega-rich Waltons of WalMart, to name just a few. He is massively well networked. He became the chairman of Bhs when Philip Green took it over and worked with him on a possible bid for the supermarket group, Safeway, that came to nothing. He was an early mentor (at Asda) to Andy Hornby, the wunderkind chief executive of HBOS, the bank chaired by Lord Stevenson. But it would be only a partial view to categorize him as a networker. He is a doer with an enormous gob. If David Brent, from Ricky Gervais's *The Office*, were actually any good as a manager, he would be Allan Leighton. I cannot resist quoting this passage from his recent book, *On Leadership*, which is pure Brent:

> Maybe my favourite piece of wisdom on leadership is from the book *The Wit and Wisdom of Forrest Gump*:
>> If you go to the zoo, always take something to feed the animals, even if the signs say 'Do not feed the animals.' It wasn't the animals that put them signs up.
>
> It's true. Every day we [business leaders] metaphorically decide what 'the animals' want. We don't talk to the animals enough, we don't ask the animals enough questions, and we don't listen

to the animals enough. We just think we know what to feed them. The companies who don't do that, but who ask the 'animals' what they want, are the ones that work and succeed. [*On Leadership*, Allan Leighton, 2007]

Leighton has yet to make a serious fortune for himself – and perhaps it is a little too late. What distinguishes him from his wealthier friends is his strong commitment to public service: he has made a financial sacrifice in what economists would call the opportunity cost of devoting himself to Royal Mail when he could have been enriching himself as a participant in the private-equity takeover boom. The tragedy is that his bruising encounters with a Government so pusillanimous that it wavered from one day to the next about whether to privatize or not has put off other seriously talented executives from following his example and committing a chunk of their lives to redeeming the public sector.

He has been an enormous presence at Royal Mail, unlike any of his predecessors. Partly, that is because he endeavours to use the media in a much more systematic way to set the climate of opinion than public servants normally do. And what is particularly striking about his public-relations campaigns is that he relies largely on his own powers of persuasion. He has long-standing and close relationships with a number of business journalists and is comfortable chatting frankly with them, in a way that is unusual for someone of his seniority – and ought to demonstrate to some of his neurotically media-shy colleagues that openness with journalists can yield handsome reputational dividends.

Senior civil servants do not know quite what to make of him. 'He is full of shit; you shouldn't listen to him' is the visceral reflection of one highly placed official. Another says: 'He is difficult to deal with, there's no doubt about that. But you have to take your hat off to him. He has reduced the headcount at Royal Mail by an incredible amount. That kind of thing just doesn't happen in the public sector.'

My assessment is that his record at Royal Mail is impressive, though probably not quite as impressive as is implied by the barrage of statistics he routinely flings at commentators like me about the postal service's performance under his sway. What strikes me about Leighton is that he could have had his pick of jobs in early 2002 when he became Royal Mail's chairman, but instead opted to do one where the challenges were immense, where the potential for being vilified by newspapers was huge, where he was bound to make himself unpopular with millions of customers and tens of thousands of employees, and where he took a pay cut (in 2002, he could have had his pick of seven-figure private-sector jobs; his salary at Royal Mail is £21,000, though he received a £180,000 bonus in 2005–06). And in the years that followed, the difficulties faced by Royal Mail were – if anything – even greater than he could have expected in some respects. What's more, the Government has not been consistently supportive, especially latterly. Royal Mail could, under different management, be in meltdown now. So for all the complaints that the service it offers to customers is not what it was, if you put together all the challenges it has faced – competition where previously there was none, serious over-manning, the financial burden of a chronically under-funded pension fund – it would be churlish not to applaud him.

Leighton is a tieless, stubble-chinned 54 year-old, in dark designer suit and with close-shaved pate – a bit flashier than your typical industrial grandee. His accent is a strange hybrid of Estuary and Midlands. Here's his own résumé of his background:

> I grew up all over the place. My dad was a Co-Op manager and trade unionist. He was a young, reforming trade unionist. I was born in Hereford, lived in Nottingham, Daventry, Banbury, all over the place. My accent is hard to place . . . I change my accent depending on where I am. Speak Yorkshire when in Yorkshire.
>
> I went to Magdalen College School in Brackley, outside Northampton. It was a boarding school. Was a very good school. It has links with Magdalen College, Oxford. These days it is a comprehensive. Then went to Oxford Poly for 18 months

to two years to do business studies. I did that because I could not do anything else. Wasn't sure I wanted to go into business. Then I went to work for Lloyds Bank. It was a nightmare. I was unsuited to it. This was 1974–5. It was a terrible place. I was a long-haired, bearded counter clerk. I led a strike in a branch and was singled out as a troublemaker. [Allan Leighton interview, 12 June 2006]

It was a trip to Mars which changed his life. In 1974, he applied to become a salesman at the privately controlled confectionery and pet-foods company, because – by his own account – his Mini had broken down irretrievably and he needed a job with a company car. Mars was the making of him (again by his own account). He talks of Mars, where he stayed until 1992, with the kind of gratitude and respect normally accorded to family:

Mars formed 70 per cent of what I am today. They trained me. I changed jobs there every two years for 18 years. They obviously saw something that nobody else had seen, including me.

My first job was in the sales force, selling Mars Bars to corner shops, 25 calls per day. I have probably been in every corner shop in Britain. My last job was sales and marketing director of Pedigree Pet Food. I was the youngest director in the company. I was covering Europe.

Mars taught me all the basic stuff about selection, training, motivating. I still remember it all now: 'Select, train, motivate, counsel, appraise'. It was a discipline. We were taught stuff you don't get taught these days – how to run a meeting, how to run a one-to-one. All the basic stuff which you never forget. There was none of this 'We're going to have a piece of management development, we're all going to climb Mount Kilimanjaro.' It was 'This is how you run a meeting.' Great basic stuff. [ibid.]

Leighton never thought he would leave Mars. But in 1992, he was poached by Asda, the supermarket group which was then in serious decline, as its marketing director. This was the appointment which was to build his public reputation. With Archie Norman – Asda's chief executive who then became its chairman and subsequently had a spell as a Tory MP – he transformed Asda into one of the most dynamic forces in supermarket retailing. The story of food retailing in the 1990s was the story of how Tesco and Asda gained market share by cutting prices, to a large extent at the expense of J Sainsbury. Leighton became Asda's retail operations director in 1994 and he succeeded Norman as chief executive in 1999.

Prior to joining Royal Mail, if he has a place in British social and economic history it is as the individual who gave the fearsome Wal-Mart – the US retailing monster, the largest retailer in the world – an entrée to the UK:

After three years we stabilized Asda – that process was called 'Renewal'. And the next phase, which I carried out, was called 'Breakout' – which was the next three years. We were really motoring. And after that everything went for us. We became the number-two player. We were voted best place in Britain to work. It all clicked.

We were tootling along and wondering what to do next. I had thought about merging with Kingfisher [the owner of B&Q, Comet, Superdrug and Woolworth] a couple of times. I had a look at buying Safeway. I thought that would be a really good thing to do and had a couple of attempts. It didn't work. Decided that we'll merge with Kingfisher. So we are going along merrily with that transaction. Must be 1999 [it was April 1999]. But I had real second thoughts about it. The merger was going to be a problem. The chemistry between the people wasn't going to work.

They [Kingfisher] were a very different culture. It was all public [i.e. the Kingfisher deal had been announced to the Stock Exchange] and everything had been done. But I felt: 'I do not feel comfortable with this, having spent ten years here.' I didn't feel good about it. I had the business with the best people, the most enduring business, on the fastest track. So I thought: 'I don't want to do this now.'

So I phoned Rob Walton [S. Robson Walton, Wal-Mart's chairman] and told him that I didn't feel comfortable with what we were doing, but I would feel comfortable with him. I'd been very close to Wal-Mart for a period. They always thought we were more like bloody Wal-Mart than they were. Perhaps this was his last chance. A week later we did the deal. It was an amazing week. [ibid.]

On 14 June 1999, Wal-Mart announced it was buying Asda for £6.7bn, comfortably more than what was being offered by King-fisher. It was almost universally seen as one of the most significant takeovers that had ever taken place in the UK. At the time, Wal-Mart was regarded by the Treasury and by 10 Downing Street as a force for good. This was before Wal-Mart's reputation was tainted by negative publicity concerning the low wages it pays US shop staff, the damage it is perceived to wreak on local communities in North America when small shops are driven to the wall by its superstores, and allegations that it turned a blind eye to unac-ceptable working conditions at overseas suppliers. In particular, Gordon Brown, then Chancellor of the Exchequer, was convinced that any intensification of competition in food retailing would be positive, by bringing down the price of food and other consumer goods. In fact, as it turned out, it is Tesco that has gone from strength to strength in the UK. Under Wal-Mart's ownership, Asda has had downs as well as ups – though it has maintained its position as the UK's number-two supermarket group and is currently enjoying one of its more successful phases.

But the deal was important, not least *pour encourager les autres*: in its wake there has been a stream of takeovers of great British businesses by overseas interests. And Leighton says he had a good time working for the leviathan – although he wanted out surpri-singly quickly:

They were brilliant – forget what everyone wrote at the time. They said, 'We'll learn,' and they meant it. They kept the Asda name. We had a fantastic 12 months, the business was flying.

They then all came over for a board meeting. I got a call from Lee [Lee Scott, Wal-Mart's chief executive] in the morning. I'd had a party at my house the previous night – they had all come. Lee said: 'Come into Asda House.' They said: 'Everyone is really impressed; we think you are really important; and we would like you to sign a five-year contract; and think about coming to Bentonville [Wal-Mart's HQ] for a bit and running the US.'

To be honest, that had the reverse effect on me. I thought: 'Do I really want to do this?' Though I am still on really good terms with them all. I had a think about it and I thought: 'Actually, I can't do this.' I thought: 'Probably it's time to move on.' So I said I would do six months and then move on. So that was it. [ibid.]

It was September 2000. What came next was that Leighton turned himself into a lifestyle brand:

My idea was not to do anything probably for a year and just chill. I'd made a few bob. Kate Rankine [who was then a *Daily Telegraph* journalist] rang me up and said, 'Have you been fired, are you getting any money?' I said, 'No, I haven't been fired and I am not getting any money, I'm not even getting a clock.'

She said, 'What are you going to do?' And into my head came: 'I'm going plural,' and she wrote: 'Leighton going plural.' And then this whole 'plural' thing took off. So I registered the name ['going plural']. And I was offered a few jobs. [ibid.]

Leighton – aka www.going-plural.com – became 'portfolio man'. Or, to put it another way, he held more positions at one time than most people do in a lifetime. He has held directorships at BSkyB, the leading satellite broadcaster, Leeds United football club, lastminute.com, the online travel business (where he was chairman), Wilson Connolly, the housebuilder, Dyson, the maker of the revolutionary vacuum cleaner, Bhs, Selfridges

and George Weston, the giant, family-controlled Canadian baker
and retailer.

Joining the Dyson board was an exercise in mutual admiration:

Got to know [James] Dyson because I read his book on holiday
and thought it was very interesting. He said in his book that
when anyone joins his company, the first thing they do is make a
vacuum cleaner, on day one.

I thought: 'What a brilliant idea.' That's how everyone knows
they are in a vacuum-cleaner business. My equivalent of that
was checkouts. So after that, everyone who joined Asda, the first
thing they did was to work on the checkout. Whoever they were.
And at Royal Mail everyone has to work as a postman [including
Leighton himself, who delivered letters when he joined]. [ibid.]

Other jobs he was sounded out about were the vacant position of
chief executive at Marks & Spencer ('I decided I didn't want to do
it') and an unspecified senior role at the National Health Service:

I got a call from a headhunter saying the Government was
looking for somebody to sort out the NHS. It was interesting.
Went to talk to Alan Milburn [then Secretary of State for
Health]. And in-between time the same headhunter said the
Government was looking for someone to look at the Post Office.
I knew Stephen Byers [then Secretary of State for Trade and
Industry].

Net net, I ended up coming in to be a non-executive on the
Consignia Board [which was what Royal Mail was then called],
but was really looking at the Post Office side of the business
because of my retail experience. And when I came in, I thought I
had never seen such a shambles in my life. [ibid.]

This was 2001. On 2 April that year, Leighton joined the board
of Consignia. He was appointed interim chairman on 8 January
2002 and chairman proper on 25 March. Leighton inherited a
mess that was hard to beat.

The business had become something of a national laughing stock in January 2001, when it announced a change of name from 'The Post Office' – which had served it perfectly well since 1635 – to Consignia. At the time, 'corporate rebranding' was all the rage: Andersen Consulting became Accenture; British Gas became Centrica; British Steel became Corus; Grand Metropolitan became Diageo. There was an epidemic of silly corporate identity changes. Was 'Consignia' any worse than 'Diageo'? The Post Office's then chief executive, John Roberts, said that research had shown that Consignia was regarded as 'modern, meaningful and appropriate'. He told the *Financial Times*: 'To consign means "to entrust to the care of" – which is what each of our customers does every day.' Apparently, 'The Post Office' just would not cut it in all the overseas markets the business wanted to conquer. What's more, the business was about to obtain new commercial freedoms by acquiring corporate status: it was to become a 'PLC', but an unusual one in that it would have a single shareholder, the Government. The incorporation happened in March 2001, when it also became answerable to a regulator, Postcomm. And what better way to mark the rite of passage than by a rechristening?

Well, a series of letters to *The Times* eloquently put the arguments against:

> Sir, The Post Office of this country is a name with a long and honourable tradition. All the more reason in the present climate (New Labour/Cool Britannia?) to ditch it for a senseless neologism: Consignia. One could weep at the official blather put out to justify the change: 'The name itself researched extraordinarily well with business customers as well as a wider research group of adults, both in the UK and abroad.'
>
> Yours etc.,

> Sir, In your reporting on the rebranding of the Post Office, many definitions of the word 'consign' were listed, all conferring notions of reliability, trust and safe delivery.

Sadly, as soon as I saw the word, I was minded of that application reserved for burials at sea.

Yours etc.,

Sir,
About that new designia
The Post Office has got.
Will anyone resignia?
I rather fancied not!
Yours faithfully,

The cost of the renaming was to be an estimated £500,000 – which may seem a great deal, but it turned out to be nearly irrelevant in the context of a horrendous financial black hole that was threatening to consume the business. Consignia was in a terrible state – which became clear when results for the year to March 2002 were published. These showed that losses before tax had soared to £1.1bn, including massive costs associated with redundancies and the reconstruction of the business. What was totally unsustainable was the large recurring loss from providing the postal service. The company told newspapers the daily deficit was running at £1.2m, which turned out to be only a slight exaggeration. The hideous figure for 2001–2002 extrapolated from its published accounts – and excluding supposedly one-off or exceptional costs – was a loss of around £1m per day (the total operating loss for mail, parcels, counter services and 'other' businesses was £317m).

But, amazingly, in the course of this mayhem, the Department of Trade and Industry hit upon the brilliant wheeze of selling the company to the Dutch postal service, TPG. When he found about it, Graham Corbett, the inaugural chairman of Postcomm, the newly formed regulator of the postal industry, was horrified. Corbett, a former accountant, is not a man given to temper tantrums. It would be hard to find a more level-headed individual than this urbane watchdog:

There was a proposal for a merger between the Royal Mail and TPG . . . but it was such a political hot potato that no one dared mention it. We took a very clear position that there was no evidence the merger would produce the benefits for the users that we wanted. [Graham Corbett interview, *Sunday Telegraph*, 25 January 2004]

Patricia Hewitt, then Secretary of State for Trade and Industry, asked if he and his fellow board members intended to resign. Corbett: 'I said, "We won't resign, you will have to sack us." ' [ibid.]

At the same time, Leighton was concerned that the merger was utterly impractical, for the simple reason that it was impossible to value the Post Office: it was in such a mess.

It became patently clear to me that not only would this business never hit any of its numbers, but they were in this transaction called Olympus which was about selling the Royal Mail to the Dutch. They were well down the track, had been talking for nine months, but it was shambolic because none of the numbers were right. So I said there's no way this transaction would ever happen. There was no value. I could not see how it would work. Because the unions had gone on strike [though the unions did not know about the transaction, according to Leighton].

I thought this was crazy. The Government finally came to the same conclusion. And the contract of the chairman, Neville Bain, was coming to an end. They did not renew it. Government said they would get a new chairman and recommended me as a stopgap. I got asked to do it. [Allan Leighton interview, 12 June 2006]

For Leighton, there is no doubt it was his toughest assignment ever:

Royal Mail is the most challenging thing I have done. Everything was wrong. It was heading south in terms of financial performance. It was kidding itself it could do a transaction with the Dutch. It completely lost the plot.

Ron Dearing had been chairman for six or seven years [Dearing had been chairman of what was then called the Post Office from 1981 to 1987]. He was a very good man with a good team, who were on top of stuff. And then it all fell to bits. No one was running it except for the unions. There was no leadership. What happened was that Downing Street, the Treasury and the DTI all thought they were running it. Postcomm appears on the scene, so the regulator thought he was running it. It became a PLC but did not act like one. And I didn't think leadership was up to much.

It was a classic case of too many cooks and no leaders. For me, it was a one-off opportunity. [ibid.]

The winter and spring of 2002 was a turbulent time for Consignia. Leighton was negotiating the terms of a rescue package with the Government. Various numbers were bandied about in the press about the scale of redundancies and branch closures that were needed to return Royal Mail to some kind of financial stability.

And there was a public dispute between Consignia and its regulator, Postcomm, about when it would be ready to cope with the introduction of competition in the commercial business of making bulk deliveries (of mostly junk mail) for businesses. All European Union members were obliged to break the monopolies of their national postal services. But Leighton argued that it would be disastrous if Royal Mail were to lose its valuable grip on the market before it had a proper chance to modernize and become more efficient. After all, it had become fat and lazy – a cash cow for the Government – after decades of being protected from competitors, able simply to put up the price of stamps when ministers needed a fatter dividend (over the previous 20 years, Royal Mail had paid the Exchequer £1.8bn in dividends). It could not become a leaner, meaner company overnight – which Postcomm acknowledged in its eventual ruling. In May 2002, the regulator announced that competition would be introduced in phases. The timetable would be faster than for the rest of Europe. But that was par for the course in the UK, which sees itself as the evangelist for competition in an EU wary of liberalized markets. For Royal Mail, competitive market conditions would be phased in from 2003. Around 30 per cent of the market, or the biggest bulk mailouts, was liberalized first. The target for full competition was April 2007, but in the event it was brought forward to 1 January 2006.

At the time, Corbett felt under great pressure – from the DTI and from Leighton – to be a spineless regulator. But he had been given enormous power by the Government to make independent judgements about how the postal market should operate and to ensure that Consignia did not abuse its dominant market position. And since the DTI had given him all this power, he certainly wasn't minded to hand it back.

> They [the DTI] did have a tendency in the early days to wait until a consultation was nearly over and then tell us what they wanted us to do . . . I told Patricia Hewitt that I had no problem with them making their views known, but through the consultation process so we could put their submission on our website. [Graham Corbett interview, *Sunday Telegraph*, 25 January 2004]

That is regulator-speak for 'hop off'. And over three years, he kept the Trade and Industry Secretary at bay and had a series of public punch-ups with Leighton, especially over his attempts to limit tariff increases (in his typically florid way, Leighton said in a press release on 14 November 2002 that Postcomm's price constraints would be 'fatal' to the company's recovery plans). When he stepped down in 2004, Corbett was philosophical about these disputes:

> The moment that Patricia Hewitt appointed Leighton she wanted someone who really lived and thrived in a competitive environment. You have got to accept that a lot of the high-

volume noise that was coming out of Leighton was part of a gladiatorial contest. [ibid.]

It was in June 2002 that Leighton unveiled the final details of his three-year 'Renewal Plan' to restore Consignia to health. And one of the few elements that proved almost universally popular – even though there would be an implementation cost of around £1m which the company could ill afford – was that the name 'Consignia' was to be consigned to the grave, and replaced with the historic 'Royal Mail':

> That's when I did the deal with the Government. I said, 'Look, it's very straightforward: we run the company and will hit the numbers; you can blame us for everything; but don't send anyone in and don't call; those are the rules.' And Patricia [Hewitt], Gordon [Brown] and Tony [Blair] agreed that. And off we went – I think largely because they didn't think we had a cat's chance of achieving what we said we would.
>
> The agreement meant we stopped dividend payments to Government, got the social-network payment [a £150m per year subsidy to help cover losses of rural offices], there would be 34,000 redundancies, 3,500 post offices would be closed. We told them about everything – said the redundancies would cost them £2bn.
>
> When I took the job, it was on the basis of the plan – which also required Parcelforce to be returned to profit. For GLS [the company's European parcels business] it was scale or sale [he opted for expanding it].
>
> And I changed the entire management and the whole board. [Allan Leighton interview, June 12 2006]

In fact, the redundancy number that was announced was 30,000 and around 3,000 urban post offices were to close (one of Leighton's great skills is to talk with enormous conviction about numbers, even though in contiguous conversations he often makes different, sometimes contradictory, statistical statements). Perhaps most controversially, the company said that the scale of the cost savings it needed to make – £1.4bn over three years – required a decision that many customers would not like: the introduction of just a single daily home delivery, in place of two.

> On the second delivery I just said: 'Pull it.' 'We are out of here,' I said. A typical home might have got one second delivery once a week – that was the reality of it. There was no regulation stopping me doing it. We had to slay all those things. [ibid.]

At the time, Leighton and Royal Mail made a series of claims about the impact of abolishing the second delivery. They said that second-delivery post covered just 4 per cent of 81 million letters delivered each day but accounted for 20 per cent of costs and 30 per cent of delivery times. And it said that there would be savings of £350m every year from cutting the second post [Royal Mail press release, 8 October 2002]. But in the event those savings turned out to be chimerical, or so the regulator says. This is what Corbett's successor as Postcomm's chairman, Nigel Stapleton, told the House of Commons Trade and Industry Committee on 7 November 2005:

> The fact is that we all thought single daily delivery was going to be a major move to improve efficiency. It was marketed on the basis of 20 per cent of the costs are incurred on 4 per cent of the volume and we all thought it would be a major extra efficiency which would strengthen the universal service. Royal Mail thought they were going to save £118m a year [rather less than the £350m in its 2002 press release] from single daily delivery. The numbers they have given us say that it is costing an extra £109m a year when it is fully implemented. We have had the renewal programme, this was the major initiative of the renewal programme and their delivery costs have not come down, they have gone up.

Or, to put it another way, the reduction in the quality of service to customers brought about by the end of the second delivery has not, apparently, yielded cost benefits. And there are plenty of other statistics available with which to beat Leighton across the head. For example, he talked of headcount reductions of 30,000 (or 34,000 in his interview with me). But Royal Mail's annual report shows that it had 13,000 fewer employees in March 2006 than its average headcount in 2001–02, or 209,000 versus 222,000. Now, direct comparison is complicated by the changing shape of Royal Mail, but it is hard to establish on the basis of published audited numbers that headcount has fallen quite as sharply as Leighton said it would.

So does that mean Leighton's period at the helm has been characterized by hot air and not much else? I don't think so. A balanced assessment is positive for him. First of all, he talked directly to staff in a way that had not happened before:

> After three months, I got all 1,700 delivery office managers together for the first time, over two days. 99 per cent of them – most had been in the company for 20 years – had never seen anyone from the board in their lives. Just unbelievable. They run the people – 160,000 people are run by them. They were 17 layers down . . . In a commercial world we were just going to get turned over. [Allan Leighton interview, 12 June 2006]

In fact, the anecdote he thinks best sums up the challenge he faced relates to his unannounced visits to sorting offices:

> I had just been appointed acting chairman and the next day I turned up at Mount Pleasant [a huge sorting office in central London]. And I couldn't get in. So I got to the gate and I said to the guy, 'I'm the chairman, can you let me in?' And he says, 'Piss off, mate, everybody's tried that one.' And I said, 'No, I really am the chairman.' So then he says, 'Bloody hell, it really is him.' So he says, 'Hang on a minute,' and he rings the duty manager. So he phones Harry, the duty manager, and Harry says, 'Piss off, everyone's tried that one.'

Anyway, eventually I persuaded them that I am the chairman. And the reason they didn't believe me was because it was 5.30 in the morning. But I went in and got everybody together and realized that nobody had ever talked to them before. And there were lots of good people with good ideas. But there was a complete disconnect between the bloody management and the people in the company. And having read the day before data saying that only 20 per cent of employees felt valued and over 25 per cent felt they had been bullied and harassed within the year, well that was it really. [Allan Leighton interview, 2 October 2006]

And when he looked further at employee relations, he was horrified by what he found:

I got this employment-opinion survey. Employee morale was terrible. More than 20 per cent of our people thought they had been bullied or harassed in the previous 12 months. It was terrible. I'd hear all this stuff about people being beaten up and cars being trashed. Then this West Indian lad hung himself for being bullied. Then there was this lad with cerebral palsy who was picked on and stabbed in the back with a pair of scissors. They stuck him in a mailbag and put him in the back of a car and drove him around London. Terrible stuff. I got them prosecuted. It was assault. I blew up. Just showed all the things that were wrong about the company. The union was in denial. Claimed it didn't happen. In fairness, the union has been as strong on this [as me] since then. [Allan Leighton interview, 12 June 2006]

There is also a way of looking at his cost-cutting record which looks better for him. The reduction in headcount in just the basic UK business – as opposed to the group as a whole – may, in fact, be more than 30,000. The group figures for numbers employed are distorted by a significant growth in its overseas operation (its successful and valuable European parcels business, GLS). But, there is still a bit of funny accounting in Royal Mail's claims to have cut jobs, in that it has 'outsourced' supposedly non-core services, such as catering and building maintenance, to subsidiaries partly owned by outside interests. These 'partially owned subsidiaries' employ 4,852 people, compared with zero in 2002. And the services they provide to Royal Mail have a cost to the company, whether or not the staff delivering those services are direct employees. More impressive – for me, at least – is that Royal Mail's bill for wages and salaries has fallen from £4.8bn in 2001–02 to £4.5bn in 2005–06, a drop of 6 per cent. Such a reduction in the wage bill in the public sector is almost unheard of. On the other hand, overall operating costs have risen in the same period from £8.5bn to £8.7bn. But it is hard to get worked up about that or accuse Leighton of having sold the Government a pup: a 3 per cent increase over four years is minimal, far less than inflation and *de minimis* compared to what has happened to the wage bill and overheads in most of Whitehall.

The other reason Leighton deserves great credit is for a financial turnaround in the face of great odds. Over the past four years, Royal Mail has had to cope with the onset of competition. And the impact of the internet has been bad and good: e-mails have replaced letters; but vast numbers of books, CDs and clothes are increasingly bought online, which is great for Royal Mail's parcels operation. It has also seen vast amounts of business leave its chain of post offices as a direct impact of Government policy, for example with the introduction of the payment of pensions and benefits directly into bank accounts rather than over post-office counters. Such withdrawals of the Government-related services offered by post offices – which Royal Mail is powerless to prevent – lost them transactions worth £168m in 2005–06 alone. And there is a painful knock-on in the reduction of people going into post offices, which limits Royal Mail's ability to sell commercial products and services. But, in spite of such obstacles, Royal Mail made an operating profit of £355m from its continuing operations in 2005–06, which is a notable recovery from the deficit of 2001–02. Now, I am minded to believe that Consignia/Royal Mail was motivated to exaggerate losses in 2001–02 – when it needed to provide a powerful reason for a painful reconstruction of the business – and that more recently its imperative was to demonstrate success. But even so, Royal Mail has been rehabilitated more effectively than might have been expected.

That said, Royal Mail has found itself in a bit of a mess again – though largely for reasons beyond the control of Leighton, or of Adam Crozier, the former chief executive of the Football Association who became Royal Mail's chief executive in February 2003. Its most glaring problem was a gigantic blot on its balance sheet – it had a deficit in its pension fund estimated at £5.6bn as of 26 March 2006. If anyone was to blame for this it would be Royal Mail directors going back many years, previous Government ministers, and actuaries (the professionals who advise companies on the health of their pension schemes) who consistently underestimated the liabilities of the scheme and overstated the likely returns to be made from its assets. But there was nothing unusual about their failure to properly assess the strength of their scheme. As Chapter 7 shows, more or less the whole world wore rose-tinted glasses when looking at UK occupational pension schemes in the 1980s and 1990s.

What is really striking about the Royal Mail pension deficit in 2006 is that it increased by more than £1.6bn during a year when the stock market was booming and the value of its assets rose very sharply – when there should, in theory, have been a shrinking of the pension-fund hole. The reason there wasn't such an improvement in the state of the fund is because its trustees suddenly realized that current and future pensioners were likely to live much longer than it had been anticipating. It had hitherto been assuming that a 60-year-old male pension-fund member would typically die and stop drawing a pension when he was 82, or 22 years after becoming a pensioner. But it now recognized that he would probably peg out after 26 years. That increase in longevity was cripplingly expensive – it meant that the costs of paying a pension to that 60-year-old were 18 per cent more than the scheme had been estimating.

The correction of this error in the pension scheme's mortality assumptions sent a seismic shock through the company. Which is clear from this little-noticed statement in its 2005–6 annual report:

> Royal Mail Group plc has net liabilities at 26 March 2006, primarily because of the pension deficit within its main pension plan, the Royal Mail Pension Plan. Consequently, Royal Mail Group plc is in default of its borrowing facilities with Government, but has received formal waivers from the Department of Trade and Industry, in its capacity as lender.

In other words, Royal Mail's finances were a disaster yet again: net assets were minus £3.3bn. If Royal Mail were a normal plc, rather than a Government-owned one, it would have been bust – because it needed to inject hundreds of millions of pounds into its pension every year, while also spending £2bn over four years on modernizing its operations to help it survive against competition from more efficient rivals. Some of its sorting offices look like Victorian workhouses, with rows of men and women putting letters into cubby holes by hand. It is almost a matter of life or death that it replaces such manual sorting with computer-controlled machines. If it doesn't, its automated competitors – whose running costs are much lower – will simply steal its most valuable commercial customers. But Royal Mail does not generate sufficient cash from its operations both to shore up its pension fund and to invest in the business. So it has been wholly reliant on the Government agreeing to provide a new financial support package – which had been under negotiation since 2005, but was subject to endless delays and prevarication by ministers.

In a way, it is a wonder that Royal Mail is not in an even greater mess. The point is that a new set of price controls, limiting the amount by which it can increase charges, came into effect on 3 April 2006 and will last for four years. And in May, Royal Mail and the DTI reached agreement in principle on a new financing framework. But for more than half a year it was not signed off and Royal Mail operated without the certainty of having formally agreed a new budget. The delay was mostly down to the inability of Alistair Darling, who was then Trade and Industry Secretary, to reach a decision on one element of Royal Mail's new financial package: a controversial transfer of shares to a trust for the benefit of Royal Mail's 200,000 employees.

Leighton was insisting that this award of shares to staff was vital to the next phase of Royal Mail's development, and therefore had to be seen as an essential part of the financing framework. The reason is his obsession with trying to create a performance-based culture within an institution which for years could not make up its mind whether it was a business, a public service or some kind of Utopian cooperative. This ambition lay behind an incentive scheme through which all staff received a payment of £1,074 in 2005 as a reward for the successful implementation of a three-year Renewal Plan. And again in 2006, each postman, sorter, sub-postmaster and manager at every grade received £418 – a so-called 'Share in Success' payment relating to the achievement of group financial targets. But Leighton wanted to take this system of linking remuneration to Royal Mail's performance a step further, by making all staff owners of the business. His recommendation was that the Government transfer 20 per cent of Royal Mail shares to a special trust for the benefit of employees – which would have handed a valuable asset (worth an estimated £5,000 per employee) to some 200,000 staff on relatively modest pay. You would have thought the postmen and sorters would have loved that. However, the share transfer was implacably opposed by the CWU trade union, which is anachronistically powerful within the company: the CWU saw the share transfer as a stepping stone towards full privatization of Royal Mail, which it viewed with horror.

The opposition of the CWU was shared by many Labour backbenchers, which made it harder for ministers to support Leighton. The DTI, in particular, was terrified of the thought of a postal workers' strike over the issue. And at a time when Labour was effectively bust – having mortgaged its future to a series of wealthy lenders in its desperate attempt to fund the 2005 general election campaign (see Chapter 8) – the CWU had clout over the party as a generous donor. From 2001 to 2006, which more or less coincides with the Leighton years at Royal Mail, the CWU gave Labour £2.1m. This is cash that Labour could ill afford to lose – so there was a powerful financial incentive to spurn Leighton's partial privatization.

However, the main concern of the Treasury about the proposal was that it was technically very difficult to achieve: valuing a company that was effectively bust would not be easy. And even if that obstacle could be overcome, there were significant implications for the public finances. If Leighton was correct and the shares would be worth £5,000 per employee after around four years, the Government would have been giving away an asset worth around £1bn, which might not have delighted all taxpayers. Leighton's counter argument was that without the share transfer, and the incentive it would give to employees to support painful plans to reorganize the business (including huge redundancies), Royal Mail would not be able to break out of a spiral of decline and could end up being worth nothing.

In June 2006, Leighton was becoming really infuriated at the failure of the Government to agree to his share scheme. He felt he had the backing of Gordon Brown and Tony Blair. In 2005, when Alan Johnson had been Trade and Industry Secretary, he had indicated support for it. But formal agreement just was not forthcoming. At the time, Leighton was so livid he said this to me about ministers:

> They tried to be clever and it's always the same. So I thought: 'Fuck you.' If they are not going to say, 'You guys have done a great job, we are very supportive of this, we buy these numbers, let's get on with it' – if instead they say, 'We think you can do it this way' – I say, 'Fuck you, I'm going to get you boxed in in such a way that you have nowhere to go . . . I'm going to get cash, you are going to take Post Office losses and I am going to get shares, and it's all going to be in one wrap, and you are not going to be able to pick your way out of it.' [Allan Leighton interview, 12 June 2006]

In the end, Leighton sacrificed his point of principle. When a comprehensive package to refinance Royal Mail was announced on 8 February 2007, there was no transfer of real shares. The CWU had won. But Leighton was less downhearted than I had expected – largely because he pulled off a neat bit of financial engineering, which meant that he ought to be able to create a share-owning culture within Royal Mail even without his cherished partial privatization. He persuaded the Treasury to sanction a 'phantom' share scheme to reward 190,000 employees. These phantom shares are proxies for real shares. In theory, they behave like real shares, although they contain no rights of ownership. The idea was that 20 per cent of the value of Royal Mail would be allocated to staff in this way – and the aim was that £1bn would be distributed to staff over five years if 'modernization' targets were reached. Since every employee would have exactly the same allocation of phantoms, that was equivalent to £5,300 per person. In its way, it was revolutionary – and dangerous for the CWU, and public-sector unions in general, because it gave each employee a direct financial interest in helping the organization to cut costs. There was no precedent for it in the public sector. And with the Government facing some difficult decisions on how to increase the efficiency of the National Health Service, as just one example, the phantom-shares scheme could turn out to be a model for securing employee cooperation for other kinds of public-sector reorganizations.

The rest of the new financial framework was gripping partly for what it said about Royal Mail's future, and also for how different interpretations put on it show the very different mentalities of private sector and public sector. Its main elements, which were finalized on 8 February 2007, were these: borrowing facilities of £1.2bn were put in place to modernize Royal Mail operations; £1bn was to be put into an escrow account, where it could not be touched by Royal Mail for normal business purposes but would be available to the pension fund in an emergency (to provide reassurance to the pension trustees that the fund could not collapse); and the Government undertook to take full financial responsibility for the network of 14,300 post offices (whose weekly losses were running at a crippling £4m per week), at an aggregate cost of £1.7bn for closing 2,500 post offices and for some investment.

When all the elements were put together, what was this package worth? Leighton has the optimism of an entrepreneur, always seeing the bright side, always accentuating the positive. He claims the deal is worth many billions to Royal Mail: 'It is £3bn, actually more,' he says. In contrast, the official line from Government officials was that a sizeable proportion of this money was simply an extension of facilities and subsidies that were already available to Royal Mail. They insisted that the new money was no more than half what Leighton thinks it is, perhaps even less. Here is the essence of the differing psychology between private and public sectors. For Leighton, the imperative is to give hope to staff that there are great opportunities in the brave, new competitive world. For all his belief that staff numbers will have to fall sharply in coming years, he is essentially a creative person, always looking for opportunities to build up Royal Mail (especially outside the UK). For the Treasury, priority number one is to limit the liability of the Exchequer and keep a tight lid on public spending – and, failing that, at least to create the impression that the public finances are not being stretched. My instinct had been that Leighton's natural exuberance had got the better of him, and that the Treasury's more conservative evaluation of the resources available to Royal Mail was nearer the truth. However, an unguarded admission by a senior Treasury official proved to me that I was wrong. 'We were absolutely furious when Leighton started mouthing off that he had got three or four billion pounds,' the official said. 'He was right, but he was under strict instructions to keep his mouth shut.'

But for all Royal Mail's new financial resources, the next few years are going to be tough. In 2006–7, the business went backwards. Profits for the group as a whole fell sharply. And it actually made a small loss, of £12m, on the part of its operation subject to price controls imposed by the regulator. That represented a sharp reversal of fortune, because it had made a profit on these price-controlled services in the previous year. Much, but not all, of that profit slump was due to increased losses on what it calls 'down-stream access'. This is when it takes mail through its own network on behalf of competitors, which it is obliged by Postcomm to do for a fixed tariff. Royal Mail estimates that it loses 2p on every letter it handles for its rivals in this way. And those pennies add up: in the year to March 2007, it helped to deliver more than 2.4bn items for these competitors, compared with 1.2bn in the previous year. So with the forced connivance of Royal Mail, other mail companies have now captured around a quarter of the profitable bulk-mail market. To add injury to insult, Royal Mail estimates it is losing 6p for every ordinary stamped letter it delivers, at a time when overall volumes in the mail market are falling. It is therefore putting as much pressure on the regulator as it can to allow it to put up prices by more than current agreements allow and to give it more free-dom to charge differential prices to business customers.

Leighton and Crozier have identified the need to renew and reconstruct Royal Mail once again in a very fundamental way. They intend to reduce the headcount yet again – by tens of thousands – and to introduce more flexible working practices, so that they can reap the efficiency savings of the automated sorting machinery which they plan to install. And they have been determined to limit the annual pay rise of postal workers – who don't exactly earn a fortune, but apparently do earn more than employees of Royal Mail's rivals – to more or less the rate of inflation. Also, they have attempted to limit the financial burden of the huge final-salary pension scheme by preventing future employees from joining it. That last ambition sent tremors throughout the public sector, because until then closing a pension fund was something only the private sector did. State schemes were sacrosanct – even if their liabilities were cripplingly expensive.

As a package, the plans were not exactly a cushy number for Royal Mail's staff. Inevitably, therefore, Leighton and Crozier found themselves at loggerheads with the CWU, the postal work-ers' union, in the summer of 2007. A majority of 127,000 union-ized postal workers voted for industrial action and then downed their postal bags in a series of one-day strikes. The periodic

disruption over several months was horribly damaging for Royal
Mail. Business clients deserted to rivals. Many of the rest of us
resorted to using e-mail even more than we had been doing. There
was a short-term financial cost stemming from revenues lost by the
strike and a longer-term one in respect of alienated customers and
business moved elsewhere which will never return. For that,
Crozier and Leighton deserve some blame. A deterioration in
relations with a workforce on that scale does not reflect well on
management. But the settlement, when it finally came in September – and only after Brendan Barber, the general secretary of the
TUC, forced the warring camps to listen to each other – preserved
some honour for the CWU while giving Crozier and Leighton
most of what they felt they needed to re-make the business yet
again.

Leighton and Crozier must wonder how many titanic battles there
are still to be fought and won before they can be confident that
Royal Mail has a sustainable future. There would have been a
period in 2007 when Leighton surely questioned whether he had
achieved anything since 2002. He is the corporate Sisyphus,
struggling on, never seeming to lose heart, but never able to say
that the job is done. What the business may need is a short, sharp
revolution, which would end, once and for all, Royal Mail's culture
of management-versus-unions and unions-versus-management. It
is hard to see how that can be achieved without privatization, either
full or partial. The status quo damages the authority and autonomy of management because the workforce can always appeal
above the heads of the directors to a shareholder, the Government,
torn between seeing Royal Mail as a business, a social service or
simply an institution arousing great passions among voters. Or, to
put it another way, continued public ownership at a time of full
competition in the postal market makes it much harder for Royal
Mail to thrive.

   Leighton and Crozier are like the pilots of a supertanker whose
hull is constructed with gaping holes in it. The ship moves forward
at a snail's pace, manoeuvring is close to impossible, and most

hands are set to bailing out water. The Government's refusal to privatize highlights the contradictions in Gordon Brown's and the Treasury's industrial policy. Brown has encouraged the excesses of liberal-market capitalism by providing hugely generous tax breaks to private-equity firms. But he would not allow Royal Mail's management the managerial and financial freedom that comes with privatization and proper access to capital markets – without which Royal Mail is very unlikely ever to become a world-class distribution business, as opposed to a rickety, second-class social service in long-term decline.

Here is another illustration of the cost to the Treasury of its feeble-mindedness. The Government has been trying – and failing – to recruit a top-class successor from the private sector to replace Leighton. The outstanding candidate was Sir Philip Hampton, chairman of the supermarket group J Sainsbury. But Hampton decided to steer well clear, having concluded that Royal Mail would be unmanageable over the longer term without privatization.

In many ways, Leighton's denouement at Royal Mail is a sorry one. When he arrived, he was a poster boy for ministers: the private-sector hero who brought answers, not problems, to Westminster and Whitehall. Now he is the nagging conscience of ministers and officials, a voluble reminder that they have ducked the difficult decisions. But they will pay a price for their cowardice, Leighton believes:

> I've gone from hero to villain. They [ministers] think now the business is okay, actually it might be a bit better if those guys [Leighton and Crozier] weren't there – because actually they are a pain in the arse, so it might be a bit easier. And in that is the reason why people never end up doing these jobs. [ibid.]

CHAPTER 10

WHO RUNS BRITAIN?

On Friday, 1 June 2007, there were four seemingly unrelated articles on the inside pages of British newspapers that in combination tell one of the big stories of our age. There was a description of a Xanadu being constructed by Mukesh Ambani, the multibillionaire chairman of Reliance Group and India's richest man. He was building a 570ft tower block in Mumbai to house his family and staff. With a value of more than £500m, it would have 27 storeys, though would be the equivalent of a 60-storey building because the ceiling-to-floor drop would be unusually large. It would be a vertical palace for a prince among the mega-rich, complete with hanging gardens, helipad, health club and theatre. That is one in the eye for his great friend Lakshmi Mittal, the Indian steel magnate who lives in London and paid £57m in 2004 for an 18-bedroom neo-Palladian mansion in Kensington Palace Gardens. Which by 2007 looked like a snip: there were a few residential properties under development in the UK for sale at £75m plus. I visited one, Updown Court in north Surrey, which has five swimming pools (one for the owner, one for his offspring, one on the roof, and two enormous ones in the grounds). The running costs of Updown Court, just to keep it heated and in decent nick, are well over a million pounds a year.

Then there was a report in the *Financial Times* about how hedge funds were becoming very angry with US banks for not throwing delinquent borrowers out of their homes. It was the height of the crisis in the market for sub-prime loans. Hedge funds had been buying up derivative contracts that pay investors when bonds backed by these sub-prime loans run into trouble. So the difficulties in the sub-prime market, as homeowners found it difficult to keep up their loan payments, should have been very good news for the hedge funds. There was only one problem: the banks were rescheduling some of the sub-prime loans, such that the borrowers could stay in their homes. Most of us would have viewed this as an example of socially responsible banking. But not the hedge funds. The apparent altruistic behaviour of the banks meant that payments to hedge funds under the derivative contracts were not being triggered. The hedge funds could not make the profits which were their due without causing homeowners misery – so they were grumpy, with apparently no concern that they might be perceived as making Ebenezer Scrooge look like a Victorian philanthropist.

Also that morning, every newspaper reported the concerns of the trustees of Boots's pension fund, which has 66,000 members, over what would happen to the fund following the takeover of the healthcare retailer by the leading US private-equity firm, Kohlberg Kravis Roberts. Shareholders had approved the £11.1bn sale to KKR, in advance of any agreement between KKR and Boots's trustees about how the viability of the pension scheme could be guaranteed over the long term. KKR insisted it would not leave Boots's pensioners high and dry – and, in the end, agreement between the pension-fund trustees and KKR was reached. But members of the pension scheme were horrified that the first priority of Boots's board was to secure the best possible sale price for Boots's shareholders, and that it was left to the trustees of the fund to defend the financial interests of 66,000 past and present Boots employees.

The main reason that pension trustees are usually concerned when private equity buys their respective parent companies is that the debts of those parent companies typically increase very sharply after a takeover – because private equity finances most of the cost of these deals with borrowed money. And if a company such as Boots is under pressure to pay the interest and principal on billions of pounds of debt, there may be less cash available for investment in the pension scheme.

These are real risks and a firm like KKR, filled with fearsomely bright financiers, would not take them on lightly. So why were there so many private-equity takeovers? Well, the final story of 1 June gave an explanation: British banks were falling over themselves to finance such deals. Figures released by the Bank of England showed that UK-based banks were providing incredibly cheap loans to private equity and hedge funds. Although the risk of lending to hedge funds and private equity is significant – which would normally mean that interest rates on the relevant loans would be relatively high – private-equity firms and hedge funds were actually able to borrow from banks to finance their deals at rates normally only available to those whose risk of default is negligible. With the cost of money for private equity and hedge funds so cheap, they would have been fools not to take it.

When you put these news stories together as a sort of jigsaw, what was the landscape that was revealed? It was a world awash with money, which could be scooped up and invested by those with the right financial credentials. The source of this money was the commodity-rich economies of the Middle East and Russia and the manufacturing powerhouses of China and Asia. All that lovely cash was then put to work by clever bankers and financiers in the US and Europe. And then the money was lent, and lent again, and then lent again far too many times, largely because of the foolish decision by central banks to cut interest rates to ludicrously low levels a few years before. The loans went to homebuyers in the US and the UK, to private-equity firms buying huge companies, to specially created financial entities which, on an industrial scale, idiotically embarked on alchemy, trying to turn low-quality loans into high-quality ones.

Plenty of bonuses, fees and capital gains stuck to clever-clogs bankers, hedge-fund founders and private-equity partners. They joined the class of the super-rich. But the debts and risks were piled on real companies with vast numbers of employees, and on hundreds of thousands of naive and hopeful individuals in the US with low-paying, unreliable employment but a desperation to own their own homes. The global financial markets evolved into a complex, Heath Robinson machine for enriching the few while loading debt on to the many. In the process of providing seemingly unlimited resources to hedge funds and private equity, the financial security of millions of ordinary citizens has been undermined. Ask Boots's pensioners, or US householders having difficulties keeping up payments on their sub-prime loans, whether they feel better or worse off as a result of the frenetic investment activity of private equity and hedge funds. US marital lawyers, however, were major beneficiaries of the hedge-fund and private-equity boom – it was all the rage for the titans of these industries to obtain post-nuptial agreements from their spouses, preventing them from seizing their interests in their firms if all the lovely money they earned could not stop their marriages falling apart.

Now, there is an argument, put forward by the bankers who grease this money-recycling machine, that all this mad lending has a socially useful purpose. In the US and the UK it gave those on low incomes and with uncertain prospects access to credit that had not hitherto been available, giving them the opportunity to accumulate property and to finance all sorts of desirable purchases. Which is true, up to a point – except that quite of lot of them are now losing their homes, having been unable to keep up the payments. Also, there is no doubt that all that financial business accelerated economic growth in the US and the UK. But a year or two ago, when the lending machine should have gone down a gear, it went into overdrive. Cheap money was spewed out and lent in terrifying quantities to individuals and businesses whose ability to repay was predicated on self-delusion. Finally, last August, when many of the providers of the cash realized their extraordinary fecklessness, the whole machine came to a juddering halt. And at that point, when it became impossible to repay one load of debt by borrowing another bigger load even more cheaply, all sorts of banks, financial institutions, companies and homeowners had a frightening realization that they had accumulated huge and horrible liabilities.

We are still living through the implications of all this. But it is already clear that credit for everyone – from you and me to big businesses – is becoming harder to obtain and more expensive. There is something of a hangover after the party. But what many will find offensive is that just as the spoils of the boom were disproportionately accumulated by the super-rich, so the costs of the subsequent bust are being heaped on all of us. Fortunes have been made by the hedge-fund and private-equity superstars that will withstand any economic shock. Their future is secure. But that is not true of the millions of homeowners who may have borrowed too much, or the employees of businesses loaded up with debt by private-equity purchasers.

What a brave new world. But any critique of the rise and rise of the super-rich must not be based on the politics of envy. I have few qualms about celebrating the creativity of capitalism and capitalists. It may not be pretty but, on the whole, greed is good. Organizations that operate in a competitive marketplace and where success is closely correlated with financial rewards tend to be more efficient and usually serve the public interest better than those run in the public sector by bureaucrats with more amorphous goals. Who in the UK can honestly argue that our competitive telecoms market – which has engendered both massive deflation in the price of services and tremendous innovation – is inferior to the pre-privatization world of British Telecommunications as a state-owned, arrogant, monolithic monopolist? Is it likely that the broadband internet would be as widely available as it is, and at such low prices, if entrepreneurs like Charles Dunstone at Carphone Warehouse or James Murdoch at British Sky Broadcasting were not endeavouring to make fortunes for themselves and their businesses by connecting up as many homes as they can in record time?

That said, there are plenty of times when capitalism and free markets fail to serve the public interest – which is why we have governments and regulators to protect us. Thus, any business that acquires the power of a monopolist usually needs to be reined in, for fear that it would overcharge customers or stifle competition. As an example, simply privatizing British Telecommunications or British Gas did not at a stroke make all of us better off. They faced inadequate competition, which meant that they were in a position to set prices at an excessively high level. So, for years, they were rightly subject to regulatory controls on what they could charge consumers. British Gas was subsequently broken up and other telecoms and energy companies started to win customers. And at that point, regulatory constraints on both of them could be relaxed.

Also, there are some products and services – such as education and health – where the free operation of the market tends to lead to unequal outcomes which most of us regard as unacceptably unfair or indeed damaging to the wider interests of the economy. It is palpably in all our interests for the state to provide minimum standards of healthcare and education for all of us. The rational debate is about where that minimum should be set and about the nature of public-sector structures for providing it. And, right now, the same kind of arguments apply in the UK to the media, where the BBC – which employs me – is a beneficiary of the notion that high-quality, politically neutral, public-service broadcasting can only be sustained by public subsidy.

During the late-twentieth-century face-off between state control and free markets, the winner by knockout was liberal capitalism. The big advantage of allowing market forces to distribute resources was that it was much more efficient than allowing those resources to be allocated by politician or bureaucrat. And this efficiency tended to outweigh any resentment about the widening gap between rich and poor that was precipitated by the triumph of markets. For most of the twentieth century, there was a reduction in inequality. But even when the gap between rich and poor started to widen again after 1979, following the election victory of Margaret Thatcher's Conservative Party, there were benefits for the vast majority of us, thanks to the way that improved financial incentives for wealth creators spurred them to manage businesses better. Apart from anything else, the massive injections of cash into schools and hospitals by the Government of Tony Blair and Gordon Brown were made possible by a rise in the productive potential of the British economy. And that was the consequence of a private-sector renaissance engendered by the previous Tory administration. These were examples of deferred dividends eventually paid to everyone out of the Thatcherite rise in inequality.

But the British economy – and perhaps the global economy – is at a crossroads. The private sector has been in rude health, especially in London and the south-east. But it is no longer quite so clear that the kind of society being created passes the fairness test or the efficiency test. Just how socially and economically beneficial is it for billions to be amassed by a tiny number of individuals? Can most of them really be expected to deploy their wealth in a useful way other than to preserve it for themselves and their offspring? The ferocity of the forces of globalization and their impact on the distribution of riches mark the difference between the Britain of the 1980s or 1990s and today.

In the UK, there are three relevant trends. First, there is our competitive advantage in financial services, the astonishing international success of the City of London. This is a winner-takes-all industry, in which fabulous rewards accrue to the most talented individuals. Then there is the belief – which has become more ingrained under New Labour – that individuals are more important than teams in the success of an organization, that those with rare and productive skills can sell themselves for a fortune anywhere in the world, and that therefore it is in the interest of the UK to be seen as a haven for the super-rich or the aspiring super-rich. The widening in the gap between the rich and poor has taken on a new slant under Tony Blair and Gordon Brown. The maximum spoils have gone to those at the very apex of the income and wealth league tables: a new plutocracy has been born. Finally, there is the

UK's openness to immigration from the new Europe of Poland and the Czech Republic, the more recent members of the European Union, which has created spare capacity in the jobs market and reduced the bargaining power of British-born employees – which keeps a lid on the pay rises of the majority of workers in the UK.

Why should any of that matter? If London is the plutocrat's home of choice, isn't that just wonderful for the UK? Doesn't it mean that the British economy is benefiting from their wealth-creating prowess? Don't capital and jobs follow them wherever they go? So shouldn't we simply say hooray for the proliferation of the super-rich in the UK?

The Prime Minister certainly thinks it should be a cause of national joy that the UK is in a way a gigantic tax haven for the internationally mobile business elite. Since about 2000, Gordon Brown – as both Chancellor and Premier – has tried to be as welcoming as possible to hedge funds and private-equity firms. The superstar of their ilk, Damon Buffini – who runs the only European private-equity firm in the global premier league, Permira – is on Brown's Business Council for Britain. Its members, who were invited to the Prime Minister's country residence, Chequers, at the end of September 2007 for a lavish lunch in honour of Alan Greenspan, the former chairman of the US Federal Reserve, have an explicit mandate to stop the Government doing anything to damage the competitiveness of business. Perhaps the most famous member of the Business Council is Sir Richard Branson, the creator of the Virgin empire, who is a great believer – as he has argued to me – that low taxes are ultimately in the interests of any economy, because they encourage productive activity. The highly successful private-equity player, John Moulton, founder of Alchemy, told MPs on the Treasury Select Committee that:

> Lines are really difficult in tax. There is white, there is grey and there is black. Different people have different views on where it lies. We have a country where people like Sir Richard Branson, who is widely respected, yet his business empire is reported to be

largely offshore: a low tax bill but widely respected. [John
Moulton to Treasury Select Committee, 3 July 2007]

Brown's views on all this have changed – which is not something
that happens often. In the 1990s and even in his early years as
Chancellor, he argued vigorously and passionately that the super-
rich living here should pay their fair share of taxes. Subsequently,
he has been careful to the point of neurosis not to change the tax
system in a way that might drive them elsewhere.

In that context, there has been widespread misunderstanding of
a controversial increase in capital gains tax and changes to rules
relating to those not domiciled here for tax purposes, which were
announced in the autumn Pre-Budget Report of 2007. In a
staggering example of the kind of spin which Brown has supposedly eschewed, the reforms were presented by the Chancellor,
Alistair Darling, and the Treasury as somehow introducing justice
to the taxation of private equity. And that is how they were
reported in much of the media. But they were in part designed
precisely so as not to impose a prohibitive rate of tax on partners in
the largest, most international of the private-equity firms. Those
private-equity partners who had organized their tax affairs so as to
pay little tax at all here would be largely untouched. And those who
do pay most of their tax here were delighted that the big source of
their remuneration – their 'carry' or share of the gains on big deals
– will be liable to a tax rate of up to 18 per cent (and the effective
rate will probably be a lot less thanks to the careful construction of
contracts with sources of finance for private-equity deals on how
the costs and gains should be divided). The important point is that
this 'carry' has many of the characteristics of income rather than a
capital gain, and yet the tax payable is well under half the 40 per
cent top rate of income tax paid by millions of British people.

A debate about the implications of the ascendancy of the super-
rich has begun in the British media. The *Daily Mail*, in particular,
gave tremendous exposure to remarks made to me in a BBC
interview by Sir Ronnie Cohen, the private-equity pioneer, in
which he said that the widening gap between rich and poor is

'something we should be concerned about' and that 'when economic situations get bad, it takes a spark to ignite a violent reaction'. Which was striking because the airing of such concerns would seem to be counter to the interests of the controllers of some newspapers, such as the Murdochs at News International, the Barclays at the Telegraph Group, Richard Desmond at the *Daily Express* and, indeed, the Harmsworths at Associated Newspapers, owners of the *Daily Mail*. To state the obvious, it might look as though these newspapers were attacking their respective owners, since all are fully paid up members of the plutocracy – although they are of differing vintages, with the Barclays and Desmond counting as members of the new super-rich.

That said, newspapers have for years routinely given a good kicking to executives at quoted companies whose rewards seem disconnected from the performance of their respective businesses, perhaps in part because of a British sense of fair play. But when the boss of a supermarket group, bank or pharmaceutical company receives a drubbing for allegedly being paid too much, it is a relatively harmless lightning rod for public unease. Those who run listed businesses, in the very biggest FTSE 100 companies, earn a fraction of the rewards that are reaped by the buyers and sellers of whole companies in private equity, or the adventurers of global financial markets who control hedge funds. Press criticism of so-called fat-cat PLC pay is the equivalent of a campaign against the earnings of footballers at a middle-ranking club like Sheffield Wednesday or Ipswich, while the remuneration of David Beckham and Wayne Rooney is ignored. It would not unduly worry media tycoons if their publications undermined confidence in the professional managers of listed businesses. After all, these tycoons typically represent a competing model of corporate stewardship, that of the owner-entrepreneur rather than of the paid professional manager. Only more recently has there been substantial press coverage of the implications for the UK of the growth of the elite that includes the media moguls, that of the immensely wealthy individuals who typically work outside of public companies.

Even so, you will be hard-pressed to find in their publications much consideration given to the idea that the growth of the super-wealthy class is contributing to the fragmentation of society. There is much wringing of hands in newspapers about the collapse of the ties that bind us together. Every other page contains an indictment of the anti-social behaviour of young people, the putative threat to our way of life from the influx of illegal or legal migrants, the assault on 'Britishness' of those with a different dress code or religious outlook from our own. Which is all very well. But what about our duty to make a proper financial contribution to the society which allows us to prosper? Why is the propensity of the super-wealthy to shelter the great bulk of their income and capital gains from taxation any less reprehensible than other manifestations of disdain for the norms of citizenship?

I am not arguing for a super-tax or any kind of special tax on the wealthy. But most of the super-wealthy would not have been able to accumulate or sustain their wealth without the stable infrastructure provided by the UK – and by a 'stable infrastructure' I mean an educated workforce, a National Health Service that sustains that workforce, roads, rail, police, a justice system safeguarding property rights, a fire service. None of that is provided by the tooth fairy, though the super-wealthy often act as though they think it is. And if headmasters, senior policemen, civil servants, junior executives and so on pay 40 per cent tax on all their income, shouldn't those who earn a great deal more do the same? But the pattern in the UK is that those on lowest incomes pay no tax and those on the highest incomes generally pay minimal tax. In Brown's Britain, the rule is that if you don't want to pay tax, be impoverished or obscenely wealthy.

This horror of paying taxes would matter less if there was a strong culture of charitable giving in the UK. But, compared with the US, that barely exists either. I've noted in this book the generosity of Sir Tom Hunter, the Scottish magnate – who made a fortune from sports retailing and is now committed to giving away at least a billion pounds to anti-poverty initiatives in Africa and educational projects in Scotland – and of Chris Hohn, the remarkable hedge-fund manager. But they are still the exceptions. The UK has returned to the nineteenth century in respect of the opportunities to make vast fortunes. But the habit of philanthropy, lost when the welfare state took on the responsibility for looking after the neediest, has not been re-acquired.

That said, partly I think out of a sense of self-preservation, many entrepreneurs have begun to talk the talk of 'giving something back'. To state the obvious, no British entrepreneur is nearly as wealthy as Bill Gates, the founder of Microsoft, or Warren Buffett, the world's greatest investor. So, by definition, when those bridge-playing chums decide to give away their fortunes, no one in the world can match their munificence. But, according to the *Chronicle of Philanthropy*, the median donation among the top 60 most generous US donors in 2006 – excluding Buffett, who pledged to give away $43.5bn – was $60m and there were 21 gifts of at least $100m. If there have been 21 gifts of at least $100m by British citizens in the past 21 years I would be very surprised. There may have been a handful of that magnitude – and the decision by Lord Sainsbury of Turville, the supermarket billionaire, to give away more or less his entire fortune over the coming years is an impressive future commitment. A huge amount of publicity was given in 2007 to a donation of £5m to the Tate Gallery by the banker John Studzinski. But guess what? Studs, as he is known, is American.

My criticism of the obsessive desire of most of the new generation of super-wealthy to hang on to every last penny of what they have pocketed would be mean-spirited if it was obvious that their activities were of themselves in the public interest. But, as I hope this book has shown, the argument that the activities of hedge funds and private equity are somehow greatly to the benefit of the vast majority of us is for the birds. Their spoils are usually an opportunity lost to the pension funds on which most of us depend for our retirement income. The companies they either buy or boss around may sometimes be strengthened in a really fundamental way. But frequently they are reconstructed to generate massive short-term gains, with little positive long-term benefit. Worse still, private equity and hedge funds are a manifestation of the era of cheap money which has undoubtedly been a source of great harm to the economy.

This came to a juddering end in the summer of 2007 and has left us with an overhang of expensive debt. That poisoned legacy undermines what had been the best argument for private equity and hedge funds, which is that they improve the productive potential of the economy by directing capital in a more efficient way to the businesses with the best long-term prospects. That happened, to an extent. But their success spawned a massive industry of copycats and their activities contributed to a massive and generalized inflation in asset prices, to conditions which turned out to be a bubble. Or, to put it another way, despite their propaganda to the contrary, their frenetic investment behaviour contributed to the seizing up of money markets, from which few of us are likely to escape unscathed.

That Gordon Brown presided over a tax system that encouraged the creation of this bubble should embarrass him. But what is perhaps even more remarkable, given his One-Britain rhetoric, is that his policies may have exacerbated the economic fragmentation of the UK. He has been a lifelong advocate of reducing the UK's dependence on London and the south-east and has long wanted to narrow the income gap between North and South. However, the great success of the City of London and the triumph of the super-rich are two sides of the same coin. The City provides the services which help the super-rich augment their wealth. And the financial services industry is the most propitious breeding ground for new members of the super-rich. It is an industry in which the UK has a real, global competitive advantage – for better and worse (a good thing for generating economic growth; perhaps less beneficial in the way that its success has sucked talent and capital from other parts of the economy).

In the last few years, Gordon Brown has tended to see primarily the advantages of a strong City, even to the extent of abandoning an almost religious contempt for the big banks and what he had earlier perceived as their near-collusive behaviour in the way they price their services for individuals and small businesses. Brown's pragmatism in providing a welcome for the super-wealthy encouraged a City boom, which helped to sustain above-average economic growth in London and the south-east – and, for all the ability of the super-rich to pay little or no tax, the prosperity of the South has generated the tax revenues that have financed public spending throughout the UK.

As a direct result of Brown's policies, the economic gap between North and South has widened. But he has then tried to narrow this gap through public spending in less prosperous regions. Almost everywhere has become more dependent on subsidies from the South. The scale of the resource transfer has been calculated by the consultancy the Centre for Economics and Business Research (CEBR). It estimates that public spending represents just a third of the economy in London and the south-east. But state expenditure is equivalent to more than 70 per cent of the Northern Ireland economy, 64 per cent of Welsh gross domestic product, 56 per cent of Scottish GDP and 63 per cent of north-east England's output.

It is just about possible to characterize Scotland and Wales as Scandinavian-style, Utopian socialist economies – with superior schools and hospitals provided by a public sector that accounts for more than half the local economy – while London is a booming capitalist enclave, a land-locked Hong Kong. Although those analogies may be overstated, the economic disparities between Scotland and the South do not look sustainable. In Scotland, there is a palpable and growing annoyance at the idea that it is an infirm economy that requires crumbs from the plate of wealthy London to survive – which partly explains the popularity of the separatist Scottish National Party. As for southerners, a growing number are irked by what they perceive as the handouts they give to Scotland. And it is doubly irksome for many in England that Scots have all the best jobs in the UK Government – and that Scottish MPs at Westminster can influence how public money is spent in England while there is no reciprocal right for English MPs. Here's the contradiction that our Scottish Prime Minister has generated for himself. He has a long history of proselytizing for the Union and for bridging the North–South divide. But his enthusiastic promotion of the City, and the evolution of London into the capital of a stateless world peopled by the immensely wealthy, is widening that divide and risks fracturing the Union.

Even if – which is debatable – the productive potential of the British economy has been improved by the demonstration that ours is a country where entrepreneurialism can be rewarded with wealth on a scale that's difficult to comprehend, the positive effects may be short-lived. Apart from anything else, there's simply the waste and opportunity cost of so many billions of pounds being in the hands of relatively few people. Having taken their dividends and cashed in their investments, what is the general benefit of their propensity to recycle their gains into overpriced modern art or control of a football club? And is there much likelihood that the thousands of trust-fund inheritors they've spawned will show much entrepreneurial flair? Or is it more likely that they'll follow the example of previous dynasties by either engaging in a fairly useless frittering of their inherited wealth or attempting to convert financial power into political power – in a manner that could be profoundly anti-democratic.

We've witnessed in the past decade the way that all the main political parties have been prepared to grant access and influence to those with the wherewithal to fund their operations. Even with reform of the system of funding political parties, the wealthy will always find a way to buy political power – whether through the direct sponsorship of politicians and parties, or through the acquisition of media businesses, or through the financing of think tanks. To put it another way, the voices of the super-wealthy are heard by politicians well above the babble of the crowd. That should concern us, especially at a time when apathy among the electorate is high and participation in the democratic process is worryingly low. It means we are more vulnerable than perhaps we have been since the nineteenth century to the advent of rule by an unelected oligarchy. Brown would die rather than see his Business Council for Britain in that light. But, on his watch, the super-rich and heads of multinational businesses have gained more direct access to Government than they have enjoyed at any time for decades.

To admit to concerns about the rise and rise of the billionaire class is not the manifestation of an atavistic socialist prejudice. And if the leaders of the Tory and Labour parties were not so thoroughly frightened of being tarnished as anti-wealth creation, they would express such concerns. Is it really the *sine qua non* of a successful modern economy that there should be no limit on the wealth which any individual can generate and retain?

My view, having observed the super-wealthy and pusillanimous politicians at close quarters for twenty years, is that the great new nonsense of our age is that we should take nothing but pride in the proliferation of billionaires and never suggest that they are parasitic. Their charitable contributions in the United Kingdom are *de minimis* compared with their peers in the United States. And, as I have said, it would be a welcome change if the billionaire class simply paid the same tax as a proportion of income and capital gains as the rest of us.

If we and other developed economies continue down the path of giving a free pass to those who have most it may undermine the fabric of the democratic nation state. More and more individuals have been earning sums that make it realistic for them to threaten to become tax exiles if they are not given privileged tax treatment in the UK. Perhaps it is time to call their bluff – or endeavour, against the instincts of many of us, to properly streamline and harmonize tax rates in countries across the globe, so that nowhere is a hiding place from fair taxation.

Failing that, here is a possible United Kingdom in ten years, on current trends. Public services would be creaking for lack of resources, as the burden of tax fell on a dwindling number of private-sector employees whose skills weren't quite rare enough or valuable enough to take them into the top league of globally mobile earners. And year after year, the real disposable income of the majority would be squeezed ever so slightly, because that would be the only way that they could keep their jobs in the climate of intense international competition endured by their respective employers. Meanwhile, the plutocrats who own these businesses would shuttle from London to Monaco to Moscow to Mumbai to Shanghai to Rio and back again, refusing to pay the subscription price to belong in any meaningful sense to any nation or community, except the global community of the super-wealthy. In that world, elected politicians would seem less and less relevant to the daily lives of the majority. The potentates would be the stateless plutocrats.

These are the conditions in which millions of citizens could ultimately feel dispossessed, alienated, powerless – especially if there were a global recession. The fracturing of our society is no less dangerous simply because it is occurring at a time of prosperity. We ignore the seemingly unstoppable rise of the super-rich at our peril.

INDEX

ACKNOWLEDGEMENTS

I spoke to hundreds of entrepreneurs, chief executives, bankers, politicians, private-equity partners, hedge-fund managers and civil servants – *inter alia* – over the three years this book has been in preparation. I am immensely grateful to all of them for their insights, their time and their tolerance of my endless tiresome questions.

Kate Jones of International Creative Management has been an invaluably wise and supportive partner in this enterprise from first to last. Rupert Lancaster of Hodder & Stoughton has been a rock (solid Hereford stone, not a Northern Rock). And big thanks are due too to Lucy Hale and Bill Jones, both of Hodder.

Ron Emler was the consummate professional, as ever, in copy editing some initial chapters. My friend Guy Dennis read an early draft and gave sterling advice.

This book would have been impossible to complete without the support and love of my wife, Siân Busby – a brilliant writer, not a journeyman like me – and my son, Maximilian. Although the book is dedicated to my parents, it is for Siân and Max too, if they want it (but they would probably prefer I spend a little less time at the laptop, which I will try to do).